THE GREATEST
BLEEDING HEARTS
RACKET IN THE WORLD

Irish Hospitals Sweepstakes

THE GREATEST BLEEDING HEARTS RACKET IN THE WORLD

Irish Hospitals Sweepstakes

DAMIAN CORLESS ❧

Gill & Macmillan

Gill & Macmillan Ltd
Hume Avenue, Park West, Dublin 12
with associated companies throughout the world
www.gillmacmillan.ie

© Damian Corless 2010
978 07171 4669 7

Index compiled by Cover to Cover
Typography design by Make Communication
Print origination by O'K Graphic Design, Dublin
Printed in Great Britain by MPG Books Ltd, Bodmin,
Cornwall

This book is typeset in 12/14.5 pt Minion.

The paper used in this book comes from the wood pulp
of managed forests. For every tree felled, at least one
tree is planted, thereby renewing natural resources.

A CIP catalogue record for this book is available from the
British Library.

5 4 3 2 1

For Martin and Kathleen

CONTENTS

Chapter 1 ∾

A FIENDISH CRIME AT OUR DOORS

It was the early afternoon of Thursday 10 October 1918 and the Dublin offices of *The Irish Times* newspaper were in a hubbub. Copy-boys scurried between the smoke-filled editorial offices which should have been emptied for lunch, but which were instead a noisy blur of confusion as sketchy reports dribbbled in of a tragedy at sea.

In the eye of this breaking crisis, someone with a cool head and a cold heart spied an opportunity. The call came down to the compositors to hold the front page. That call didn't come from the editor, but from the advertising department. In 1918 newspaper front pages were still entirely given over to adverts, mainly of the small classified variety.

But this front page was going to look out of the ordinary. A new advert was hurriedly made up, much larger than was usual, and placed top centre to catch the eye. In large bold type it addressed itself to 'Passengers to London and England'. The message to these passengers was 'Protect Your Dependents'. In smaller type it went on: 'You should make provision for your families or dependents in case you meet with a Fatal Accident, owing to a War and/or Marine peril.' It concluded that full particulars of this fatal accident cover were available from the Motor Union Insurance Company in Dublin.

The oversized advert was a cryptic pointer to the lead story being pieced together for page 3. The finalised headlines would scream: 'Irish Mail Boat Sunk. Torpedoed by German U-Boat in Irish Sea. Heavy Death Toll—Over 500 Victims'. Even before all the facts were gathered, the tone of the editorial was set: 'The people of Ireland and, indeed, the whole of the English-speaking world, will learn this morning with a thrill of horror of the latest fiendish crime which has been committed almost at our very doors by the Germans.'

As part of the United Kingdom, Ireland had been on a war footing for fully four years. The Irish Sea had earned the name U-boat alley because of the number of German submarines on the prowl, but no passenger mailboat had ever been attacked. So as the word spread that the *Leinster* had been sunk, a shudder ran through the capital. The vessels of the City of Dublin Steam Packet Company provided a busy shuttle service between Ireland and Britain. Sailing between Kingstown (now Dun Laoghaire) and Holyhead, they connected families, friends and businesses on opposite sides of the Irish Sea.

The first rumours to circulate, around noon, suggested that the *Leinster* had been hit and damaged but was still afloat and being towed back to port. That story quickly dissolved into wishful thinking. The mailboat went under within five minutes. The *Leinster*'s sos had been picked up by its sister ship, the *Ulster*, which was passing in the opposite direction and within sight. Under wartime Admiralty rules, however, the *Ulster* was forbidden from sailing to its rescue for fear of providing the U-boat with an easy second kill. The *Ulster*'s captain sent out a telegraphed sos in all directions, which reached the Admiralty at Kingstown.

As every available vessel was being dispatched from Kingstown Harbour on a rescue mission, the car owners of the greater Dublin area were press-ganged into providing emergency transport. Some who resisted the chance to play the white knight had their vehicles commandeered. Volunteers of the Red Cross and St John Ambulance Brigade made their way to Victoria Wharf in Kingstown, where boats of all sizes arrived from afternoon till late at night bearing the living and the dead. Frozen survivors were given warm clothing and blankets and revived with Bovril, coffee and spirits. The critical and the dead were conveyed to the local hospital. The traumatised were taken to recoup at the Royal Marine and Ross's hotels.

A reporter on the scene wrote: 'A great deal of anxiety was displayed by a crowd of persons who had come from the city and other places to inquire about their friends or relatives who were passengers on the *Leinster*. A few ladies who failed to discover any trace of their relatives were overcome with grief and had to be attended to by the nurses at the Admiralty shed.'

One grief-stricken man was Richard Duggan, a 40-year-old Dublin bookmaker who, only hours earlier, had seen off a group of friends sailing on the *Leinster* to a big race meeting in England. Over the following days and weeks, the papers carried notices of contributions to the Lord Mayor's *Leinster* relief fund. Big companies including Jameson Whiskey and Bank of Ireland were joined on the list by football clubs such as Bohemians FC and members of the aristocracy. Special collections were held at theatre matinées and sports events. These were hard times in a world racked by years of war, which excuses the letters sent to the press a fortnight after the tragedy from residents of Kingstown seeking the return of blankets and other items given to the shivering survivers.

The well-heeled bookmaker Richard Duggan was in a giving mood. He decided to organise a lottery to help out families of the dead. It was an age when those without means of support could end up in the penal squalor of the workhouse. Duggan's target was to raise the handsome sum of £1,000, returning only £100 in prizes and distributing the rest to the needy. His draw was a roaring success, far exceeding his expectations. His subsequent activities give firm grounds for suspecting that Duggan helped himself to a personal profit from the *Leinster* draw; but if he did it was never disclosed.

Like *The Irish Times* advertising man, Duggan was quick to turn the *Leinster* crisis into an opportunity. There were other opportunities out there ripe for the plucking, although the bookie took another couple of years to exploit one that was already in plain sight in October 1918 when the *Leinster* was sent to the bottom of the sea. *The Irish Times* that month carried a notice headlined 'Urgent Appeal for Funds'. The appeal in question was from the Coombe Lying-In Hospital. The Dublin maternity hospital was a massive £7,000 in debt; the trustees only had £3,110 in the coffers and the banks were saying they would not honour the hospital's cheques.

When the penny dropped that Dublin's debt-ridden hospitals could be harnessed to a money-spinning scheme, Duggan acted on a grand scale.

Chapter 2

MATERIAL GAIN AND SORDID PERSONAL ADVANTAGE

Richard Duggan's second coming as the bookie with the heart of gold took place in 1922. Ireland was still in the grip of war, but this time it was a vicious Civil War between the two sundered halves of Sinn Féin. The party had amassed a landslide majority of Irish Westminster seats in the first post-war general election held just weeks after the sinking of the *Leinster*. Duggan was now living in a liberated 26 County state, but the action hero men and women who had secured it were now at each other's throats, with gunfire on the streets an everyday event. It was not the best of times to be a bookmaker, even one who carefully honed the image of a pious, dapper, trustworthy and charming gentleman. On the racecourse he traded under a banner carrying the cheery message, 'Whatever Duggan Lays He Pays'.

Nor was it, in 1922, a good time to be ill in Ireland, but very many were. Much of rural Ireland was dirt poor and hungry, but many Dubliners lived in a squalor which condemned them to lives even more nasty, brutish and short. The capital's slums were the poorest in the British Isles, with a death rate 33 per cent higher than the worst parts of London. The inner city was crowded with livestock kept in filthy, undrained dairy-yards and laneways, and the sound of animals being slaughtered rang from countless backstreet abattoirs. Offal, blood and excrement splattered the pavements.

Disease plagued the slum tenements where one in three families lived in one room. Henrietta Street near O'Connell Street was now a byword for wretchedness, with some 800 people squashed into 15 formerly grand houses originally built to house just one upper crust family each. Out the back there was a piggery. Dublin Corporation's efforts to improve conditions were feeble, not least because a significant number of the corporation members were themselves the slum landlords collecting rents from the crumbling tenements.

And as disease raged and infant mortality in particular soared, the new State's hospital system was falling apart. Inflation during the Great War had eaten away at the value of the charitable endowments supposed to fund the voluntary hospitals, while a host of other financial afflictions were adding to the death rate.

There had been sporadic attempts to fix the problem, but nothing had worked. In 1920, shortly before Independence, a public meeting had been held on Dublin's Kildare Street 'for the purpose of inaugurating a fund to meet the urgent needs of eleven of the voluntary hospitals in the city'. The combined debt hanging over these institutions was estimated at £100,000.

Lord Powerscourt took the podium as president 'of this gigantic scheme'. 'He thought he was right in saying that nothing had ever been done in Dublin before on such a scale—to raise £100,000 to pay off all the debts of practically all the hospitals.'

The meeting heard that the Royal Dublin Society had supplied its Ballsbridge grounds for a large fête. Football clubs, swimming clubs and other sporting bodies were urged to have a flag day during Horse Show Week. The society's chancellor was reported as declaring: 'The time had come for all those hospitals, in conjunction with some of their leading business citizens, to put their heads together and tell the public what they proposed doing in the future if the public came to their rescue now and relieved them of the burden of debt.'

Whatever plans the hospitals may have outlined, they came to nothing because a cash-strapped public failed to find the required £100,000 to rescue the dire situation. The new Free State government had neither the funds, nor to some extent the inclination, to pour cash into the health system. In recent decades the British had dampened down dissent by pumping generous subsidies into Ireland's local authorities. The result was that the country's parish pump politicians had never had it so good, dispensing state-funded patronage and jobs in their cushy fiefdoms, including clusters of local hospitals. The puritan reformers of Sinn Féin took a very dim view of what they regarded as widespread gombeenism. The visionaries of a new Ireland thought it a waste of money to fund a multiplicity of small hospitals with too many staff and too few patients.

The Dáil had recently sent an inspector to investigate whether the sick and the needy of the underpopulated county of Monaghan really warranted four hospitals and a workhouse. The inspector reported back that Monaghan County Council was carrying far too much deadwood and that the hospitals in Carrickmacross, Clones and Castleblaney should all be shut down. It was decided that the hospital in Monaghan town itself was more than adequate to meet the needs of the whole county.

In the capital, meanwhile, the problem was radically reversed and the need for more hospital beds was pressing. Richard Duggan stepped up to the mark. In the autumn of 1922 a series of enticing newspaper adverts began appearing for a £10,000 Mater Hospital Sweep to be run on the Manchester Handicap of 25 November. The notice said: 'Organized by Mr RJ Duggan, 38 Dame St, Dublin. The draw will take place at the Mansion House, Dublin, on November 23rd, under the supervision of the Right Hon The Lord Mayor, with whom the prize money has been deposited.'

Duggan's fundraiser for the *Leinster* four years earlier had been a straight lottery draw with the prizes going directly to the holders of the tickets drawn. A sweepstake, on the other hand, was a two-tier gamble. Ticket duplicates (or counterfoils) would be signed by the buyer and would then go into a drum, with the buyer keeping the original. The small number of tickets drawn from the drum would then be matched against the field of horses in a specific race. In other words, the first stage of a sweepstake was a lottery in which the prize was a bet on a horse. After that, the size of the prize depended on the performance of the holder's horse. In the circumstances, a contestant whose ticket was matched to one of the favourites could savour the anticipation of a likely big prize.

Sweepstakes had been outlawed almost a century earlier under British rule and remained illegal both in Ireland and in Britain where Duggan's chosen race was to take place. However, the prohibition had been more honoured in the breach than the observance. In fact, in the period since the troops returned home from the trenches of the Great War, sport and gambling entwined in a gaming boom as the people of both islands tried to shake off the horrors of slaughter on an industrial scale.

Duggan was first out of the traps with his scheme for a sweepstake hitched to a good cause in a proud but poor newly independent Ireland. He was, quite literally, banking on generating strong sales among the community of Irish economic exiles in Britain. In the summer of 1922 he made the Mater Hospital an offer it could not refuse. If the Mater would sign up as the good cause and promote the venture, he would guarantee a payout of £10,000—enough to wipe out the hospital's debts. In parallel, he would guarantee a highly attractive prize fund totalling a further £10,000. Duggan was placing a massive £20,000 bet on the gamble of his life.

But Duggan soon learned that good ideas travel fast. Shortly after the first advert appeared for his Mater sweep, a rival popped up trumpeting 'The Chance of a Lifetime' to win some cash while raising funds for St Mary's Hospital for Tubercular Children, Cappagh, Co. Dublin. John Foley's rival sweep was being run out of 15 College Green, about 200 metres from Duggan's HQ. But while Duggan was peddling ten shilling tickets with the first horse home bringing its ticket-holder a £5,000 fortune, Foley's lesser resources were reflected in a £1,100 first prize for a one shilling flutter in his Great Cappagh Sweep.

Meanwhile, a couple of minutes' walk away on Ormond Quay, James J. Kearney was attempting to get in on the act with his Oliver Plunkett Sweep, named after the martyred Catholic archbishop who had been beatified by the Vatican just two years earlier. The latest arrival was met with a distinct lack of Christian charity by a rival or rivals unknown, and Kearney was forced to place the following advert in the papers. Headlined 'Oliver Plunkett Sweep, Important Notice', it read: 'Owing to various rumours having gained currency regarding the Oliver Plunkett Sweep, and in answer to numerous inquiries, we wish to announce that the sweep will be held exactly as announced on the tickets. Those who have purchased tickets need have no apprehension therefore.'

Other sweeps were now in motion, but it was obvious that all were low-budget sideshows to Duggan's main event to be held at the Lord Mayor's official residence under the supervision of the capital's first citizen. Everything was going nicely to plan until, with just weeks to go, a TD pitched an awkward question to Home Affairs Minister Kevin O'Higgins in the Dáil. The deputy asked O'Higgins if he had seen the adverts for a 'monster sweep' to be held in November in aid of the Mater Hospital. Questioning the legality of the sweep, the deputy asked if O'Higgins would 'cause to have published by the promoters a full and certified statement by a reputable and recognized public auditor, showing receipts and disbursements in connection therewith, so as to safeguard the charitable and philanthropic public from being exploited under the guise of praiseworthy charity'. He went on to suggest that the real purpose of Duggan's monster Mater Sweep was 'for the material gain and sordid personal advantage of an individual or combination of individuals'.

O'Higgins's suspicions that charitable lotteries and sweepstakes were indeed a vehicle to gain 'sordid personal advantage' were well known in the tight circle of Dáil deputies. However, the Home Affairs Minister's clear hostility to Duggan and his rivals was countered by cabinet colleagues who supported legalisation as a welcome money-spinner. Taoiseach W. T. Cosgrave (his title of the time was President of the Executive Council) stepped in to settle the matter. Cosgrave said he had met with a deputation from the Mater and they had persuaded him that Duggan's guaranteed £10,000 was a gift horse that should be given a run. He went on: 'The deputation assured me that they are quite satisfied with the bargain they made with Mr Duggan. It is understood that the accounts will be submitted to audit. In the circumstances, I see no reason for interfering with the holding of this sweep.'

The draw for Duggan's Mater Sweep took place at the Mansion House on 23 November 1922. It was presented to the audience, seated in their Sunday best, as a piece of light entertainment. Under the headline 'The Great Mater Sweep', the next day's *Irish Independent* carried photos of a large brick-shaped glass drum on a stage, flanked by a podium for the master of ceremonies and other speakers. The report, headlined 'Enthusiasm at Draw', explained that 'two little blind girls' named Nora Brady and Annie Hughes had drawn the tickets. One had pulled 25 tickets naming horses, while the other drew out the 25 lucky holders who would have a chance of hitting the jackpot on the Manchester Handicap to be run within days. The lord mayor, who was supposed to oversee the probity of this event, which was still illegal despite the endorsement of the country's leader, sent his apologies for failing to show, saying he was ill. Nevertheless, the *Independent* was able to report: 'The proceedings were marked by great enthusiasm and general approval of the manner in which they were conducted.'

Blind children were chosen as a vouchsafe that there could be no peeking at the tickets being drawn. Of the 25 lucky names drawn by the two girls, 15 came from England, four from Ireland, four from Scotland and one each from Wales and Canada. When, at one point, it seemed that every ticket being drawn was from England, deputy lord mayor and master of ceremonies Alfie Byrne raised a chuckle from the audience with his quip: 'If this continues I won't be elected next year.' In fact, Byrne's long career as an elected cheerleader for Duggan's enterprises had only just begun.

When the race was run, the £5,000 first prize went to Northern Ireland, the second of £2,500 to Scotland and the third to England. By far the biggest winner, as intended, was Richard Duggan, whose mountain of cash now resembled a Swiss Alp. In the circumstances, Switzerland with its lax tax laws seemed a much better location for his next sweeps operation than Dublin's Dame Street, where the forces of law and order could come knocking any day. So that's precisely where he set up shop to begin work on his next Sweep.

But even as Duggan was finalising things with his Swiss estate agent, there were signs that he might soon fall victim to his own success, as a feeding frenzy erupted in Ireland for a bite of the sweepstakes cake.

Chapter 3 ∾

MY GOOD CAUSE IS BETTER THAN YOUR GOOD CAUSE

By the close of 1922 many of Ireland's bookies had developed a profound concern for the shortcomings of the health system and a steely determination to give it a much-needed dig-out. Hard-pressed hospital managements kept a welcome on the mat for prospective suitors.

The governors of Dublin's Jervis Street Hospital lent their name to an advert for a sweep on the Epsom Derby, urging: 'We trust no rival sweep will be run on the same race.' Their hopes were to be dashed within days when the trustees of St Patrick's Infant Home announced the inaugural Save The Child sweep to be held on the same fixture. The mortal survival of the toddlers of Dublin was said to be at stake as the trustees of the Infant Home added that they 'must raise the money or suspend activities'. Other charitable causes, not all of them hospitals, joined what began to look like a very unseemly free-for-all.

Once again there were questions in the House. Inspired by Duggan's extraordinary success, a lobby had sprung up to legalise not just sweepstakes, but casinos. During a Dáil debate in January 1923, Labour leader Thomas Johnson told Minister for Home Affairs Kevin O'Higgins: 'There is developing a belief that Ireland is to become an enlarged kind of Monte Carlo, and I would like the Ministry to give us an idea of their policy on this question.'

It was O'Higgins's stated belief that the government shouldn't be wasting time on the issue of sweepstakes while still fighting a vicious civil war, but he took time to give Johnson 'a short historical sketch' to preface his answer to the Labour man's question. He explained that in the years prior to 1907 'it was not the practice' of the authorities in Ireland to shut down lotteries 'so long as they were *bona fide* in aid of charitable and philanthropic objects, and so long as they were not run in the interest or benefit of individual promoters'. The authorities turned a practised blind eye to 'sweepstakes on races such as the Derby, and for which the tickets were mostly purchased locally. Sundry fraudulent sweeps then crept into existence, and tickets began to be broadcast throughout the United Kingdom.' The minister continued: 'That was about 1907. Questions were asked in the House of Commons as to the legality of Irish lotteries, and replies thereto given. The Irish Government (within the UK) were then compelled to take action, and proceedings were instituted against fraudulent promoters. At the same time a warning was issued that no further sweeps or drawings would be allowed, and the clubs and associations who had tickets in circulation were compelled to sign undertakings that they would not hold similar enterprises in the future. The effect was that sweepstakes and lotteries remained dormant in Ireland for practically a decade.'

Concluding his history lesson, O'Higgins said that sweeps on horse racing sprang up once again in Britain as the Great War wound to a close in 1918, with 'many complaints being addressed to the British Home Secretary of the breach of the law in Ireland'. In 1920 a ban was placed on sending sweep material through the post, which had little or no effect. What finally did work was an instruction to the postal service to open all mail suspected of carrying sweep material. That was in March 1921, four months before the War of Independence ended in an uneasy truce between Ireland and Britain.

But no sooner had statehood been hard won, complained O'Higgins in that 1923 Dáil debate, than 'on the assumption the Provisional Government would take no action, sweepstakes were again revived'. The unedifying sight of bookies playing a game of my-good-cause-is-better-than-your-good-cause had given O'Higgins the moral clout to impose a blanket ban on all sweepstakes, though he granted the exemption that those already in motion would be allowed to conclude their business.

He added: 'Charitable interests must find other means of support. It is not for me to say what those means ought to be, but this evil—and I am perfectly satisfied in my own mind that it is an evil—is spreading, and things had gone long past the stage when sweeps were being run in the interests of charitable institutions. What was happening was this. These people came along to a charitable institution and said, "You could do with £5,000, and we could do with £10,000. What about lending us your name for a sweep?" It is very hard to exercise discrimination. To put it vulgarly, how am I to know who is a crook and who is not a crook?'

The minister said that the crackdown would begin straight away under the current laws. He added that if there was a public mood to change the laws to permit sweepstakes, some deputy should table a Private Member's Bill so that the matter could be put to a vote. The pro-gambling faction in the House went to work on just such a bill.

Richard Duggan's sweep on the spring Grand National was already well advanced and so was exempt from the immediate ban. So too was the sweep of another bookmaker, P. L. Smythe, on the Lincoln. Both offered a £10,000 prize fund in aid of cancer hospitals. Duggan's vehicle was the Hollis Street Cancer Hospital. Faced with the possibility that this might be his last payday before the government shut him down, he cheekily claimed the backing of the State. One advert proclaimed: 'Final days of Duggan's Great Sweep. No time to lose. Sanctioned by the Irish Government. The only sweep for which the Lord Mayor holds the prize money.'

Smythe had also originally signalled that he would have the endorsement of Dublin's lord mayor, but the established player Duggan secured the services of the mayor, leaving Smythe with egg on his face and Dublin's High Sheriff as the next best thing. Smythe's advert read: 'Lincoln Meeting 1923 will be forever memorable. Why? Because PL Smythe's Great Lincolnshire Handicap Sweep of £10,000 is associated with it. And because the object is to assist suffering humanity against its deadliest enemy—cancer. Be sure to catch the post with your counterfoil and remittance.'

The draws for Duggan and Smythe's sweeps took place within a day of each other, and the outcomes were similar, with most of those drawn coming from Britain and North America. In the event, the lord mayor again failed to show, leaving his deputy, Alfie Byrne, to once again do the honours as genial wise-cracking host.

Duggan and Smythe went to work on new sweeps. But these were now subject to O'Higgins's crackdown. One of Duggan's next big paydays was to be on 17 October 1923 with a sweep on the Cesarewitch in aid of Dublin's Coombe Maternity Hospital. O'Higgins wrote directly to Duggan warning that he would disrupt any post to or from Duggan's operation suspected to relate to the sweep. At the same time the minister sent a memo to the General Post Office which had reported the interception of 'an undisclosed postal packet containing tickets in respect of a lottery' in aid of the colourfully named 'Cosy Nook Stall at the Coombe Lying-In Hospital'. The minister instructed: 'All such packets observed in the post should be confiscated.' There was some success in intercepting such packages, as later in the year the Minister for Finance sanctioned the payment to the Post Office of £87 1. 3 for costs 'incurred by the PO in connection with the detention of postal packets relating to sweepstakes'.

The Irish postal clampdown persuaded Smythe to get out of the sweepstakes racket, as he lamented that 'the hospitals didn't get one tenth of the letters they should have got', leaving him £30,000 out of pocket. On 8 June 1923 the British Home Office warned the Irish government that if action was not taken to shut down Duggan's operations, it would attempt to do the job itself by intercepting post from Ireland into Britain. The implied threat was that all mail from Ireland would be stopped as suspicious, which would have a debilitating and demoralising effect on the fragile newborn nation. Duggan by this time had opened his new office in Switzerland for tax purposes.

The British threat was issued between two Dáil debates on the merits of legalised gambling. In announcing his get-tough approach to sweepstakes, Minister O'Higgins had challenged the pro-gambling lobby to produce a private member's bill. It appeared very quickly, in February 1923, under the title the Charitable Hospital Bill. By the start of June the bill to legitimise the golden goose looked like a dead duck. Although Richard Duggan was never referred to by name, there were several hostile references to Switzerland and 'a man from Switzerland'.

At one point in the passage of the bill, one TD contested that a young man buying a ten shilling sweepstake ticket might be started on a career of crime that would lead to him putting his hand in the till of his employer. Sir James Craig said he thought that this was a tad far fetched. He explained that he had initially voted in favour of the bill but had since done a U-turn, persuaded by the arguments of O'Higgins that the business was open to fraud on a grand scale. Even where there was no illegality involved, Sir James feared, the scope for immorality was too great. He explained: 'One of the great objections I have to this measure was that it is possible for a private individual to say that he was going to support a charity, that he was going to give, say, £5,000 towards a charity, but that by running a sweepstake a man might be able to pocket perhaps £30,000 or £40,000, and I object to it entirely if there is anything of that nature going to be done.'

Anti-Semitism was rife in the new and avowedly Catholic Free State, as can be gauged from the contribution of Deputy Gorey, who opposed the bill with the following: 'Of every £1,000 worth of tickets sent out £400 goes to the Jewman and £600 comes back to the fellow who posted them from here. £10,000 is given in prizes, and we are told that anything from £30,000 to £90,000 is made by the men who run the scheme. I call that a public scandal and a swindle in every form. I will oppose it tooth and nail, and I will oppose the Jewmen and what they are getting out of it. You cannot go into any city or racecourse in England but you will have these fellows chasing round after you to buy these tickets. They would not do it unless they were getting £40 out of every £100. You are keeping swindlers and loafers supported all over the country by this method.'

Two of the most damning condemnations of the bill during its ill-fated passage came from Labour leader Thomas Johnson and its most powerful critic, Kevin O'Higgins. Observing that approximately 95 per cent of all the money generated came from abroad, Johnson lamented: 'It's a shameful proposition. Self-reliance? Sinn Féin? You throw yourself on the mercy of an alien administration.'

Most scathingly of all, O'Higgins snarled: 'The carpet in my office has been worn out by people whom I never suspected of being philanthropists. They wept about the condition of medical charities. They told me one little sweepstake would prevent them from being closed down.' There would be no official sanction for sweepstakes. From now on, declared O'Higgins, the law would be strictly enforced.

In November 1924 Duggan appeared in court charged under the Lotteries Act for running a venture called Duggan's Dublin Sweep. He was found guilty, fined £50 and bound over to keep the peace for a year. He was also obliged to solemnly swear that he would not organise any more sweeps. The Irish Revenue also targeted Duggan, serving him with a tax demand for £40,000. Duggan brazenly rebuffed the tax authorities, claiming that the proceeds of illegal schemes did not fall within the remit of Ireland's tax laws. The authorities found themselves forced to agree and initially dropped their claim before taking it to the High Court, which found against the bookie, before the Supreme Court finally ruled in his favour.

Richard Duggan's pledge to run no further sweepstakes was an empty one, and he was back to his old ways in 1927 with a sweep on the Epsom Derby conducted from his new headquarters in Liechtenstein. Others were quick to fill the vacuum left by Duggan during his brief absence. In 1926 the British authorities complained to the Free State government that the number of Irish gambling tickets had actually increased since the supposed crackdown of 1923.

Chapter 4 ～

| THE GO-BETWEEN

Less than five months before the MV *Leinster* was sent to the bottom of the Irish Sea, it had carried a distinguished and deeply unwilling group of passengers from Ireland to Britain. They included Sinn Féin founder Arthur Griffith and several of his key confederates, including Éamon de Valera, Constance Markievicz and 31-year-old Joseph McGrath.

Under the front page headline 'Sinn Féin Leaders Arrested and Deported', *The Irish Times* reported: 'The Lord Lieutenant on Saturday issued a proclamation announcing the discovery of a German plot in Ireland, and the intention of the Government to adopt drastic measures to put it down . . . Joseph McGrath was arrested at his home, 13 Ruttledge Terrace, Donore Avenue, Dublin. He was deported after the [1916] Rebellion and subsequently released.' Indeed, it had been just 11 months since McGrath and a group of fellow Easter Rising rebels had sailed triumphantly into Kingstown Harbour bellowing out 'The Soldier's Song' following their release from British jails. McGrath had put years of dedicated effort into becoming one of the usual suspects routinely rounded up by Ireland's Crown authorities, and he would be rounded up once again in Feburary 1920.

As a boy, McGrath paid his way by selling newspapers on the street corners of his native Dublin. Having learned the fundamentals of chartered accountancy, he secured a job with the Irish Transport & General Workers' Union sorting out members' insurance. There, he fell under the spell of the union's charismatic founder, Jim Larkin. The newly politicised McGrath cut his teeth as a front-line activist during the callous 1913 Lock-Out, in which workers who wished to unionise (and others who had no strong view) were locked out by employers in an attempt to crush the organised labour movement at birth. The willingness of the bosses to use hired thugs and imported scab labour, and to let countless Dublin women and children go hungry, only confirmed McGrath in his new-found radicalism.

A strapping 6' 2", McGrath was valued by his comrades as much for his physical prowess as his nimble mind and forceful personality. In 1912 Larkin co-founded the Irish Labour Party with the like-minded James Connolly, and Connolly made McGrath one of his trusted bodyguards as he printed his seditious and highly illegal Workers' Republic pamphlets.

By the start of 1916 McGrath was a zealous member of the oath-bound Fenian sect that called itself the Irish Republican Brotherhood. When the IRB staged the Easter Rising that year, McGrath took part in the fierce fighting at Marrowbone Lane, where the rebels dug in at a distillery. After their inevitable defeat, commander Eamonn Ceannt was executed, while Cathal Brugha, W. T. Cosgrave, McGrath and other survivors of the siege were transported to Britain, with Brixton Prison their final destination.

McGrath first met Michael Collins before the Easter Rising when they both worked in the accounting firm of Craig Gardiner. During his periods of freedom over the next few years, McGrath became a close confidant of Collins, who was shortly to become both President of the IRB secret society and Director of Intelligence of the Irish Republican Army. As sorcerer's apprentice to the master of deception, McGrath immersed himself in the dark arts of deceit that would serve him well in times to come.

Following the round-up of May 1918 to thwart a supposed 'German plot', Joe McGrath was behind bars in Britain when he learned he had been elected an MP in the general election of December that year. When the dust had settled on that momentous campaign, newcomers Sinn Féin had wiped out the old order, sweeping up 73 of the 105 Irish seats in the Westminster Parliament. Refusing to sit at Westminster, they declared themselves Dáil Éireann and sat for the first time at Dublin's Mansion House in January 1919. McGrath was otherwise detained at His Majesty's pleasure, and remained so until March 1919.

The Crown forces immediately declared war on the first Dáil and its declaration of a republic, and the guerrilla war that began in January 1919 lasted until a truce was called in July 1921. During that conflict McGrath proved himself a brave and able commander who masterminded many successful bank raids to fund the rebels. Stories persist that he and his men would always award themselves a percentage of the haul for a job well done. Captured once again in January 1921, he sat out the last six months of the freedom struggle in an English jail.

When the ceasefire between the British and rebelling Irish was called, McGrath was released to rejoin his Sinn Féin colleagues now faced with coming to peace terms with Lloyd George's government over the future shape of Ireland. During the negotiations on what was to become the Treaty, McGrath acted as an envoy between Sinn Féin and Lloyd George, and later between the London delegation led by Michael Collins and Dublin where Sinn Féin President Éamon de Valera remained in the role of self-styled puppet master. One of the messages McGrath brought home to de Valera was a protest, signed by all the members of the delegation, that Dev the puppeteer was pulling the strings so slyly and tightly he was tying their hands behind their backs.

The strings snapped. In December 1921—eyeball to eyeball with the world's greatest Empire threatening a return to dreadful war—the London delegation signed the Treaty accepting self-rule for a 26 County Free State. Back home, the puppet master bayed betrayal.

The sense of mutual betrayal was as thick in the air as the smoke that filled the Dáil chamber as the ratification of the imperfect Treaty was debated. Those who supported the Treaty argued that it bought 'the freedom to achieve freedom', and was the best deal that could have been secured. To oppose it would be an act of mindless vandalism that risked bringing down the full wrath of the British Empire. Joe McGrath followed the 'freedom to achieve freedom' argument. He spoke in favour of ratification and acted as Griffith's whip in the debate. Two months later he again defended the achievements of the London delegation as the only show in town. He told the Dáil: 'They accepted the Treaty as part-payment on a debt long overdue. They knew their own strength during the peace negotiations and they knew how far they could go.'

The Sinn Féin family split bitterly, almost down the middle, with the pro-Treaty faction carrying the day by 64 to 57. Party president Éamon de Valera marched his faction out of the Dáil and they took up arms against the pro-Treaty members of their own party who now styled themselves the Provisional Government of the Free State. As the Civil

War raged, Joe McGrath found himself holding down the civilian portfolio of Minister for Labour and the military post of Director of Intelligence. He was then given charge of the government's Criminal Investigation Department (CID).

Created by Michael Collins shortly before his death in August 1922, the CID was a parallel police division to the unarmed and uniformed Civic Guard. Armed and plain clothed, the CID's mission statement was to take the dirty war to Dev's so-called Irregulars. At its peak in early 1923, the CID had a strength of 350 heavily armed men and a handful of women. Under McGrath, the unit was accused of brutal torture and numerous assassinations.

Many years later McGrath told historian Tim Pat Coogan that he took it upon himself to restrain his detectives from 'taking care of the Long Fellow', meaning de Valera. McGrath added: 'A life meant very little to some of those men.' One killing in which McGrath would find himself publicly implicated was that of Noel Lemass, brother of the future Fianna Fáil taoiseach Seán Lemass.

Noel Lemass was captured by members of the CID on 3 July 1922. It was known that Michael Collins had suspected Lemass of opening his mail in the past, and there was a belief he had been involved in the killing of Treatyite TD Seán Hales as he left the Dáil. It was months before the body of Noel Lemass was found in the Dublin Mountains. Family members said it was badly mutilated and covered with the tell-tale marks of brutal torture. When the Civil War ended, it was deemed there was no place for a state-terrorist force like the CID in a stable democracy, and it was disbanded in October 1923.

For Joe McGrath, however, the deeds of the men under his control would bring him eventually to court—in Britain. In February 1927 McGrath stood in the London High Court taking a libel action against a *Morning Post* journalist named Bretherton who had written a book entitled *The Real Ireland*. At issue was the following passage: 'Lemass, for example, was known to have ambushed a Ford car containing three Free State soldiers and an NCO near Leeson Street Bridge, a bomb being thrown which killed three of the occupants of the car and wounded the fourth. Responsibility for the murder of Lemass was brought home with reasonable certainty to Joe McGrath, then Free State Minister for Labour, and head of the Free State Military Secret Service.'

The trial was over before it began as the ruling establishments in both Dublin and London closed ranks in a protective cordon around McGrath. The book's publishers agreed to pay over the substantial sum of £3,000 in damages. McGrath's King's Counsel, Sir Patrick Hastings, put the following statement on the court record: 'Both the English and the Irish governments are here represented, if necessary to claim privilege in respect of any matters that might arise, that many wider interests are concerned than merely with the personal character of Mr McGrath. It would be in these circumstances most unfortunate if any attempt were made on any side to revive matters that are far better forgotten and dead.'

By the time of that 1927 court case, Joe McGrath had been out of politics for two years, following a series of resignation threats, an actual resignation from his party, and a final exit from the profession. He had been a reluctant minister from the start. It had been the plan of Collins and Griffith to bring the Labour Party on board the first provisional government by offering the Labour portfolio to a Labour Party nominee. With his impeccable credentials as a sidekick of both Larkin and Connolly, McGrath was picked to act as go-between, and when he reported back that Labour wanted no hand or part in such a deal, he was asked to take the job himself.

The first of his several threats to resign came in early 1922 when postal workers went on strike. His colleague J. J. Walsh, the Postmaster General, wrote to his British counterpart looking for a list of strike-breakers who would come to Ireland and put the native mailmen in their place. The union man in McGrath was incensed, but he stopped short of going through with his threat to quit.

There was a marked shift in McGrath's attitude to the postal workers six months later. When they went on strike for a second time, the Civil War was raging and he was charged with handling the disruption to communications in his capacity as Director of Intelligence. Put on the spot, he dispatched force to harass and arrest Post Office union activists. Decades later his cabinet colleague Ernest Blythe said that McGrath 'shared the indignation felt by most of us because of the fact that workers who had never struck against the British should strike almost immediately they came under the authority of an Irish Government'.

In October 1922, as Joe McGrath was going about the business of suppressing the postal strike by fair means or foul, Richard Duggan was generating a lot of publicity for his 'monster sweep' to raise £10,000 for the Mater Hospital. President W. T. Cosgrave fielded questions in the Dáil from deputies who wanted to know why the illegal venture was not quashed. According to Arthur Webb, writing in 1968: 'He [Cosgrave] said he had discussed the matter with a member of the Dáil—many assumed he meant Joe McGrath, the Minister for Labour—before the sweepstake was initiated. The President did not give the sweep an official blessing, but he implied that he had no personal objections to the sweep being promoted by Mr Richard Duggan.' Historian Marie Coleman has written that McGrath was the key go-between who secured Duggan's audience with Cosgrave in 1922, and that the two men's acquaintance 'probably stemmed from a shared love of the turf'.

When McGrath gave his endorsement to Duggan's unlawful monster sweep of 1922, he could have had no idea that by the end of the decade the pair would be engaged together on a sweeps project that would make Duggan's big 1922 bonanza look like small change. The countdown to McGrath's departure from politics started when, with the Civil War safely over, the impoverished Free State decided it neither needed, nor could it afford, a standing army of 55,000 troops.

But the process of slashing the numbers in the army by over one-half was fraught with risk for a State which had yet to prove, even to itself, that it was a stable democracy. The army was riddled with factions, and each of these factions had its counterpart in the elected body politic, leading to a bamboozling state of affairs in 1923 and 1924 when the so-called Army Mutiny festered and burst.

The tensions and divisions in the ranks triggered by massive lay-offs on to a jobless jobs market were intensified by ideological rifts. In particular, there was the resentment of old associates of Collins that true republicans were being sidelined in the army and that the officer ranks were being systematically packed with pro-British individuals. They grumbled that Collins's 'freedom to win freedom' long game was being abandoned and that the 26 County state was becoming an end in itself.

McGrath had some sympathy for the complaints of this faction, which organised itself into a body called the Irish Republican Army Organisation (IRAO), but his stance set him at odds with others in the cabinet who feared the destabilising effect of the IRAO.

The beginning of the end came when two dissident officers

absconded, taking with them arms and ammunition. Under the terms of the Treaty, the British kept three deep-water ports for maritime security purposes. One of them was at Queenstown (now Cobh) in Cork. A boat carrying a party of British men, women and children was fired upon at Queenstown, wounding over 20 and killing one. Shell-shocked members of the cabinet linked the shooting to the missing officers.

The army mutiny became official on 6 March 1924 when the IRAO handed President Cosgrave an ultimatum at Government Buildings. The mutineers challenged the entire direction the new State was taking and demanded the suspension of the army reforms and redundancies. The following night the military authorities ordered that McGrath's home be searched for the two fugitive officers. When he refused to let them in, the soldiers took his word he wasn't harbouring any fugitives and left.

While McGrath, who by now was Minister for Industry & Commerce, accepted that most of his colleagues in the Executive Council had no advance knowledge of the raid on his home, he nevertheless resigned from government. In doing so he claimed that the midnight visit had been politically inspired by Defence Minister Richard Mulcahy in order to link him publicly to the mutineers. Whether there was a political plot against him or not, McGrath did become linked in many minds to the mutineers. The second point on which he won his 1927 libel trial was a line in the offending book which stated: 'It is considered pretty certain that he knows who were the men implicated in the attack made on British troops in Queenstown.'

Initially, it was McGrath's intention to retire completely from politics. He had been led to believe that the mutineers would be given a fair hearing, with a view to reinstating them to the ranks. When it became clear there would be no amnesty for the mutineers, McGrath, convinced he had been double-crossed, decided to stay on in politics and make himself a thorn in the side of the government.

McGrath founded his National Group, attracting a handful of disgruntled TDs from within and without the ruling party. The group initially seemed to pose a serious electoral threat to Cosgrave's government, but before too long it emerged that the press and the public regarded the National Group as a single-issue party with little to contribute on the broader canvas. It proved an evolutionary dead end and by the middle of 1925 ex-TD Joe McGrath was twiddling his thumbs and watching his funds dwindle.

Then along came an offer he couldn't refuse.

Chapter 5

PIGSTIES, INFORMERS AND BOGUS UNIONS

In January 1923 a brilliant and well-connected young engineer named Thomas McLaughlin made an audacious proposal to the Minister for Industry & Commerce, Joe McGrath. The other members of McLaughlin's audience included President W. T. Cosgrave, Finance Minister Ernest Blythe and the Attorney General Hugh Kennedy. To some of those present, what they heard had the ring more of science fiction than of the slump economics of 1920s Ireland. Arguing that neither peat nor coal could meet Ireland's pressing electricity needs, McLaughlin insisted that a hydroelectric damn on the Shannon could bring power to the whole State.

Still in his twenties, McLaughlin was home on his Christmas holidays from Germany, where he was working for Siemens-Schuckert at the cutting edge of new engineering technologies. Some months earlier he had been sent to Berlin to study the latest power plant designs. He wrote: 'In Bavaria I saw a network similar to our Shannon network, fed by water plants similar to the Shannon. What impressed me most, probably, was the network was supplying the province of Pomerania, a province with an area of about half that of our territory at home. Pomerania resembled our country in being almost entirely agricultural. An electricity network extended like a spider's web all over the country, supplying 60 towns, 1,500 villages and rural areas, and close on 3,000 farms. To this area I went and studied for myself on the spot, always with the query in my mind—why not in Ireland? From reading and from discussions I learned of the large-scale electricity networks of other countries. Of Sweden and Switzerland, of Italy and France, of Canada and of the United States. . . . Quickly came the determination that at home in Ireland we must have a national electricity network reaching to our cities, towns and villages, and on out to the rural areas. My country, of which I was so intensely proud, must not lag behind other lands.'

Cosgrave and other members of the cabinet were sceptical of McLaughlin's flighty scheme. Not only did they harbour doubts about the technical feasibility of it, but the men dubbed the most conservative revolutionaries in history also harboured a *laissez-faire* belief that private enterprise should supply whatever demand there was. However, it was already apparent to many that the patchwork of small private electricity firms scattered about the country was not up to the task.

The cities and larger towns were generally well serviced by private generators, but in villages and rural areas a lack of competition made electricity prohibitively expensive. Large swathes of the land had no power supply at all, severely limiting the output potential of farms and other manufacturers. The annual energy consumption per head in the Free State was almost three times lower than in Northern Ireland. Only dirt poor Portugal had a lower per capita consumption.

McLaughlin made a persuasive case for his national scheme, but even after gaining acceptance for the general principle, he had to fight for a site on the Shannon against a lobby who favoured harnessing the power of the Liffey. When word reached Britain that the Irish government was in negotiations with Siemens-Schuckert, the *Daily Mail* ran a condemnation headlined: German Intrigue in Ireland—Bid for Economic Control'. The *Mail* claimed that the 'Siemens Syndicate' was plotting to use the scheme as a Trojan Horse to set up a German-controlled state on Britain's back doorstep. First the dastardly Germans would establish an electricity monopoly, which they would use to take over Ireland's industry, which in turn they would use as a cash cow to repatriate profits into a German economy still struggling to pay back crippling reparation penalties from World War I.

Despite the taunts of the British press, the Shannon Electricity Bill passed into law in June 1925. A spot on the Shannon by the sleepy Clare village of Ardnacrusha had been chosen as the site for the hydroelectric dam, the biggest engineering project ever undertaken on the island of Ireland. In a land where job opportunities were scarce, the opening of this vast state-sponsored construction project held out the prospect of steady work and decent money. But when the adverts appeared in September seeking 3,000 labourers at a rate of 32 shillings for a 50 hour week, there was widespread dismay at the low wages on offer. Even so, by the time the adverts appeared, a huge throng of would-be workers had already descended on the banks of the Shannon.

When the unions called for a fairer deal, Siemens countered that the pay was fair. The Germans argued that the going rate reflected that of agricultural labourers and the unions' mistake was to seek parity with urban labourers who earned more than their rural cousins. The unions countered in turn that farm labourers could usually expect perks of the job on top of their wages, whereas the only so-called perk the Shannon Scheme workers were being offered was a bed for the night, which in many cases was floor space in a barn or even a pigsty.

Almost before a sod had been turned on the State's showcase scheme, a strike was called. And no sooner had the strike been called than Big Joe McGrath was summoned to fill the role of troubleshooter. According to McGrath's one-time cabinet colleague Ernest Blythe, writing much later, President Cosgrave brought McGrath into the picture because he was 'at a loose end'. According to Blythe: 'He brought with him to Ardnacrusha some of the men with whom he had been associated in Army Intelligence, or whom he had got to know at the time of the Mutiny. It was popularly believed that thereafter, a man working on the Shannon Scheme could not curse the weather without his words being reported to Joe.'

Blythe's jocular tone at a distance of decades was in jarring contrast to the dismay of the union leaders when they learned of McGrath's appointment as Director of Labour for the scheme. McGrath brought the striking Transport Union to the table, and when the negotiations stalled he went to another source of labour, paying a new influx of ex-servicemen the 50 shillings a week which would have averted the strike in the first place. Within three months of his arrival, McGrath had broken the strike. He stayed on to keep the workforce in line, in conditions never far from toppling into anarchy.

Apart from the paltry pay, the living conditions for many of the workers on the Shannon Scheme were shameful. A shanty town had sprung up around Ardnacrusha, its population swollen by hundreds of men just hanging around in the hope that a few days' work might come their way. In June 1926 a meeting of the Clare County Board of Health heard that between 12 and 14 workers had made their home in a stable at Blackwater, while a married couple were living in a pigsty attached to a labourer's cottage. On any construction scheme of such a size, there were bound to be serious injuries and other afflictions on a daily basis, and very quickly the surrounding hospitals were groaning under the strain.

The pigsty, the stable and the shantytown proved shocking images, even in an Ireland where many hadn't two ha'pennies to rub together. This was no one's vision of a new, proudly self-sufficient land of freedom. Within days the *Irish Independent* had a reporter at the entrance of the infamous pigsty.

The *Independent* reported: 'The latter accommodates a husband, a wife and two children. Some of the places in which men are sleeping are not at all fit for human beings. There was one place referred to by the Home Assistance Officer. It was merely an out-office. It might have housed horses or cattle. The beds consisted of old hay, thrown on the floor, with no suggestion of bed clothing. One of the heaps of hay was semi-covered with an old sack. This was the very place in which fifteen men slept up to a short time ago. The number has now dwindled down to eight, and those men are paying rent for the privilege of the accommodation.'

Further on, the piece continued: 'The Camp Commandant at Ardnacrusha, Mr WJ Stapleton, when interviewed on the matter, stated that it was possible there were men living in outhouses, but they were not employed on the Scheme and that it was not because of lack of accommodation . . . He went on to say that when hut accommodation was not available, the fact was stated to the men before they were employed, and as a result of the rapidly approaching completion of the temporary works at Ardnacrusha, between 200 and 300 men had been disemployed during the past month. Whilst an effort was being made to give them at least one night's accommodation after dismissal, they could not be held responsible for them afterwards.

'A further matter which he pointed out was that men were arriving at the works daily from all parts of the country, oftimes penniless, seeking to find employment and unable to find any. It was quite conceivable that those men in numerous instances were obliged to sleep out.'

The media outcry led to a Dáil debate, where McGrath's successor at Industry & Commerce, Patrick McGilligan, dismissed reports of squalor, saying: 'You may take it *prima facie* that the press is inaccurate.'

It was McGilligan who had signed the contract with Siemens, tying the Germans to the most flimsy health and safety commitments. Asked to prevail upon them now to take greater responsibility for their sick and injured, the minister said it was outrageous to think of asking such a thing.

The storm of publicity over the workers' conditions might have been expected to provide the perfect platform for the unions to raise their voice once again. Instead, their silence was deafening. Joe McGrath had done his job well. In April, two months before the story reached the press, a meeting had been held with the aim of recruiting unskilled Shannon Scheme men into the ITGWU, the union which Joe McGrath had helped to get on its feet more than a decade earlier. The recruitment drive petered out, along, seemingly, with all meaningful attempts to organise labour on the project.

According to historian Michael McCarthy: 'The apparent disengagement by the unions, following so rapidly on the heels of the strike which had held up work on the Scheme for months, may have been because at this point the unions were demoralized. McGrath had out-flanked and out-played the unions during the strike by hiring ex-servicemen from the Free State Army, including a captain as camp commandant, while excluding would be troublemakers and union organizers. The contractors also, reportedly, encouraged the formation of bogus unions in the Ardnacrusha camp, set up an effective camp-informer network, and employed a "heavy gang" to enforce law and order.'

In years and decades to come, Joe McGrath would brush off repeated charges of running a bogus union in the Irish Hospitals Sweepstakes in order to frustrate attempts to mobilise a real one.

The Shannon Scheme was officially launched on 22 July 1929 when, following a blessing by the Bishop of Killaloe, President Cosgrave threw the switch to open the sluice gates that would bring Ireland into the modern power age.

The shock-horror coverage of the summer of 1926 had long since subsided, and housing and medical conditions had improved only marginally, if at all. In 1928 one lead story in the *Clare Champion* had blared: 'Crowds in Stable—Shocking Conditions at Ardnacrusha'. Subsequent research has shown that the Germans had been willing to fund better accommodation for their Irish workers, but the government, in the person of Patrick McGilligan, was obsessed with shaving every expenditure to the bone.

McGrath and McGilligan were demonised in a piece of doggerel published in the magazine *Voice of Labour*. It began:

I am McGilligan, McGilligan, McGilligan!
Never shall you see such wonderful skill again.
I've got a plan on
Down where the Shannon
Rolls to the foaming sea.
Jealous folks say it is a bit of a gamble
But we know better, don't we?
For there's Siemens-Schuckert and Gordon Campbell,
Joe McGrath and McLaughlin and me!

Writing many years later of McGrath's four years as enforcer on the Shannon Scheme, his old cabinet colleague Ernest Blythe contended: 'He ensured that Ardnacrusha came in on time to the delight of the Government.'

On the face of it, in the autumn of 1929 Joe McGrath was once again out of work and on the look-out for gainful employment. In fact, he had already embarked on the biggest enterprise of his life, and he had every intention of cashing in on the goodwill he had stored up in the form of government delight.

Chapter 6

TUMBLING OVER THEMSELVES TO GET HOLD OF A CHARITY

When the renowned surgeon and president of the Irish Medical Board, John Shanley, died in 1996 at the age of 101, one obituary credited him with lighting the touch-paper on the Irish Hospitals Sweepstakes.

It stated: 'John Shanley, with a few colleagues and friends, discussed their [hospital funding] problems with Joe McGrath and Dick Duggan. The latter contacted Dougie Stuart, a famous Glasgow bookie. When he agreed to be the financial guarantor, W. T. Cosgrave issued a licence, so the Irish Hospitals Sweepstakes were born, with the first funds going to Cappagh and Jervis Street Hospitals.'

It was never so simple as that. Following the clampdowns in Ireland and Britain of 1923, some sweeps promoters had quit the business. Richard Duggan, on the other hand, had defied the ban by running a moderately successful sweep on the 1927 Epsom Derby from the safe distance of Liechtenstein. But Duggan had bigger fish to fry, and his roving mind kept drifting back to the banks of the River Liffey. In the doubtful event that Shanley had made the first move to contact Duggan and McGrath, it was because they had expertly cleared his path to their door. The pair had been working away behind the scenes grooming politicians, medics and hospital committees into a state of receptiveness for their Big Idea.

The big idea in question was a new sweepstakes to benefit Irish hospitals, but this time one rubber stamped by the Irish Free State. In an age of fly-by-night lotteries, any venture which could claim any sort of lawful status would have a decisive marketing edge over the competition. As with Duggan's earlier enterprises, neighbouring Britain would provide the obvious target market, but from the outset plans were laid to ensure the new venture would have a global sweep. In the summer of 1928, a full year before Duggan and McGrath began canvassing their scheme openly, they wined and dined an influential American who was passing through Dublin. Satisfied that they had found their man to get the ball rolling in the United States, they told him to leave everything with them and they would be in touch.

As for the Glasgow bookie Dougie Stuart, he was no more a real person than Ronald McDonald or the Michelin Man. Douglas 'Dougie' Stuart was the corporate creation of two British bookies, Sidney Freeman and Harry Benson, who at one point had run their own small-scale lottery into Britain from the tax loophole of Liechtenstein. Freeman and Benson saw the potential of a lawful Irish-based sweepstakes and became investors.

In June 1929 the grand scheme began to hatch. Deputy Patrick Shaw stood up in the Dáil and made the transparently preposterous claim that elaborate sums of cash were being siphoned out of the Free State into sweepstakes in Britain and other foreign parts. This piece of nonsense was simply a hook on which to hang the real meat of his set-piece where he asked the Minister for Justice 'whether he will consider the advisability of introducing proposals for legislation to permit of similar sweepstakes being organised in the Saorstát, in view of the benefits that would be derived by hospitals and other such deserving objects, in addition to providing employment?'

The minister replied: 'I have no information as to the amount of money which leaves the Saorstát for investment in British and foreign sweepstakes. The answer to the second part of the question is in the negative.' Deputy Shaw gave 'notice' that the issue would not be dropped.

And dropped it was not. Shortly afterwards, deputies found on their desks the draft of a private member's bill, entitled the Public Charitable Hospitals (Temporary Provisions) Bill 1929, sponsored by Sir James Craig, a Protestant representing Trinity College Dublin. Absent from the Dáil which debated Craig's bill were the two men who had done most to shoot down the sweeps legislation of six years earlier.

Two years previously, in July 1927, the hardline Justice Minister Kevin

O'Higgins was gunned down by three anti-Treaty IRA hitmen as he walked to Mass on Booterstown Avenue in south Dublin. Thomas Johnson of the Labour Party had been elevated to the talking shop of the Senate where he would once again wax eloquent against the legalisation of sweepstakes, but this time at a remove from the real levers of power.

As he moved the second reading of the bill in February 1930, Craig took the highly unusual step of distancing himself from the piece of legislation he was bringing before the House. He began by stating: 'In its inception I had no part. It originated with a Joint Committee of six or eight hospitals, the financial position of which was so precarious that they were threatened unless funds could be raised by some means in the near future. I understand that the combined indebtedness of these six hospitals as far as overdrafts to the bank are concerned is not less than £60,000.'

The bill provided that public charitable hospitals offering free treatment could establish sweepstake committees to submit schemes to the Minister for Justice. If the minister was satisfied that a scheme was above board, it was given legal sanction. Prize money must be lodged in a bank in advance of the sweep. Promoters were entitled to a seven per cent cut of all ticket money raised, with 20 per cent going to the hospitals. Properly audited accounts for each sweep must be supplied to the minister and every Dáil deputy within three months of the event. Concerns were raised that the promoters' seven per cent off the gross turnover was too generous, and the figure was later trimmed by an amendment in the Senate.

Craig was at pains to point out that he was just the slightly reluctant messenger. As he told it: 'The Bill was actually placed in my hands before I knew any proposal of such a sort had been adopted by these hospitals, and I may say at once if there had seemed to me any other method of securing financial aid for the poverty-stricken hospitals I should not have consented to bringing the measure before the Dáil. I have no great desire to see the hospitals supported by means of sweepstakes, but I am driven to this position, that these hospitals which are involved have practically no other means by which they are to subsist unless a measure such as I am proposing tonight passes the Oireachtas.'

The bill, drawn up by a person or persons unknown, should be given a chance as a short-term experiment, said Craig. He insisted: 'It is only a temporary measure. This is not a permanent measure. I want to lay stress on this fact.' A clause in the legislation stipulated that it would only remain in force for four years from its inception, lapsing on 1 July 1933, which was later amended to 1934.

President Cosgrave gave the bill the most lukewarm of endorsements, but the most important thing for Duggan and McGrath was that he gave no negative directions to members of his party. Cosgrave began by pointing out: 'This Bill is not a Government Bill. It is a Private Member's Bill and there is an open vote to be taken on it.' He said that government deputies had objections to the bill, not in its own right, but because it could open the door to unscrupulous promoters. His key contribution was that he was ideologically opposed to the State running the hospital system. That being the case, funding by sweepstakes seemed the lesser of two evils and should be given a chance.

In an era when anti-English sentiment was strong, there was a predictable proposal that the sweeps should be held on Irish and not English races, with the speaker contending: 'You're turning people's minds away from their affairs at home, to English newspapers. I do not like encouraging our people to be constantly reading papers that set their minds on foreign races.'

Dismissing this objection, President Cosgrave chipped in: 'I do not think there is anything in the objection that was made to sweepstakes being on English races. It has so happened that English races are particularly attractive for more reasons than one. There is a general ambition on the part of persons to own the winner of the Grand National. More horses enter here in respect of this than of any other race. It is a great feat of endurance.'

The bill faced a rougher passage in the Senate where Senator Robinson made a prescient contribution. He warned: 'I refer to the dangers that the promoters are in. Amendments introduced today by Senator Farren have obviated the danger of general or wholesale corruption on the part of the sellers of tickets. But as far as the promoters are concerned there is very little protection except the audit. There are many ways of getting around an audit.'

Now moved from the Dáil to the Senate, Duggan's old enemy Thomas Johnson once again insisted that the State would surely be dragged into disrepute by its association with sweepstakes. He insisted: 'The general scheme should not be one that, even by implication, is being run under State auspices or any auspices or authority or sanction of the Minister for Justice, especially in view of the statement made by the Minister and his predecessor as to the difficulty of providing against evil practices by law or by Departmental regulation. The feeling is that there is very considerable risk of fraud.'

The bill was being promoted as a 'temporary' measure which would elapse after a period of four years, but Johnson argued that once the genie was out of the bottle it would be out for good. He predicted with expert crystal ball gazing: 'In those four years very many sweepstakes can be promoted, all kinds of hospitals can seek the approval of the Minister for their sweepstakes. By that time the industry of sweepstakes promotion will have become established. There will, no doubt, be a considerable number of people employed as clerks, and, as I said on a previous debate on sweepstakes, vested interests, if one may so speak, will have grown up. It was put forward as one reason why these sweeps might be legitimised that there were 600 clerks employed, and if you refuse permission to carry on the sweeps you will throw on the unemployment market 600 clerks. That was the argument then used. But the establishment and legitimisation of these sweepstakes for four years will mean that there will be a considerable plea at the end of the four years for their continuation, on the grounds that otherwise you are going to disemploy a certain number of clerks.'

Warming to his theme, Johnson singled out Richard Duggan's offshore operations for special mention, saying: 'One of the members of the Dáil Committee who has a considerable knowledge of the circumstances and conditions under which these sweeps will be run informed that Committee that the probability was that a great deal of the work will be done in Switzerland, because it seems that there is an organisation available there which it was not quite convenient to transfer to this country. It is, of course, set out that the printing will be done in this country, and that is part of the bribe for the legalisation, for a specific purpose, of sweepstakes. I do not think there has ever been a bill introduced covering four or five pages and with ten or eleven sections which contained more objectionable features than this.

'There are many loopholes for fraud. There is very little in the bill to prevent fraud. Those of us who are in the way of being pestered by children and others in trying to sell to us those minor sweepstake tickets will know quite well how easy it is for fraud to be committed in this matter. You are proposing to send out, under the scheme embodied in the bill, millions of sweepstake tickets. In the case of two sweeps it was reported that not less than three million tickets had been issued and somewhere else it was reported that nine out of every ten that are issued are never returned. Is there any safeguard under this bill which will ensure that the people who buy tickets receive the chance for which they are paying? Is there anything to ensure that the person who sells the tickets will forward the counterfoil to the head office to ensure that the ticket number will be drawn? There is nothing whatever to ensure these things and I am as certain as I am here standing that there are many thousands of tickets sold all over the world to people who are attracted by the name of a hospital but whose tickets never come within the scheme and whose chances of drawing a prize are nil.'

Taking another swipe on another occasion, Johnson charged: 'The professional promoters are tumbling over themselves to get hold of a charity. They are like the professional beggar who gets hold of the most decrepit child for exciting the charity of the public.'

Johnson's contention that many tickets would never have the slightest chance of being drawn would be borne out in the very first draw of the Irish Hospitals Sweepstakes in November 1930.

Chapter 7

THEY KEPT ALL THE MONEY, OF COURSE

The third member of the Hospitals Sweeps triumvurate was, at 38, also the youngest. Spencer Freeman was dispatched from England to look after the financial interests of Dougie Stuart, the bookmaking firm founded by his brother Sidney, which was the scheme's major financier.

If Richard Duggan was the financial brains of the outfit and McGrath was the man with the contacts in the corridors of power, Freeman would quickly turn out to be the publicity genius instrumental in making the Irish Sweeps one of the showbiz wonders of the age. Welsh by birth and raised in South Africa, Freeman gave up a shining academic career at the age of 18 in 1910 to head for the United States where his ambition was to become an engineer.

He started with the Pullman Car Company in Pennslyvania on the very bottom rung, as a cleaner. After working his way up to the design office, he hit the road for Detroit where the automobile industry was in its infancy. There he got a job testing cars for faults. Pullman lured him back to Pennsylvania with an improved package, but the move was short lived.

When war was declared in 1914 he sailed for England and enlisted as a private. Within a year he had risen through the ranks from corporal to second lieutenant. He found his ideal job behind the lines in France, taking control of the Rouen depot of the Royal Army Service Corps which repaired motor vehicles and got them back into active service. His reward was another swift promotion, this time to captain. On a tour of inspection, the press baron Lord Northcliffe gave Freeman's operation a glowing commendation, describing the young officer as 'a round peg in a round hole'.

Back on civvy street, Freeman became an entrepreneur, sourcing or manufacturing materials and goods to meet gaps in the market. It was a precarious existence, however, so when the call came from Duggan and McGrath to join their ambitious sweepstake scheme, there was little hesitation in saying yes. A sweep of the scale Duggan and McGrath envisaged needed an organiser. Bookmaker Sidney Freeman said his younger brother was the man with the skills. It would turn out to be an inspired choice.

In the summer of 1930 the Public Charitable Hospitals (Temporary Provisions) Act was signed into law. Even before that happened, Duggan and Co. were certain they had a done deal. Before it was formally passed, Duggan, McGrath and Freeman had six needy hospitals on board and had set up a limited company in order to be first out of the stalls. A Hospitals Committee was set up packed with right honourable gentlemen to show that the new venture was one of impeccable respectability, but the Hospitals Committee, while it was good for photo-opportunities and speech-making, was good for little else. The real business of the Hospitals Sweepstakes was run by Hospitals Trust Limited controlled by Duggan, McGrath and Spencer.

From the outset, based on the success of Duggan's monster Mater Hospital Sweep of eight years earlier and others, it was clear that Britain was going to be the main target market. Duggan had assembled a mailing list of Irish migrants across the Irish Sea who had bought tickets for his earlier sweeps. Those migrants could hopefully be relied upon to act as a ready-made distribution network operating beneath the radar of the British authorities.

In a 1968 book written in lavish praise of the Hospitals Sweepstakes organisation—it was entitled *The Clean Sweep*—author Arthur Webb cited another factor the trio were gambling on. He wrote: 'Another great asset they had was the Sweeps Act itself. Sweepstakes did not enjoy Government patronage. Indeed the Act sternly prohibited any suggestion that they were held under their auspices. But the Government had to endorse all arrangements. With the percentage of profit and prizes fixed by the Government, the funds banked under the Government's eye and balance sheets published for the Government to inspect, the public had a complete picture of where the money would go and possibly found it hard to distinguish between such close supervision and outright Government sponsorship. This would be a really clean sweep!'

The previous year, 1929, TD Seán Lemass had memorably described Fianna Fáil's relationship to the State as being that of 'a slightly constitutional party'. The Irish Hospitals Sweep could have been described in similar terms, but Webb was emphatically correct in saying that the new enterprise would immediately be seen, at home and abroad, as an arm of the Free State. However, Webb was outlandishly wide of the mark in claiming that 'the public had a complete picture of where the money would go'. Nobody would ever have a complete picture of where the money would go, most likely including Duggan, McGrath and Spencer. That's how the business was structured.

The trio set up an office in a large empty house on Earlsfort Terrace in central Dublin. With the Great Depression becoming ever greater by the day, their adverts for female staff brought a queue quickly to their door. It was the summer of 1930. They had selected the Manchester Handicap in November as the big race around which the first sweep would be staged.

The process now was this. Books of ten shilling tickets would be printed and mailed to 'agents', mostly meaning the people on Duggan's list who had participated in earlier sweeps. The tickets were elegantly produced to resemble banknotes. Each book of ten tickets would be sold for £5. An inspired move was to put 12 tickets in each £5 book, giving the agent the choice of selling the extra brace of tickets for a profit, or keeping them to have a free flutter. Each ticket was made up of the ticket itself, which the buyer would keep, and a peel-away counterfoil which would be self-addressed and mailed back to Dublin for the big draw. Counterfoils would be shuffled and mixed before being funnelled into a big cylindrical drum sitting centre stage on a podium. Each ticket drawn from the drum would match a horse running days later in the Manchester Handicap.

By the middle of October the three promoters realised they had backed a runaway winner. The trio's original hope had been to generate £100,000 in ticket sales. The target was soon upsized to raising a prize pot of £100,000. As they intensified their press advertising campaign through October and the cash and counterfoils blew in like a paper blizzard, the prize fund grew beyond their wildest ambitions. By late October the pot had ballooned to £150,000. A fortnight later they were taking out full page adverts exclaiming: 'There is no doubt that more than £200,000 will be available as prize money. Someone is going to win a first prize of £100,000. Your chance of winning an immense fortune is slipping away. What about that house, that car, those friends you would like to help? Money to accomplish all you desire may be yours.' The prize fund soared to a jaw-dropping £300,000.

As the prize bonanza grew and grew and the Manchester November Handicap aproached ever nearer, the British authorities couldn't help but notice that something was afoot. There were questions in the House of Commons, and reports that the British Post Office was under orders once again to intercept mail from Ireland. But as the big race neared, it became clear that the authorities had been wrong-footed by the crafty audacity of the heist through Britain's back door.

The supreme showman Spencer Freeman went to work making sure that news of the first Irish Hospitals Sweepstake would travel far and wide. He sent out personal invites to Britain's most powerful newspaper executives to come to Dublin for the grand draw. He brought over the top writers and editors and wined and dined them in the finest style. The most celebrated guest lured by the offer of an all expenses-paid trip to Ireland was the prolific novelist, playwright and scribbler Edgar Wallace, who happened to be Sidney Freeman's best friend. The two had shared a tent while fighting the Boer War 30 years earlier. The hard-living Wallace was in his element on the Dublin junket, quipping: 'I am a journalist. I have the greatest objection to paying my own expenses.' On his return to Hollywood the following year, Wallace would write the original screenplay for the movie classic *King Kong*.

While the international newspapermen in Dublin were being seduced into sending out glowing reports, some stranded at home took a dimmer view of the new sweep. Days before the draw one British paper suggested that the sweep could be the ruination of horse racing there by encouraging unscrupulous ticket-holders to bribe equally unscrupulous owners to run nags that had no hope of competing.

The writer argued: 'It is possible that a horse which has been drawing a roundsman's van, which has never been in training, and which has never jumped a fence, may be one of the starters for the Grand National next March. This alarming possibility is foreshadowed by the effect which the Irish Hospitals Sweepstake has had on the Manchester November Handicap, for which a "record" field is expected to go to the post on Saturday. The prize for a runner is so much greater than that for a non-starter that the drawer of a horse still left in that race is in a position to offer its owner a substantial inducement to run. There is nothing to prevent a horse with no pretentions of jumping from being entered in the Grand National, providing it has been registered.' Supporting that contention, Lord Decies said there could be 100 starters in the next Grand National as against the normal 30, as owners entered 'dud' horses in the hope of extracting a pay-off from a ticket-holder.

In plain English, the argument was that owners would enter completely unsuitable horses in the knowledge that someone would draw a ticket bearing the horse's name. If the owner scratched the horse on the grounds that it was useless, the bearer of the ticket would receive the consolation prize of £491. However, if the horse merely turned up on the day and set its hoof over the starting line, the ticket-holder was automatically entitled to a payout of £2,004. The incentive for hatching underhand deals was obvious. Under pressure from the turf industry, the Hospitals Trust subsequently virtually abolished the difference in prize money for starters and non-starters.

The day before the big race, American newspapers which were lapping up sweeps-related stories, ran a variation on the theme under the headline, 'Racketeers Threaten Sweepstake Entries'. The sub-headline expanded: 'Two Holders of Tickets in Irish Prize Contest Told to "Pay Up or Your Horse Won't Run".' The report read: 'A new problem of turf racketeering has arisen from the big Irish sweepstakes which have attracted world-wide attention to the Manchester November Handicap to be run tomorrow, weather permitting. At least two holders of tickets for horses still left in the race are reported to have been threatened with the words: "Pay up or your horse won't run." A share of the winnings is being demanded from them. Whether a horse runs or is scratched means the difference between $48,370 and $2,670 [the newspaper got these figures wrong—DC]. The ticket-holder whose horse starts will get the former, while the ticket-holders of the non-starters will receive the latter amount. The proposed launching of other big sweepstakes means that jockey club stewards will have an entirely new situation to face, it being obvious that some changes in the rules will be necessary to cope with it.'

In Dublin, meanwhile, on the eve of the race as the journalists' jamboree was winding down, circus master Spencer Freeman was basking in the satisfaction of a job well done and all eyes were turning to Manchester. The draw at the Mansion House had gone swimmingly, and pictures had been wired around the globe of the line of little blind boys plucking counterfoils from the big cylindrical drum under the watchful eyes of Police Commissioner General Eoin O'Duffy and the ever reliable Alfie Byrne, now at the start of a long reign as Dublin's Lord Mayor.

Seventy-nine tickets were pulled and matched to the 79 horses originally entered in the Handicap. All but 28 of these named horses, for a variety of reasons, were non-runners, but even a non-runner paid out the substantial sum of £491. A beaming Lord Powerscourt, chairman of the Hospitals Committee, announced that the six hospitals who had lent their name to the sweep would share a very welcome £131,798. Duggan, McGrath and Freeman of the Hospitals Trust shared a windfall of £46,085.

But that was only half the excitement, because even these two phenomenal figures combined would not come near the £204,764 which would be paid out to one of the 28 ticket-holders with a starter in the big race. When race day came, Manchester became the focus of the whole world's attention.

From the furthest point on the globe, Australia's *Melbourne Argus* began its extensive coverage: 'Twenty-eight horses stampeding in the mud in the Manchester November Handicap completely changed the future lives of many Irish Sweep ticket holders. A Belfast civil servant, being unable to sell the last of his book of tickets, shared it with two local barmen and drew the first prize of £204,764. As they [had previously] sold one half of the ticket for £3,000 their net win was £102,382. They made the night journey from Belfast to see the race, and quietly went for a drink when they saw Glorious Devon win. "My greatest immediate need," said the civil servant, "is a good sleep, for I have had bad nights ever since we drew the horse."'

At the Dublin draw the ticket bearing the name of Belfast man Frank Ward had been matched to the heavily fancied Glorious Devon. In fact, Ward and two barmen had each put in a third of the ten shilling ticket price. Had the three sat tight and held their nerve, they could have picked up the whole winning prize of £204,764, enough to keep all three in luxury for several lifetimes. On the other hand, a single slip or stumble on the greasy winter turf could leave Glorious Devon outside the top three finishers and the northerners' reward slashed a hundredfold.

This was the dilemma posed to the three by bookmakers Ladbrokes, who were on Ward's Belfast doorstep in record time with a poser for him. Ladbrokes would pay the three men the small fortune of £2,500 upfront for a half-share of the ticket, plus another £800 if Glorious Devon won. After much brain-rattling, the three agreed to sell a 50 per cent share. Other holders of tickets on fancied horses were also approached by Ladbrokes and other bookies. Some sold; others opted to keep the whole ticket and take their chances.

What the bookies already knew from earlier sweepstakes run by Richard Duggan and others, was that sweepstakes were a boon to the bookmaking profession. At the very heart of that profession is the ability to calculate the odds so that, no matter what the outcome of an event, there is less paid out on winning bets than is taken in on losing bets. In the case of the Manchester November Handicap, bookies would attempt to lay off their liabilities by paying a few thousand each for shares in tickets on runners with a prospect of winning.

Glorious Devon was heavily backed by the punters. If the horse won, the bookies would have to pay out large sums to the betting public. But by buying a half-share in the sweeps ticket on Glorious Devon, it didn't matter to Ladbrokes if the horse won, because the bookmaker would have £102,000 to meet those payouts. If, on the other hand, an unfancied runner won, that didn't matter either, since in that case there would be few bets to pay out. It was a win-win situation for any bookie who could catch up with the ticket-holders first.

That fact was well known to ace bookmaker Richard Duggan and to the Spencer brothers of the hugely successful Dougie Stuart bookmaking firm. Not only were they bookmakers, but they were now bookmakers with an inside track. Over the next couple of years they would become the undisputed world heavyweight champions of a caper they called 'plucking the chickens'. But more of that later.

There was no time for Duggan, McGrath and Spencer to rest on their lavishly upholstered laurels. The women in their employ were already at work in preparation for the second Irish Hospitals Sweepstake, on the Aintree Grand National of the following spring. Flush with money, the promoters decided that the grand spectacle of the second draw would make the acclaimed first carnival look like the dress rehearsal of a village amateur dramatic society. Among Spencer Freeman's pressing priorities was the need to replace the cylindrical drawing drum with an upgrade of much greater capacity. Because at the heart of the glowing global triumph of the first Irish Hospitals Sweepstake lay a dark secret not to be let out.

Early in his book, *The Clean Sweep*, Arthur Webb wrote of Richard Duggan and Joe McGrath: 'Neither had any reason to suspect that their paths were to meet and merge and become a highway thickly carpeted with the world's money.' That thickly carpeted highway was laid down at the first attempt, on the evidence of the first Irish journalist to properly investigate the Sweeps.

Decades after that momentous week in November 1930, veteran reporter Joe MacAnthony revealed: 'There was a bookmaker, and his son told me that the bookmaker went to see them [the promoters] on the day of the first lottery in 1930. And they were in the room, and the room floor was covered with money. They were walking in money. They had bags of tickets upstairs. Tens of thousands of tickets that never went into the drum. The drum they had designed just wasn't big enough. They had no idea they were going to hit the level that they did. So masses of the very first people never got into the drum. And they kept all the money, of course.'

Chapter 8

PROTECT ME FROM ALL EVIL CHARMS

Duggan, McGrath and Freeman had created a monster. Now they had to harness it, control it and milk it for all it was worth. And that was precisely what they went about doing.

With their first sweep they had struck a chord that chimed sweetly through the gloom of the Great Depression. The $2 million prize fund—the biggest ever heard of—found claimants on four continents. From Adelaide to Anchorage newspapers splurged on the pageantry of the Dublin draw, on Glorious Devon's romp to victory, but most of all on the dream-come-true stories of everyday folk made rich beyond imagining.

Britain had accounted for 40 of the 79 tickets drawn from the drum and the buzz there proved contagious. The whole British nation launched itself gleefully into the throes of sweepmania. Cinema audiences lapped up the fairytale beginning, middle and ending with ravenous eyes. Newsreel films of the big Dublin draw were repackaged with footage of the Manchester race, and then rerun again with shots of the prizewinners receiving their cheques. It wasn't yet December 1930, but already the scramble was on to procure tickets for the second sweep on the 1931 Aintree Grand National. For millions of people around the world bewitched by the double-barrelled extravaganzas of Dublin and Manchester, the Grand National in March couldn't come soon enough.

Meanwhile, Dubliners marvelled as a second, even greater deluge of cash began pouring down on their backwater city early in the new year of 1931. Ticket applications for the second sweep clogged the mail service. Overnight the new enterprise had leapfrogged the Guinness brewery to become the country's biggest cash turnover business. The

Bank of Ireland had to recruit extra staff to cope with the haystacks of international banknotes coming from far and wide.

From the United States, the *Catholic Bulletin* condemned the Hospitals Sweepstakes as 'a great international scandal, a malignant menace, a putrid pool, a giant evil'. No one in Catholic Ireland was reading the *Catholic Bulletin*. Doctors, nurses, politicians, lawyers, judges and even parish priests were among the pillars of Irish society only too willing to provide 'depot' addresses for Sweepstakes-bound post. Because participating in the Irish Sweep was illegal in Britain, North America and many other places, anyone so foolish as to address a missive to 'Irish Sweep, Dublin, Ireland' was inviting confiscation and prosecution before it had even travelled beyond their own borders. So the Sweeps promoters set up scores of bogus depot addresses to get the precious incoming post to within a few miles of the Earlsfort Terrace HQ without arousing the suspicions of snoopy foreign postal workers.

Irish postal workers, on the other hand, were known to earn a little backhand bonus by ensuring that the foreign mail travelled safely those last few miles to Dublin's city centre. This thriving nixer culture was well known to officials in the upper echelons of the Irish postal service, which found itself in something of a bind, given that the vast mailshots from Earlsfort Terrace provided a huge boost to revenue. With airmail in its infancy, post travelled by sea, and the newspapers carried 'Notes on Foreign Mails'. Tuesday was the biggest mailing day of the week. This was when the post was shipped to the US and Canada via Southampton, and the day it went to Cyprus, Zanzibar, the Dutch East Indies and all points east via Marseilles. On Saturdays it went to the South American staging posts of Colombia, Mexico and Ecuador, sailing from Cobh.

Some of the Sweeps-bound incoming mail caused an amount of head-scratching. The *Donegal Vindicator* reported that one letter arrived addressed to Hospitals Trust Ltd, Duragla-la-Pharie. According to the newspaper, the clever postman deciphered that Duragla-la-Pharie was the sender's stab at spelling Dun Laoghaire. He then obligingly sent it on to Earlsfort Terrace.

Many of those sending money off to Dublin for tickets couldn't have identified Ireland on a map of the British Isles, never mind one of the world. Others didn't have the foggiest as to what the Irish Hospitals Sweepstakes could in reality do for them. But then, the whole thrust of the Sweeps propaganda machine was that a ticket could change reality and make dreams come true. It was a potent magic brew which led to some truly weird and wonderful customer requests.

The *Donegal Vindicator* reprinted a letter sent by a tribal chief on Africa's Gold Coast, together with a 12 shilling postal order and a strip of material cut from his Sunday coat. The Gold Coast lies due south of Ireland, but the chief's application travelled over a thousand miles west to Calcutta before arriving in Dublin via a firm of general merchants there. In his poignant long-distance request the chief explained that he wanted 'three talismans' by return post. He then set out what these talismans should grant him.

> That I will command respect on all my subjects to be loved by them. Also to gain respect with the government and much promotions in my State.
>
> To become wealthy on races, lotteries and sweeps, and to gain back all my heavy business losses.
>
> To gain back my house that was sold by auction.
>
> To protect me from all evil charms. To gain sound health and long life.
>
> You offer one talisman free when buying three at a time. I wish you therefore to prepare that in the name of my wife to protect her also from all evil charms.

By the early spring of 1931 Sweepstake HQ on Earlsfort Terrace was creaking under a bountiful harvest of envelopes even greater than the first. Even the garden of the big Georgian building had to be pressed into service as an *ad hoc* sorting factory as tickets went out, cash and counterfoils came in, and receipts went out again. McGrath erected a terrace of huts on the lawn to house 800 young women working long shifts to process the applications and counterfoils in good time for the Grand National in March. On smoggy spring evenings scores of young men milled about on the broad footpath outside No. 13 awaiting the release of their wives and girlfriends. McGrath joshed about building 'an extra hut to accommodate the sweethearts', but with money to burn, the notion must already have been forming of an upwardly mobile move to a new location purpose built for processing millions of transactions against tight deadlines.

The 1931 Aintree Grand National was set for Saturday 27 March. The gala draw would take place in Dublin three days earlier. As the double deadline approached, the hype snowballed. The Sweeps promoters took out full-page adverts in British and Irish newspapers. 'Will It Be A Million?' the big type tantalised, hoping to sway waverers. Yes, a million and the rest. The prize fund closed at a breath-taking £1,181,815 (nearly $6 million), triple that of the previous November's inaugural draw. The cartel of hospitals sponsoring the event would share £438,990, while the winner of the first prize would land almost as much, pocketing a staggering £354,724.

Advertising copywriters piggybacked the craze: 'You Don't Need to be the Winner of a £1,000,000 Sweep to Own an Austin Seven—£153.' And the morning after: 'Let's Have a Consolation Draw—Let's Draw a Paddy Whiskey.'

In Dublin, extra trains were laid on to accommodate the last-minute dash of ticket-buyers arriving from Britain. Two-thirds of the tickets for the second draw were sold in Britain, where the jobless figures were creeping ever nearer the three million mark. For the British authorities this siphoning of hard cash from a crippled economy was a deplorable scandal. For the millions of Britons hell bent on having a flutter, the Sweep was a spellbinding chink of light at the end of a long dark tunnel.

The morning of the big draw arrived. 'The World's Eyes on Dublin Today' proclaimed *The Irish Times*, without fear of contradiction. The paper added that 'phone lines between Dublin and London will be almost entirely monopolised' by the events taking place in the Mansion House, official residence of the city's Lord Mayor. In anticipation of another global spread of winners, the promoters had a United Nations of linguists on standby to wire off the good news to lucky punters in the four corners of the globe.

This time out Spencer Freeman choreographed a far more lavish parade, which for its duration transported the cheering crowds from dank, chilly Dublin to the rapture of a Rio carnival. Once again the great and the good lent the affair a veneer of respectability—the Lord Mayor, Ireland's Chief of Police, government ministers, sporting heroes—and the world's press chronicled the motorised floats, the weaving procession of clowns, acrobats, ancient Grecian maidens, and a host of other exotic new attention-grabbers dreamed up by Spencer Freeman. Conspicuous by their absence were the little blind boys who had picked out the tickets for the inaugural draw. Their place on the platform would be taken this time by pretty nurses all in a row, in short sleeves to show they couldn't be masking an underarm ticket. This sexy makeover, together with the cast-of-thousands spectacle worthy of Cecil B. De Mille, invited comparison with François Rabelais' Gargantua. 'The appetite grows by eating', wrote Rabelais of his insatiable fictional giant. After getting their first taste of global fame and fortune the previous November, Duggan, McGrath and Freeman were giving notice that their appetite had grown with the eating. It would continue to grow.

The spectacular parade snaked its way to the Mansion House. The dignitaries and reporters were ushered inside for champagne and canapés, while the heaving crowds outside made do with a loudspeaker feed and packed lunches. Up on the stage the big steel drum gleamed like a miniature submarine in dry dock. Inside the capsule were three and a half million tickets. The drawing of the tickets took place military style—the port-holed drum rotating, the nurses plucking and showing with synchronised smiles, the exercise repeated again and again. As the names were matched with horses, the details were wired to newsrooms in London, New York, Rome and all points of the compass, where newspaper staffs awaited the news to fill special editions that would hit the streets while the Dublin bubbly still fizzed.

The draw reduced the three and a half million tickets down to the few dozen that mattered. A handful of individuals and syndicates remained in the reckoning, and they were now plunged headfirst into 72 hours of unrelenting madness before the moment of truth, the race itself. Every newspaper wanted a posed photo, some background and a quotable quote. Neighbours and well-wishers laid siege. Long lost relations came out of the woodwork. For the ticket-holders this was limbo in a goldfish bowl. They were celebrities but not real celebrities, not the finished article. They were each on the cusp of incredible riches, but most of them would end up with a consolation prize that was a handsome enough sum in itself, but alongside what might have been would seem a mean pittance.

The race favourite for the 1931 Grand National was Easter Hero. The ticket that had drawn Easter Hero belonged to Bob Berkley, a colliery weighman from Co. Durham in England. Several hundred miles south, in the London suburb of Battersea, a middle-aged Italian café owner called Emilio Scala had drawn another of the fancied runners, Grakle. With the Great Depression deepening, Emilio's business was just about ticking over. In a good week he might take £20 at the till.

Scala, like the other drawers of likely horses, was besieged the next day by pressmen and photographers wanting pen-pictures of his life. They found out he had arrived in England as a small boy, sold ice-cream from a pushcart in his teens, married and opened his now struggling café which specialised in his home-made ice-cream. He decided against making the long trek to Liverpool to see his horse run, preferring to stay at home and keep shop.

Thousands of miles away in North America, millions wished they could be in Aintree to witness the final episode of this soap which had come nicely to the boil after a four month run. *Time* magazine provided them with a breathless report that expertly captured how the Irish Sweeps had instantly turned the world's most celebrated race into something much bigger than a mere sporting event.

'By 9 am the trams were crowded and along the roads to Aintree lumbered buses filled with girls nibbling chocolate bars, clerks in their Sunday suits, gentlemen with binoculars who made notes on the margins of their form charts. By 11 am the bookmakers were on their platforms shouting odds soon to be changed: "Fifty-to-one against the field except Easter Hero!" All morning there were long lines of betters at the windows of the new "tote" [totalisator] machines.

'The sky, which had been misty, brightened before the trippers opened their sandwich baskets. On a barge moored in the Leeds & Liverpool Canal near Valentine's Brook, the Duke of Westminster and his friends quaffed scotch & soda. They were watched, from the Royal stand built several years ago for the Prince of Wales, by a wide-eyed group of Swedish excursionists. The grandstand and enclosure were nearly filled toward noon, when an agitated hare came humping down the home stretch, crossed the finish line and dodged into the paddock.

'In the paddock, the horses stood easy and quiet. Cyril R Taylor's Grakle, a brown gelding nine years old who had run in the Grand National four times and only finished once, nibbled wisps of hay in comparative obscurity; he was a 100-to-6 shot. Gregalach, the chestnut gelding who won in 1929, pawed the ground without enthusiasm while his fanciers flocked around. Thickest of all was the crowd looking at John Hay Whitney's Easter Hero, favourite at odds of 8-to-1.

'The warning bell rang and the horses danced slowly through a lane in the crowd from the paddock to the track—Easter Hero first, then Glangesia, Ballasport, Kakuskin and 39 others.

'Watched by 300,000 people (100,000 of them women) they stood for a few seconds jostling at the line, then broke in the confusion of a false start. A moment later the field broke again, this time gathering speed and narrowing together as they went past Sefton Yard. Every horse went over the first fence. At Becher's Brook, Swift Roland fell and was killed when the horse behind him landed on his head. The first time past the stands, Easter Hero was ahead, with Gregalach second and Grakle, Shaun Goilin, Solanum, and a half-dozen others bunched close behind.

'In the grandstand, a British radio announcer tried to tell the world about the finish. "Grakle is still there. Grakle is still there. Grakle is out in front. Gregalach is second and Ballasport third. Grakle is there and Gregalach is there. It is a terrific race. No, I think Grakle will win it. It is a terrific race. Gregalach will win it. Grakle has got it. Gregalach is second. The official result has been put up. The winner is Grakle. Second horse is Gregalach. Third horse is Annandale."

'The three persons most concerned with the result of the Grand National were not at Aintree. One was Emilio Scala, the proprietor of a coffee shop in London, who had Grakle's ticket in the Irish Hospitals Sweepstakes. Another was Clayton C Woods, the woodwork inspector at Fisher Body's Shops in Buffalo, NY. The third was George P Dyamond, who runs a hotel in Cape Town, South Africa and who, because he had been unable to sell a half interest in his ticket on Annandale, won $590,905.

'When informed that he had won $1,723,083, Emilio Scala shouted: "Now I will go to my village of Isola and settle down." He said he would share his winnings with the 39 members of his family who had pooled $2.50 to buy the ticket, and employ physicians for his ailing wife.

'In Buffalo, Clayton Woods, who with four other members of his family held Gregalach's ticket worth $886,360, explained that he had been unemployed for a week because, after it was known his ticket was for Gregalach, "my fellow employees would not let me work. They congratulated me and promised me everything and the boss told me to get out." Workman Woods announced that he would purchase his wife "an Easter outfit" and "buy that horse Gregalach and keep him in a velvet-lined stall", and give up his job.

'Next day Workman Woods paid a long visit to a barber shop, then inspected his letters. Said he: "A lot of them have been from women who want to know where they can buy tickets on the race next year. There are a whole lot more women after that information than men."

'Also after lottery information were Buffalo police who arrested one William H Paschal, charged him with being chief agent for the quick distribution of $50,000 worth of tickets in the Kentucky Derby Sweepstakes.

'In London, J Harpman, half-owner of the Irish Sweepstakes ticket on Easter Hero, was told the favorite had not finished. "Well, never mind," said he. "Now, someone give me a cup of tea."'

Appended to the *Time* piece were a couple of public information notices relating to the Irish Sweepstakes. The first warned prospective US ticket-buyers that, in the event they were to win a prize, the US Treasury Department would issue a tax demand for almost a quarter of the sum, and the winner's State of residence would take a chunk of what was left.

The second was a reminder that mailing lottery literature or tickets was an offence in the United States under the Federal Criminal Code. However, there was a 'but'. The notice continued: 'But US periodicals are, by Federal indulgence, allowed to break the letter of the law and send through the mails news accounts of lotteries. This year the Irish Sweepstakes were the world's largest. Irish Sweepstake tickets were peddled in the US by racetrack bookies or by salesmen who brought them over from Dublin in books of twelve at $2.50 each, the salesman receiving two tickets free from each book sold.'

As the *Time* magazine account hit the news-stands, Emilio Scala was already getting used to his new life as a global celebrity. Mobbed by reporters at his café just minutes after Grakle crossed the line, he assured them: 'I'm not letting this go to my head. I'm still drinking lemonade and my wife is still washing the dishes.'

He didn't let it go to his head, but he began to act in keeping with his new station in life and everything he did was eagerly covered by the newspapers and newsreels. True to his word, he spread some of the wealth across his extended family. Some of them thought of this as their entitlement as much as an act of benevolence on Emilio's part. As soon as the news of his gargantuan win reached his home town of Isola del Liri, his brother Mario declared that his ship had come in too.

In an age of heavy Italian emigration, Mario had remained in the little village to care for his parents. Now, he cheerily told invading reporters: 'When we heard of Emilio's good fortune I went to [the printer's shop where he worked] and quit. Everybody was drinking his health. Wine never tasted better. Now we are rich I might marry. I've been working forty years and it's time to have a rest.' Sadly, his next act was to lay his mother to rest. Emilio received the shocking news that she had died of a heart attack when told of his massive win. In his own words, 'she died of too much happiness'.

The cameras followed Emilio when he visited the town of his birth, its populace swelled by crowds streaming in from far and wide to cheer their world-beater. In the initial euphoria of his win, Scala had reportedly said he would return home to settle, but after his visit there he thought better of swapping the bright lights of the world's capital city for a sleepy hamlet in the middle of nowhere.

Scala had bought a 33 horsepower luxury touring car for his trip home, and a state-of-the-art movie camera to record the event. Once back in London he was in the news again when he acquired a 23 room mansion looking down on the city. Once installed there, he kept open house for his extended Anglo-Italian family. There was more publicity when he went to the police reporting an attempt by Mafia hoods to extort money from him. The international media also followed him to Dublin where he went to court to successfully repulse the claims of two acquaintances that they owned shares in his winning ticket.

The two seen off in court did not have a claim on his huge win, but others did. The fact tended to get buried in the cult of personality that shot up around Emilio Scala, but the really big winner of the 1931 Grand National was local bookmaker Arthur Bendir who had made it hotfoot to Scala's café once his name was drawn, and offered him an irresistible £10,500 for three-quarters of his ticket. In fact, Emilio Scala's actual payoff from the sweep of some £100,000 barely exceeded the amount that went to third placed George Dyamond in South Africa, who couldn't get anyone to buy a share in his ticket. But that disappointingly plain truth was not allowed to get in the way of a good story.

The world loved Emilio Scala, who would pop up again and again over the decades as an ambassador for the Sweeps. The publicity feeding frenzy surrounding Scala's monster win ensured that the next event would be even bigger. However, the scale of his prize was so huge that it represented the very real threat that the Irish Sweep could fall victim to its own success. Duggan, McGrath and Freeman calculated that, at the rate the prize fund had been growing to date, the first prize would quickly exceed £1 million and rising. This, they reckoned, would not bring them good publicity but bad. They foresaw that with critics branding it an obscenity that any one winner should bank a million pounds, the authorities in Britain, North America and elsewhere would redouble their efforts to wipe out the Irish Sweeps.

So it was decided that for the next sweep on the 1931 Epsom Derby there would be many more prizes, but much smaller ones. The millions of ticket-holders would from now on face less astronomical odds of winning just three astronomical prizes. Under the new regime there would be 20 chances to win a first prize of £30,000, a second prize of £20,000 and a third prize of £10,000.

Chapter 9

THE LAW IS IN A STATE OF CHAOS

rom the off, Britain was an open door just waiting to be pushed by anyone offering attention-grabbing prizes and an official-sounding guarantee that everything was well regulated and above board.

By the dawn of the 1930s the popularity of staged sporting events was soaring to heights never before witnessed. To this day, the biggest ever attendance for a club football match in England was at Maine Road in March 1934 when Manchester City and Stoke entertained a crowd of 84,569. Many of the all-time biggest attendances were recorded in the early 1930s. Other sports had experienced a similar expansion in popularity in the post-war years, including horse and greyhound racing.

Hand-in-hand with this upsurge of enthusiasm for all things sporting went an expanded appetite for gambling on sports. Littlewoods, Vernons and Zetters all rolled out football pools in the decade from 1923 to 1933. The Tote was created in 1928 by an Act of the Westminster Parliament. Shortly after, the first Horse Race Totaliser Board was set up by Winston Churchill for the purpose of providing a safe, state-controlled alternative to illegal, fly-by-night off-course bookies, and to ensure that some of the money gambled was funnelled back into the sport. The first major race meetings with tote betting were at Newmarket and Carlisle in July 1929.

Such was the craze for gambling that an attachment to sport was optional. One rage that swept Britain and Ireland in the 1930s was for a game called House, which was essentially bingo nights for men. In one incident recorded in central Dublin, a man was fined the hefty sum of £5 for permitting a social club to be used for the purpose of this unlawful pursuit. The arresting officer said he found between 40 and 50 men playing, with the defendant shouting out numbers. One of the men yelled 'House!' and went up to the platform to collect three shillings as a prize. The prosecuting official said the game of House was becoming far too common, pointing out that the police were being swamped with complaints from the wives of these men who were blowing the housekeeping budget on gambling.

Despite the much publicised clampdown on illegal sweeps and lotteries by the British and Irish governments in 1923, the British authorities lacked sufficient will and resources to fully stamp them out. Most were trifling affairs not worth the manpower to investigate and prosecute. The glaring exception to these petty raffles was the Calcutta Club's annual sweep on the Epsom Derby which, for years, had been the world's richest. In 1922 the winning ticket in the Calcutta Sweep was worth an enormous £116,000. An exclusive private members' club based in India, the Calcutta Club had been founded by the British Viceroy, the Earl of Minto. As a result, British high society had always been extremely permissive when it came to the Calcutta.

In a Commons debate of May 1930, months before the Irish Sweep made its first public appearance, an MP named Harry Day asked the Home Secretary if he was aware that tickets for the Calcutta Sweep were available on every street corner, and whether the police had been instructed to take action? The Home Secretary replied: 'No evidence of the commission of any criminal offence has come to my notice.' A third MP then informed the Home Secretary that Day, who had raised the issue, had a personal interest in whether the law would be enforced, as he had bought tickets for the sweep himself.

The advent of the Irish Sweeps shortly after would shake up for ever the cosy relationship between the British establishment and the illicit sweep of the Calcutta Club established by one of their own. To that same establishment there was a world of difference between a sweep to benefit one of the most prestigious gentlemen's clubs of the Empire, and one that was starting to leech millions from a depression-hit British economy to aid a State which had violently, and ungratefully and unforgivably renounced its membership of the United Kingdom.

Unfortunately for both the establishment and the Calcutta Club, the law was not able to reflect that world of difference. In April 1931, with the Calcutta Club and the Irish Hospitals Trust both planning rival sweeps on the Derby, Harry Day again wanted to know if the law against sweepstakes would be enforced. The Home Secretary's fudge was: 'I do not propose to discontinue the existing practice.'

Sir Patrick Hannon then cut to the chase, asking: 'Will the Right Honourable Gentleman tell the House whether there is to be one law in relation to the Calcutta Sweep and another in relation to the Irish Sweep?'

The Home Secretary replied: 'All sweeps which are illegal are treated in exactly the same manner by the Departments concerned.'

By way of underlining that one sweep enjoyed less exposure to the law than the other, Sir Patrick asked: 'Is the Right Honourable Gentleman aware that I, a humble citizen and a Member of the House, can obtain tickets for the Calcutta Sweep without any difficulty whatever?'

Harry Day closed off the debate by telling Prime Minister Ramsay MacDonald that 'the present condition of the law with regard to sweepstakes is holding this country up to great ridicule'.

While the politicians dithered and dawdled, the common people of Britain got on with the sunny business of seeking out and sending off tickets for the Irish Sweep on the summer Derby, their enthusiasm fanned by blanket media coverage. For the Dublin draw, Spencer Freeman had once again excelled himself, staging his most dazzling extravaganza yet.

The man sent over from the *Daily Express* was bowled over by the spectacle, which now ran for two days and would soon be expanded into a three-day affair. The man from the *Mail* gushed: 'I will see tomorrow the most spectacular lottery in all history, the spectacle of nearly two million pounds vanishing with the revolutions of a drum. In three short months and in spite of nearly every government's prohibition, money poured into Dublin at a rate unprecedented in the history of sweepstakes, of £100,000 a day until the Hospitals Trust said, in effect, no more, and put away in the strong rooms of its bank a sum of nearly three million pounds subscribed by people in every corner of the Earth.'

He continued: 'Dublin has seen many strange processions, but none so strange as that which I saw at twenty minutes past nine this morning when 6,500,000 pieces of paper carrying the hopes of probably three times as many people was borne under police escort along the city streets to the historic Mansion House. I sat in one of the trucks in this remarkable convoy, an armed detective on my left, a chartered accountant on my right, and beneath us the hopes of you and I and all of us.'

Having chronicled in detail the elaborate mixing process which left the 250 female mixers in a state of exhaustion, another visiting writer from the *Express* recorded how the millions of tickets were bundled into the drum where they would remain overnight under armed guard. When the draw commenced the following day: 'White faces stared at the brilliantly lighted platform on which the great drum revolved, the portholes like the eyes of some fabled monster.'

Countless other pen-pictures carried the message back to Britain that the Irish Sweeps was the greatest show on earth, and, to the ruination of the Calcutta Sweep, the only show in town. The Irish in Britain were usually the first point of contact on the underground distribution network. With millions on the breadline in the depression-hit United States, the 1930s saw a rise in the numbers of Irish migrating to Britain in search of work rather than crossing the Atlantic.

But the Irish were just a conduit to the plain people of England, Scotland and Wales, who didn't need any hard sell to part with their money. Tickets, and shares in tickets, found their way into the most stately of homes and the most humble of hovels. The application of the law was uneven and often half-hearted. The ambivalent attitude of the authorities was illustrated when the question arose as to whether Emilio Scala was liable to pay income tax on his huge illicit windfall. The question went all the way to the House of Commons, where the answer, 'No', hardly signalled a hardline approach from the lawmakers themselves.

The credibility of the legal system took a further blow in May 1932 when the Mayor of Rye in Sussex, sitting in his capacity as a magistrate, imposed a fine on local businessman Ernest Long for selling Irish Sweep tickets. Long got off lightly with a penalty of just one shilling. Then, within days, it emerged that a syndicate of Rye Freemasons had scooped £30,000 on the sweep. It was bad enough that a group of society's most eminent citizens would be involved in an illegal activity, but much worse when it turned out that one member of the charmed circle was none other than the same Mayor of Rye, a distinguished retired headmaster.

The *Daily Express* turned the parable into an editorial. It said: 'About three million pounds was sent from here to Ireland to be invested in the Derby Sweepstake. Part of the sum which will come back will be paid to an English magistrate who had a share in a winning ticket. Before the race was run he had to fine a man who was charged with selling such a ticket. The fantasy of this occasion is multiplied a thousand times each day. It is now plain that the people of this country do not regard gambling as a crime. Yet most of those who gamble must break the law to do it. If they break the law for one reason they will in time acquire the habit of breaking it for less harmless reasons. Laws which outrun public opinion or lag far behind it are bad laws, for they bring the general rules of order into the same contempt.'

In the early 1930s around two out of every three tickets going into the drum were sent from Britain. It is estimated that in 1932 the proportion from Britain peaked at three out of every four. With over five million tickets going from Dublin to Britain, it was clear to the authorities that smuggling in bulk was afoot.

One tale, which sounds more like a good yarn than a done deed, has it that a shrewd operator in Dublin purchased a job-lot of plastic fish, slit them open and stuffed books of tickets inside. The fake fish were then taken to sea on a trawler which met with a Welsh fishing boat and transferred the haul. The plastic fish were concealed in crates of real fish and landed without arousing suspicion.

Fake fish which *were* intended to be detected were at the heart of an imaginative publicity campaign which proved a spectacular success. Years after the event, the *New York Times* fondly recalled: 'The Sweeps committee dispatched a trawler to the edge of the English coast and dumped hundreds of bottles shaped like fish over the side. Each bottle contained a note bidding the finder to write the Irish Hospitals Trust and give the name of their favourite pub. Seventy-seven bottles washed ashore at Sennen's Cove in Cornwall, or so the receipts indicated, and the committee promptly sent five shillings per person to each pub cited and invited the correspondents to have a drink on the Irish Hospitals Trust. A fellow turned up in New York harbour with a bottle and the hospital people stood him a drink at Jack Dempsey's. The luck wasn't so good at Bournemouth, England, however, where the police kept an avid watch on the shoreline and seized every bottle that washed in with the tide.'

Ferry crewmen were obvious recruits for those in the business of smuggling tickets. In 1932 customs officials searching one vessel found four suitcases and 40 large packages crammed with books of tickets. There was so much contraband that when the ship's wireless operator was hauled before a judge, just one mailbag was used as a sample exhibit because moving the whole lot would have taken up too much time and space. The accused said he had been instructed to deliver his smuggled cargo to the left-luggage office of a Liverpool railway station. He could offer no clue as to where they would go from there.

At the lower end of the criminality scale, many tickets were smuggled into Britain by freelancers carrying dozens of books rather than thousands. When customs officers began routinely searching the luggage of passengers arriving from Ireland, the MP Colonel Charles Howard-Bury took grave exception and initiated a full-blown Commons debate entitled 'Irish Sweepstake Tickets (Customs Seizure)'.

Born in County Offaly in 1881, Howard-Bury notched up many achievements during his long life, the most enduring of which is that he indirectly gave the world the term 'Abominable Snowman'. In 1921 he led the Mount Everest Reconnaissance Expedition which was to prepare the way for the first British attempt to climb the world's highest mountain. The Offaly man found footprint trails at high altitude which he put down to wolves. His Sherpas begged to differ, insisting the tracks belonged to a *metch kangmi*, meaning 'filthy snowman'. Upon Howard-Bury's return to Darjeeling, a journalist covering the story mistranslated *metch kangmi* as 'abominable snowman' and the name quickly caught on around the globe.

Kicking off the Commons debate, Howard-Bury fumed: 'Irish citizens who come over to this country, or it may be American citizens who land in Ireland and who come over to this country, are today being subjected by the Treasury to an inquisition which ought not to happen. Any Irish subject is entitled to buy a ticket in his own country. That action is perfectly legal.'

He said it was ridiculous that HM Customs were confiscating tickets on the grounds that each elaborately designed ticket was an advertisement for the Sweeps. Under Britain's Lotteries Act, it was illegal for any person to 'print or publish or cause to be printed any advertisement or notice' relating to any unapproved lottery. Howard-Bury argued that this was a ludicrous misapplication of the law. He asked of the government's Financial Secretary: 'When he buys a railway ticket, is that an advertisement of that railway? When he goes to the theatre and buys a ticket, is that an advertisement of that theatre?'

He continued: 'In this country we are not entitled to have sweepstakes for the benefit of our hospitals, and the Honourable Member is determined that the Irish Free State shall not have sweepstakes for its hospitals if he can help it. He has adopted a dog-in-the-manger attitude. He says: "We cannot benefit therefore you shall not, and we are going to take every step to prevent you." On that he is basing his action. The Postmaster General was told by the Home Office to open letters, but they found that that was not sufficient. The tickets are coming into this country. There is hardly a Member of this House who has not one of these illegal, or supposed to be illegal, documents.'

Warming to his theme Howard-Bury went on: 'I suggest that the action of the Financial Secretary is mere bluff, and that his action is not legal. I wish some rich citizen from America or the Irish Free State, who has sufficient money, or some of the leagues for freedom that we have in this country would test the case in a court of law, because it is an attack on the liberty of the subject. It needs a rich man to be able to attack the Treasury. If the point were argued in a court of law it could be proved that the action taken by the Financial Secretary is illegal. It is not doing us any good in this country, and I ask him to stop this inquisition which is going on today in all the ports adjacent to Ireland.'

The Financial Secretary, Frederick Pethick-Lawrence, was a staunch Unitarian socialist who believed that lotteries were a tax on the poor. He countered: 'Anyone who has seen one of these tickets can have no possible doubt that it is not like an ordinary ticket. It is, in fact, an advertisement and a notice of the lottery. It describes what the lottery is about. It gives particulars of the prizes. It tells how other tickets are to be obtained, and it gives all those particulars and descriptions which one would expect a notice and advertisement to give.'

Antrim-born Sir William Davison made the final noteworthy contribution to the debate, neatly summing up the status of the Irish Sweep in Britain in the early 1930s. He said: 'Before individuals coming from the Irish Free State are harassed by having their pockets turned inside out, on the suggestion that they are bringing advertisements to this country because particulars of the lottery are printed on the ticket, the Financial Secretary had better make further inquiries into the law on the subject. It only shows how essential it is that the whole question of lotteries and sweepstakes should be dealt with by the Government. The law on the subject is in a state of chaos.'

And as long as it remained so, Duggan, McGrath and Freeman would gleefully coin cash from chaos.

Chapter 10

FIRING THE AMERICAN IMAGINATION

The United States—where millions came to make their fortune but no one was allowed to gamble—was a ready-made market for an illicit flutter. And then there was the Irish factor. Of all the emigrant groups in the States, the Irish maintained arguably the closest links with the old country. Over a couple of generations, the offspring of continental European settlers would become English speakers, becoming cut off from their mother tongue and motherland. Not so the English-speaking Irish. From 1916 the IRB had organised a well-oiled collection network in the US to channel home funds for the Easter Rising and the War of Independence. By the early 1930s the machine was still in place, albeit a little rusty.

Joe McGrath personally knew many IRA/IRB veterans living in the United States who could be relied upon, but in a country run by White Anglo-Saxon Protestants (WASPs) many doors were firmly shut to those of Catholic Irish stock. McGrath keenly understood the importance of having a presence in the corridors of power, and in the summer of 1928, more than a year before the enabling legislation would go before Dáil Éireann, Richard Duggan and Joe McGrath sat down to lunch with a man they thought might fit the bill.

The son of a circus clown who reinvented himself as a lecturer, 31-year-old Andrew 'Drew' Pearson was a Quaker journalist with the happy knack of making the steepest social climbing look like a gentle spot of hill-walking. A decade earlier, visiting war-torn Serbia as an aid worker with the Quakers, he befriended Red Cross volunteers Sylvia Beach and her sister Holly. When his two-year contract on the reconstruction scheme was finished, Pearson was entitled to a first-class passage home to the United States from any port in Europe.

Surprisingly, he chose to set sail from Alexandria in Egypt, which entailed an additional trip across the Mediterranean. Eyebrows were raised when the Beach sisters announced they were going with him, and jaws dropped when gossip spread that they were going to Egypt to procure an abortion. The tight American colony was quickly abuzz with speculation that Sylvia was pregnant and Pearson was the father.

Towards the end of his life, Pearson began to talk of a passionate affair with an unnamed young woman in Serbia. Sadly, he related, she was out of his league as he had neither money nor connections nor prospects.

When Sylvia Beach resurfaced in Paris, she opened the legendary Shakespeare & Company bookshop which became a rendezvous for Ernest Hemingway, Ezra Pound, F. Scott Fitzgerald, Gertrude Stein, Man Ray and James Joyce. When no one else would touch Joyce's masterpiece, Beach published *Ulysses* in 1922. She never married. Close to death in 1971, she was asked by her adopted son if she had recollections of Drew Pearson in Serbia. Her curt reply was: 'I never knew him.'

Whether Pearson jilted society girl Sylvia Beach or vice versa, he wasn't long in once again romancing above his social station. He married Felicia Patterson, a woman so well connected that when her Polish Count father had her kidnapped as a child from his estranged American wife, US President William Taft called on Czar Nicholas of Russia to force the Count to return the child, which he did.

After a whirlwind romance and marriage, Drew and Felicia took a slow boat to China for a honeymoon-cum-journalistic adventure which took them across the Gobi Desert and on to India where he turned up on Mahatma Gandhi's doorstep in an attempt to interview the great man. It was his second attempt to interview Gandhi. On his previous visit to the Mahatma's home, he had been told that Gandhi couldn't oblige since he was in jail. Undeterred, Pearson wrote a piece anyway, using quotations he had lifted from other sources to give the impression he had spoken to the Indian refusnik. On this second occasion Gandhi was at home, but he refused to see Pearson, possibly miffed at the writer's previous promiscuous use of artistic licence.

Through Felicia, or rather through her formidable mother Cissy, Drew Pearson had an entrée into a Washington high society of politicians, diplomats and plutocrats. He began to forge a reputation as a campaigning journalist. From the outset he fancied himself as a player in the stories he wrote, regularly boasting: 'I've always gone for the action.' He told one interviewer that his best stories came from good tips from well-placed sources, or from following up on his journalistic hunches. He said: 'I operate by sense of smell. If something smells wrong, I go to work.' He outlined his personal manifesto as: 'It's the job of a newspaperman to spur the lazy, watch out for the weak, expose the corrupt. He must be the eyes, ears and nose of the American people. The nose is important for no matter how much stench a newspaperman is exposed to, he must never lose his smell.'

On their return from honeymoon, Cissy Patterson offered to settle a huge allowance on Felicia. To Drew's presumed dismay, Felicia turned it down, insisting that it was for a husband to support his wife. The marriage was an unhappy one, and by the time Pearson sat down with Duggan and McGrath in Dublin in 1928, it was already steering full steam ahead for the rocks.

Pearson arrived in Europe that year to cover a peace conference which had the laudable objective of ensuring there would never be another Great War. Most American newspapers already had correspondents in Europe, so Pearson found himself the only us correspondent accompanying Secretary of State Frank Kellogg across the Atlantic. The pair became friendly during the long voyage and continued to keep close company in Paris.

Just before the peace conference was due to begin, a newspaper uncovered a secret alliance between France and Britain which exposed their commitment to a new peace deal as a sham. Fuming at British duplicity, us President Calvin Coolidge told Kellogg to scrap a planned London stopover and sail instead to Dublin where he was to make a pointedly anti-British courtesy call on Free State President W. T. Cosgrave.

A year earlier Pearson had met the Irish journalist, adventurer and diplomat Michael MacWhite at a disarmament conference in Vienna. The Corkman had been the Free State's permanent representative to the League of Nations since the League's foundation in 1923. Joe McGrath was an old friend of MacWhite, and when Drew Pearson stepped off the boat with Secretary of State Kellogg, McGrath and Duggan were well briefed on this young Washington insider. Over dinner the two Irishmen sketched out their plans for their ambitious sweepstake. Pearson was interested. Duggan and McGrath said that nothing was settled yet, but if things went to plan he would be hearing from them.

Two years later, when the Public Charitable Hospitals Bill passed into law, Pearson received through diplomatic channels the offer of a five-year contract as Western Hemisphere director of the Irish Hospitals Sweepstake. The hefty $30,000 annual secret salary would more than take care of his money worries, and for good measure the deal included generous expenses and a chauffeur driven Lincoln Continental.

Pearson rented a desk in the seedy office of a lawyer named David Babp in the Evans Building on Washington's New York Avenue, close to the White House. He hired a former prohibition undercover agent as his sidekick. The occupants of other desks in the office were engaged in a range of nefarious schemes. At one work-station, a plot was being hatched to stir up trouble in the Virgin Islands. At another the overthrow of Cuban President Gerardo Machado was being planned. In 1933 he would be toppled by a US-backed coup.

Manning the desk, Pearson's henchman would receive regular RCA cables saying that $500 or $1,000 had been lodged into a Swiss bank account. Pearson would then meet up with him at a covert spot with large sums of money for the running of the business. The sidekick was never let in on how the money travelled from Switzerland to the United States, but he formed the impression that the Algonquin Hotel in New York was the pick-up point.

As soon as each sweeps draw was made in Dublin, Pearson's crony would receive a list of ticket-holders down the wires. The assistant would take the list to Pearson's house where scores of copies would be made for immediate mailing to the newspapers. Pearson never showed up at the office, acutely aware that parcels of illegal tickets arrived there on a regular basis, along with incriminating 'special communications' from Irish Sweeps backer Dougie Stuart.

Newly divorced and ostensibly living on a journalist's modest income, Drew Pearson's flash car and uniformed chauffeur inevitably invited comment and questions. His standard reply was that he was engaged in public relations work of a hush-hush nature. For all the millions of words he penned during his long career he was unskilled at small talk, so Drew the man-of-mystery and Drew the man-of-few-words provided back-up for each other. He was so taken with his Lincoln Continental that he decided he wanted to drive it himself and delegated his chauffeur to other chores. The new arrangement lasted until he crashed into an iron gate while driving drunk, sustaining injuries that required a stay in bed. The chauffeur was reinstalled behind the wheel.

Pearson quickly figured out that it was more productive to send his Irish Sweeps press releases to the laid-back sports desks than to the more stuffy hard news departments. A couple of tickets would often accompany the publicity material. He invested some of his Swiss money in a confidential news service circulated to Washington insiders. His commentaries on us foreign policy in particular became required reading for native politicians and foreign diplomats and helped raise his profile as a shrewd analyst.

Another key recruit made by Joe McGrath in the United States was Tyrone-born Joe McGarrity, a naturalised American citizen who made the first of several fortunes running a wholesale wine business which was shut down with the advent of Prohibition in 1919. McGarrity had joined the us Fenian organisation Clan na Gael in his teens, and rapidly rose through the ranks. In 1914 he met Padraig Pearse who was on a trip to the United States, and pledged to raise funds for the Irish Volunteers who would stage the 1916 Rising. Money he raised paid in part for the consignment of rifles and ammunition landed by Erskine Childers at Howth Harbour later that year. In 1920 Éamon de Valera made McGarrity a trustee for the illegal Republic of Ireland's government funds in the event of de Valera's arrest, imprisonment or death. He would later become godfather to de Valera's youngest son. During the War of Independence in 1921 Michael Collins asked McGarrity to source and ship 500 Thompson sub-machine guns. Most got no further than the Hoboken waterfront in New Jersey before they were seized by us authorities.

By the end of the 1920s McGarrity was broke, as is evident from letters of 1928 and 1929 thanking another prominent Irish American for substantial cash dig-outs totalling $2,000. He tried his hand as a financial broker, but was let go in May 1930 after just two months. Weeks later a letter arrived from an old Sinn Féin pal in Ireland, Dr Patrick McCartan. McCartan wrote invitingly: 'Would you be interested in a scheme to make from $50,000 to $100,000 a year for two years?' McCartan reminded McGarrity that he would be breaking the law in the United States but added that previous sweeps operated from Ireland were also illegal and 'we all bought and sold tickets'.

McGarrity turned down the stupendous offer, saying he had just been made a member of the New York Curb Exchange (later renamed the Stock Exchange). Family members and three Clan men had dug him out of his financial hole with loans. Unfortunately for McGarrity, the world of high finance induced crippling vertigo. He wrote that his expulsion from the Curb Exchange over cooked books left him 'humiliated and crushed'. In a letter to McCartan of February 1933 he lamented: 'The most unpleasant place in the world for me in one sense, at present, is Philadelphia. Some of my old friends look at me as though I had been guilty of burglary.'

McGarrity staunchly maintained that the book-keeping fraud perpetrated by his firm was the work of an associate and done without his slightest knowledge. But he was left carrying the can, his name was muck, and legal investigations were hanging over him. So in the late spring of 1933 he headed for Ireland to escape his worries. Some weeks after he returned to the United States, he broke the surprise news to a close Clan friend that he had taken up the Sweeps agency offer. He set up shop on Manhattan's 41st Street, using a restaurant as his front business.

If timing wasn't everything to the success of the Irish Sweeps in the United States, it was a key element in securing that crucial first beach-head. When tickets for the first sweep hit the East Coast ten months after the Wall Street Crash of 1929, the administration of President Herbert Hoover had its hands full fire-fighting on all fronts as the economy sank deeper and deeper into the Great Depression.

The man with direct responsibility for stamping out the illegal traffic of tickets from Ireland was Walter Folger Brown, who had been appointed Postmaster General as a thank you for his work in getting Hoover into the White House. Happily for the Irish Sweeps organisation, Brown had his eye off the ball. For years, US airlines had been robbing the Washington government blind by operating a scam involving phantom air-mail deliveries. While Brown tackled the airlines, policing of the mail for gambling-related material dropped down the priority list.

The mail service in the United States was imbued with a much greater cultural significance in the opening decades of the twentieth century than today. In a time before television, when valve radio sets were still the preserve of the privileged few, the postal service was the channel that carried news, literature, and cultural and political analysis into the homes of Americans. As an exercise in social control, strict laws were drafted to govern what could and could not be transmitted through the post.

One rule stipulated that no contraceptives, or even adverts for contraceptives, could be sent through the mail. In 1925 Carko Tresca, the publisher of an Italian language periodical, was convicted of carrying a foreign language advert for contraceptives in his magazine. During World War 1 the role of the postal service as a political instrument was demonstrated as the Postmaster General took a range of actions to disrupt the passage of anti-war material. Shortly before the first Irish Sweeps tickets began to arrive, the writer and critic Henry Mencken described the postal service as 'one of the most sinister agents of oppression in the United States'.

Transmitting Irish Sweeps adverts and tickets through the US mail was an act of subversion that could not be tolerated. Belatedly, Brown put his staff on high alert. When material posted in unsealed envelopes stopped getting through, the senders paid the extra cents to have them sealed. Letters posted from Ireland inevitably attracted attention, so large shipments were landed in Canada and Mexico and posted from there. Unprecedented numbers of prayer books began arriving in the post from Ireland. It was some time before the authorities realised the books were hollowed out to accommodate tickets.

The Post Office was fighting a losing battle with the Irish Sweeps, so it tried a switch of tactics. Department solicitor Horace Donnelly threatened that any newspapers containing coverage of the Sweeps, which he disapprovingly observed 'have fired the imagination of the people', would be denied distribution through the mail. There were howls of protest from newspaper publishers who claimed that a big win, for instance, was a legitimate news story about which the public had a right to know.

Between them, the newspapers and the Post Office contrived a fudge. Some stories deemed to have genuine news value would be let through. Some newspapers gave this loophole the widest possible interpretation and carried on their Sweeps coverage more or less as before, while others displayed more caution by splitting their print runs. One edition would go into the post with no Sweeps coverage, while a separate one carrying the latest Sweeps news would hit the news-stands. By the time Hoover was ejected from the White House and Walter Brown from the Post Office in 1933, there hadn't been a single Sweeps-related prosecution under the censorship code.

If the United States Post Office was slow off the mark with the Irish Sweeps, others were quick to place a different obstacle in the way of getting the business established. The first sweep on the Manchester November Handicap of 1930 attracted blanket coverage in the States, and within weeks the US newspapers were carrying a story headlined 'Warns of Fraud Here in Irish Sweepstakes'. The report began: 'Joseph McGrath, Director of the Irish Hospitals Sweepstakes, tonight branded the selling of Irish Sweepstake tickets in the United States by the "Irish Free State Association" as a fraud of the clumsiest sort.'

It quoted McGrath as saying: 'First of all there is no such organization as the Irish Free State Association. The tickets being sold are not in the least like the regular authorized tickets. Furthermore, they bear four flags, none of which is a Free State flag, and one of the flags belongs to no country at all. Nor is there any mention of what race they are for, although they make it understood it is the Grand National.' He further pointed out that the bogus tickets were printed on stiff card rather than on the distinctive blue paper that came in books. Counterfeiters would continue to piggyback on the Irish Sweeps over the entire lifetime of the venture. Counterfeit tickets were rarely detected because the purchaser had no further interest in the ticket if it wasn't drawn out of the drum in Dublin. Since the chances of that happening were astronomical, countless fake tickets joined the millions of genuine ones binned without a second thought.

One ticket which did arouse huge interest in the United States was that drawn on a horse called Gregalach for the 1931 Grand National. The name on the ticket was that of Clayton Woods, a motor mechanic earning $50 a week in a car plant in the city of Buffalo on the US side of Niagara Falls. A friend came to him trying to offload the last two sweep tickets in a book. The price was $5 the pair. Woods took the tickets 'to help him out', but now found he was short of lunch money. Woods's wife gave him a dollar from a kitty she had been saving for a summer dress, in exchange for a fifth share in her husband's $5 investment.

Woods's brother Kenneth offered a dollar for another fifth share, and Woods's brothers-in-law, Elmer and Clarence Batt, also pitched in a dollar each. The five were now equal shareholders in the brace of tickets.

One of the tickets drew Gregalach. In a scene that was replicated in workplaces around the world the day after the Dublin draw, the motor factory ground to a virtual standstill as Woods's workmates discussed his chances. 'So the foreman came over,' Woods later recalled, 'And he said "Clayton, you can beat it out of here. You're fired."' When he got home, Woods found a bookies' agent waiting for him with the offer of $50,000—many years' wages in the car factory—for a half-share. After some long and heated discussion, the five opted to reject the offer and take their chances on finishing with just a few hundred dollars each if Gregalach finished down the field. Decision made, the Woods and the Batts hid themselves away and awaited their fate.

On the March day of the 1931 Aintree Grand National, Clayton Woods was guest of honour at the office of the *Buffalo Evening News*. There he watched the ticker-tape machine stutter out the outcome of the big race. Grakle was the winner, and 3,000 miles away Emilio Scala was about to be mobbed. In second place was Gregalach. Woods watched in numbed disbelief as the newspaper's compositor excitedly set up the blaring front page headline: 'Woods Wins $886,630.' The Woods and Batts were instant media stars. Reporters descended on Buffalo from all directions, anxious to know how the five were going to spend their vast shared windfall. Clayton had his eyes set on France, explaining: 'I was there in 1918 and it wasn't much fun. This time I'm going to make whoopee.' When his wife and the others announced they were in the market for property, estate agents made a bee-line for their doors.

But the US government had other plans for the quintet's money. Unlike its British counterpart, the US Revenue was determined to take a hefty cut of the winnings. Playing hardball, Clayton said that if the government wanted more than 25 per cent he would make the short hop across the border and settle in Canada. The Revenue quickly issued a tax demand for more than 50 per cent of the bonanza. Another nasty surprise was sprung on the five winners when Buffalo's city fathers informed the Woods and Batts that under an old law all lottery winnings could be confiscated and used for poor relief.

The lifestyle of the rich and famous was rapidly losing its lustre for the Buffalo Five, as they had become known across America. They were snowed under with begging letters, petitions, hard-luck stories, charity appeals and investment offers. They couldn't go out the front door without attracting a scrum of reporters, well-wishers and panhandlers. Clayton's boss from the factory called on him to offer his congratulations. He found Woods fretful. 'I told him I just couldn't loaf,' said Clayton, 'and I would be back at work before long.'

It all got too much. Making good on their threat to the Revenue, Woods and the Batts made a break for the border, holing up in a Canadian backwoods cabin where they were safe from prowling reporters, taxmen, beggars and estate agents. After a few weeks in exile the five were lured home with assurances that the Buffalo authorities and the US Revenue would cut them a fair deal. After some horse-trading, Clayton got the tax bill down to around the 25 per cent he had said would be tolerable.

There was to be no fairytale ending, however. Clayton Woods and his wife split up. Kenneth Woods's wife went insane. Some years later Elmer Batt wound up shot dead in a patch of forest. His death was recorded as a hunting accident, but it was widely assumed to be suicide. A day earlier Woods had been released on bail following his arrest on charges of having sexual relations with a 15-year-old girl.

While the saga of the Buffalo Five's tussles with the authorities received blow-by-blow coverage in the American media, the ongoing adventures of Emilio Scala were not ignored. Scala's house purchase, his mother's death from 'too much happiness' at his good fortune, his trip home to Italy and his legal battle against two claimants on his ticket were all splashed on the news pages. In December of 1931 the US papers ran the headline 'Scala Wins in Court', with the subhead: 'Sweepstakes Winner Keeps All By Dublin Verdict'.

The huge sums won by Scala and the Buffalo Five in the first Irish Sweep of 1931 ensured that the second of that year, on June's Epsom Derby, would attract huge attention from the North American media. When the race was run, front pages across the continent carried news of Cameronian's win under headlines such as 'American Winnings on Derby A Million'.

In addition to the list of winners, there was one notable hard-luck story. The *New York Times* reported: 'The biggest loser on the Derby was the Maharajah of Patiala, according to a dispatch from Lahore tonight. He bought 10,000 tickets in the Irish Sweepstakes at a cost of $25,000 and won nothing. As in former years he also extensively patronized the Calcutta Sweepstakes in which he never won anything.'

Other losers on the 1931 Derby were the bookies and hundreds of on-course gamblers who got badly stung. The report explained: 'For the bookmakers Cameronian's Derby was the worst on record, for the three most fancied horses were the first three home. According to police reports tonight more than fifty bookmakers on the course failed to meet their obligations while dozens of others in the enclosures shut up shop before the last race. The police arrested fifteen welchers, but one gang with what is believed to be the first welching totalisator that has made its appearance on a British race course got away with $5,000 during the excitement of the race. The totalisator, mounted on a motor truck, arrived near Saint Dunstan's stand. Many placed bets, but after the race found the machine empty and the money gone. The crowd wrecked the truck.'

The day after the race results appeared, the papers were full of photos of America's latest sweep winners. George Hill, a 'lumberman and automobile dealer' who won $75,000 pledged that all those dollars 'won't go out of circulation'. As soon as his name had emerged from the drum he had been bombarded with 'cabled offers from England' for the whole ticket or shares in it, but he had stuck on his own. For print worker Sam Horowitz, his half-share of $50,000 would mean liberation from the burden of supporting his parents, brother and two sisters. He said that now he was a man of substance, he'd like to get married. Middle-aged Tom O'Connor had emigrated from Tralee at 17 to seek his fortune, but had wound up running the engine room of a New York hotel to support his family of six in a cramped Bronx apartment. Describing himself as a 'conservative' man who would do nothing 'foolish', he said 'after all there are few things a man of my age wants. My wife and I now can have some of the pleasant things in the world and we can live a little better than we have. We can buy a small automobile, perhaps a small house in the suburbs, and above all we can send the girls to college.'

As Postmaster General Walter Brown mounted his belated attempted clampdown on Sweeps coverage in mailed publications, stories on the subject which couldn't be interpreted as promoting gambling were still considered fit to print.

One, in August 1932, reported that the Fianna Fáil administration newly installed in power in the Free State was already displaying hostility to a business closely identified with the political opposition. According to the report: 'A charge that the de Valera government is holding shares due to hospitals from the last three Irish Sweepstakes was made at today's meeting of the governors of the North Infirmary in Cork. The governors decided to send a demand for the money which, they said, had already been handed to the government by the Hospitals Trust. Richard Anthony, a member of the Irish Dáil and Chairman of the governors, was reported as having said none of the hospitals got its share. According to the *Herald*, more than £270,000 (about $940,000) is due to Cork's hospitals on last November's Handicap. Since then the Grand National and Derby Sweeps swelled the total to about £750,000. It is understood the government wants to know how the hospitals propose to spend the money before handing it over.'

The hospitals eventually got their funds, but the report was correct in suggesting that de Valera's incoming government was giving the Sweeps a rigorous examination. The 'temporary' legislation licensing the operation was shortly to expire. Already it was evident that the Irish Sweeps were here to stay. The question now before de Valera was what tweaks should be made to the arrangement between State and Sweeps before the latter would be given a permanent framework.

While the lawmakers in Ireland were drawing up a startling sweetheart deal between the State and the Sweeps, things got even better for Hospitals Trust when, in June 1933, the *New York Times* ran the headline 'Lottery Ban Lifted by Farley'. An Irish American from New York, James Farley, was appointed Postmaster General by incoming President Franklin Roosevelt in early 1933. The report began: 'Chicago, June 1: Postmaster General Farley has rescinded a ruling issued two years ago by his Republican predecessor Walter H Brown barring newspapers from printing stories about winners of lotteries or sweepstakes.'

Good news stories were at a premium at the time. More than three years after the Wall Street Crash, the economy of the United States was on its knees. With the nation's bankers hiding behind bolted doors, there were no loans available to anyone. No one could cash a cheque or even get at their savings. Queues for a charitable bowl of soup stretched endlessly as the jobless figures shot above 25 per cent in a land where employers used to compete for manpower. Farm prices fell through the floor while countless homeowners who couldn't meet their mortgage payments loaded up their belongings and vanished down the road in the hope of making a fresh start.

Roosevelt swept to power on a promise of putting things right with a New Deal. The New Deal rested on realising what commentators dubbed the Three Rs. He would give Relief to the jobless and the devastated farmers. He would Reform the banking system with tough new laws and strict regulation. On a more touchy-feely note, the new administration would promote a feelgood factor which, in itself, would speed the nation towards Recovery.

It was as a token of this new feelgood spirit that Postmaster Farley opted to cut the Irish Sweeps and its American fanbase a New Deal of his own making. Reversing the policy of decades, the beefy ex-baseball player declared it was not the business of the Post Office to police the morals of the American people. He gave newspaper owners the go-ahead to 'print all the news about the poor chambermaid or the unemployed miner who bought a ticket for a quarter and won a million dollars'. On another occasion he expanded: 'If it is going to impair our morals to know what is going on in the world that is a problem for our pastors, not the Post Office.'

Flying in the face of the law as it stood, and incurring the wrath of his own legal department, Farrelly had opened the floodgates for a fresh deluge of Irish contraband, and his kindness would be repaid. For many years after he left his post, he was a regular visitor to Dublin where the Irish Hospitals Trust ensured he never had to put his hand in his pocket.

Chapter 11

THE WORST REVENGE ON
THE OLD ENEMY

In Dublin, at the close of a giddily successful 1931, the most coveted sweep tickets in town weren't those already on sale for the 1932 Grand National, but those for what promised to be one of the most exotic Christmas parties the capital had ever seen.

On 22 December *The Irish Times* offered a tantalising teaser of what was in store for the select band of lucky invitees. It said: 'The most novel of dances held for some time in Dublin is to be given at the Gresham Hotel tonight. It is a Christmas dance and supper, given by the Foreign Section of the Irish Hospitals Sweepstake staff. The dance will be as picturesque as it is new, and as quaint as it is novel. The supper menu is described in eight languages, and an Irish dance will be performed in the costumes of fifty different types of nationals. "John Bull", who buys so many "sweep" tickets, will be in this Irish dance. So too will Eskimos and Maoris, Red Indians and Japanese, Africans, Indians and Chinese. All will have a place in the performance of The Bridge Of Athlone.'

The Foreign Section had recruited an army of translators from all parts of the globe, tasked with sending out press releases and liaising with lucky winners in their native tongues. The United Nations of foreign speakers were not the only arrivals to find a warm welcome in Ireland. The Sweeps promoters and their bankers had to make special arrangements to cope with the assortment of weird and wonderful foreign banknotes flooding in from all parts of the world. In advance of the 1932 Epsom Derby, the *Daily Telegraph* captured the Sweeps sensation in a nutshell with the headline: 'World's Gold Pouring into Dublin.'

The *Telegraph* was just one of many publications from around the globe competing to feed the public's voracious appetite for Sweeps glamour and gossip. Or, in the words of one reporter: 'There are few places on the surface of the Earth that are not interested in this Sweepstake.' It was an age when passenger flights were rare, pricey and dangerous, but on the eve of the March draw on the Grand National, three De Havilland Puss Moth aeroplanes arrived at Dublin's Baldonnel Aerodrome packed with British press and newsreel cameramen. Within minutes of the last ticket being drawn, the pressmen were motoring back to the airstrip with their photos for the following day's editions.

In an age when millions struggled with grinding poverty, the Sweeps organisers made a publicity virtue of flaunting the wealth pouring in. One awestruck British reporter wrote of how cash was arriving into Sweeps headquarters at the breakneck rate of £20,000 per hour. Among those standing in a queue that ran out the door and down the street was 'a floor manager from a large London store' who 'brought the largest individual sum, £27,000, handed over the counters during the day'.

Another 1932 report from the British press was crowned with the triple-headline: 'Sweepstake Rush. Zero Hour at Dublin Depots. The Laggards.' It told readers: 'The six o'clock deadline for counterfoils passed with big crowds still delivering their counterfoils to various Dublin depots, so staff worked long past zero hour. Many had arrived on the evening London mailboat. The cross channel passenger vessels in the morning brought to the city many hundreds of Britishers with cash and counterfoils.'

From the outset, the Sweeps promoters had purposefully printed up their tickets to look like legal tender. Several governments made irate noises about confiscating tickets as counterfeit currency, so by mid-1932 it was deemed prudent to stamp them with the word 'ticket' in large print. But legal tender or not, for the sake of Spencer Freeman's publicity machine the counterfoils for the draw were handled as if they were worth their weight in gold.

One British newsman reported on how suitcases full of counterfoils were handed over the counter at Sweeps HQ by officials of British 'banks and business houses which had been entrusted by clients with the purchase of tickets'. The writer continued: 'To help the banks and business houses a special depot had been opened in the early morning by the Sweeps promoters. Armed detectives were on duty in all the offices throughout the day and uniformed police regulated the queues outside on the streets.'

The heavy armed security presence was really just for show. The highly visible 24 hour police cordon in case of a daring raid was pure Spencer Freeman media mastery. Even if a criminal gang did escape with the nine million counterfoils, what would they do with them? Invite some nurses and the world's media to their hideout and stage the draw there?

It was claptrap but it sent out a message that the Irish Hospitals Sweep was backed by the full authority of a widely admired plucky little state. It was swallowed whole by the man from London's *Evening Standard* who was deeply impressed by the sight of all those precious counterfoils requiring a round-the-clock armed guard. As enthralled as he knew his readers would be, he wrote: 'If Mister Joe [McGrath] wants to go into the strong rooms where the nine million counterfoils for the Derby draw are kept, he must . . .

- Get a certificate of authorisation signed by two of the senior auditors.
- Be accompanied by one of the auditiors.

'This is one of the precautions taken in the watch on the counterfoils. The robbery of a single one of them, if detected, would cancel all arrangements for the Sweep. Plain clothes detectives are keeping the building under observation day and night. And inside the building other men, in plain clothes, are lounging, but less conspicuous, about the corridors. The bulge in the hip pocket in every case is their gun.'

Freeman's set-up was pitch perfect for the year in which the movie sensation *Scarface* starring George Raft topped the box-office, following hot on the heels of other seminal gangster blockbusters such as *Little Caesar* with Edward G. Robinson, and Jimmy Cagney's breakthrough role as *The Public Enemy*.

But there was a price to be paid elsewhere for the swelling coffers of Ireland, and the *Evening Standard* concluded with a patriotic twinge of regret: 'The total subscriptions to the Calcutta Turf Club Derby Sweepstake amount to £150,000. Last year's total was £621,000. The Calcutta Sweep was for some years the largest sweep organized on the Derby but has been overshadowed since the establishment of the Irish Hospitals Sweepstakes.'

The patriotic feelings of London's *Daily Herald* were less mellow. The newspaper pointed out that millions of pounds were being drained each year from Britain's sickly economy, supposedly to provide life-support for Ireland's even sicklier health service. The *Daily Herald* and other papers ran a story detailing the huge profits being creamed off by a tiny number of private individuals for personal gain. It deplored the fact that six named shareholders in the Irish Hospitals Trust had turned an initial investment of £5,000 into a huge fortune of £370,000 in less than two years. It named Richard Duggan as the largest shareholder, while the combined holdings of Joe McGrath and his wife Eileen put them on a close footing.

Churchmen of all hues added their condemnation. The Bishop of Blackpool bemoaned that: 'The world is lost in the worship of chance, a miserable crafty way of getting money.' The *Catholic Times* condemned the 'worldwide hunt for unearned fortune'. The Anglican Bishop of Worcester did his best to stir up a patriotic backlash against the run of money out of his country, providing the papers with the headline 'Ireland's Revenge'. Arthur Perowne, whose father had been Bishop of Worcester before him, railed: 'The moral debauchment that the Irish gamble is effecting in England is the worst form of revenge upon its old enemy that Ireland could have invented. The Dublin sweepstakes may be almost compared with Balaam's indirect attack on Israel.' Ancient lore has it that the prophet Balaam led the people of Israel off the straight and narrow by seducing them with earthly pleasures and false gods.

The Catholics who made up the overwhelming bulk of the Free State's population in 1932 were very much at peace with both their God and the Irish Hospitals Sweepstakes, even when one of the draws that year was themed against an elaborate backdrop of Ireland's pagan deities rendered in large figures of wood and painted canvas. The biggest of these was a towering Manannan Mac Lir, the mythical god of the sea, at the prow of his magic boat he had made from copper. If the big drum containing the tickets was disguised as a copper ship, the cheek of the Sweeps' publicity material was unvarnished brass. Journalists were fed the line: 'He has been brought into modern life in the symbolic story, told in the setting of his travels around the world collecting treasures for the Sweepstakes.'

Behind the drum/ship was a giant rising sun. All around it, the young women mixing the tickets were dressed as fairies, princesses and warriors. The mixing system devised by Freeman involved churning the counterfoils through a factory-like process during which they were shaken, shuffled, shovelled, siphoned and subjected to a perplexing variety of other actions. With eight, nine or ten million tickets in the mix, the hoopla had now been stretched to three days. The *Irish Independent* viewed this marathon as a source of national pride, reporting: 'Captain Spencer Freeman, the Technical Director of the draw, has devised a scheme of mixing which ensures that all the counterfoils that are to be loaded into the drum are mixed together with the same care that a housewife uses to stir a Christmas pudding.'

By far the biggest event to take place in Ireland in 1932 was the Eucharistic Congress which was held in Dublin in June. The Catholic world's equivalent of hosting the Olympic Games, the Congress was attended by cardinals, bishops and other clerics from around the world and culminated with an outdoor Mass in the Phoenix Park which drew roughly one-quarter of the Free State's entire populace. In terms of crowds on the streets, the next three biggest events were the three Sweeps draws of that heady year. In terms of global coverage and interest, the Sweeps were hands-down winners over the clerical love-in.

The thrice yearly pageant orchestrated by Spencer Freeman became a tourist attraction in its own right. In 1932 the mixing and draw was moved to the more spacious Plaza Ballroom which normally hosted dancing and billiards, and which faced directly on to the capital's showpiece central park, St Stephen's Green. The park and its wide surrounding boulevards would accommodate even greater crowds and allow Freeman to further upscale his grand parades.

As the *Irish Independent* diarist observed: 'The whole town had a holiday atmosphere this week. The number of people from every part of the country and from England and Scotland who find the draw a business which entails their presence in Dublin is extraordinary. The hotels and restaurants were working at a hectic rate, the streets were packed with motor cars and thronged with visitors. All the folk in and around Dublin who are always looking for things to fill in their leisured days were having the time of their lives sitting in the Plaza for hours on end, then meeting for luncheon and seeing everybody else they knew lunching too, then returning for the draw and sitting for more hours on end and doing exactly the same thing for three days running.' The venue couldn't accommodate all those who turned up, so, as the same paper noted: 'An elaborate loudspeaker installation will enable those in the Plaza and the crowds in St Stephen's Green to hear the opening speeches and the numbers called.'

One visiting reporter wrote admiringly: 'The organization of the Irish Free State Hospitals Sweeps is the nearest thing to perpetual motion that has ever been devised.' The engineer who deserved praise for bringing military precision to a new form of showbiz was Spencer Freeman, and he wasn't shy about lapping it up. One pen-picture caught him in his element, 'sitting on a high perch in the middle of the Plaza ballroom floor, calling commands and blowing a whistle at the crowd of young women clad as jockeys who were mixing the counterfoils. The young women were pushing little boxes with horses on the outside of them round a set of rails. Captain Freeman, looking like a doctor diagnosing patients in the bulk, was dressed in morning coat and striped trousers. He is said to be the best dressed man in Dublin.'

The three-day mixathon was gruelling work for the young women who had to manually shift tons of paper in hundreds of repetitive manoeuvres. The *Irish Independent* pointed out: 'A rest room in the Plaza is provided for girls who suffer from exhaustion or minor injuries. A nurse is in attendance. The number of casualties treated here daily is about sixty.'

In the week of the Derby draw in 1932, the number of women employed by the Sweeps swelled to 4,200, making the organisation one of the biggest employers in the State. The entire civil service numbered only 19,000. Down the following decades the Irish Hospitals Trust would repeatedly use its position as a major employer in a run-down economy to extract favourable deals from successive governments. Such was the demand for jobs in the Sweeps, that the Irish Hospitals Trust set up its own counterpart to the written exams for entry to the civil service. In 1932, 1,650 current and former clerical staff were examined in 'English composition and handwriting, technical questions connected to Sweeps work and general knowledge'. While the examinations would ensure that staff were capable, it did not guarantee that women were employed entirely on merit. From the outset it was clear that many of those handed the coveted jobs were well connected to the Sweeps promoters. More than one commentator pointed out that the staff roll-call read like a Who's Who of old IRA wives and daughters.

But if favouritism was often a factor in securing a job, once employed the regime was strict and stern. Staff who arrived for work even seconds late were refused entry and docked pay. A playful list of New Year's resolutions published by the *Evening Herald* included the following: 'We even hazard a guess that a certain young lady who works in the Sweep, and who probably holds the record for being locked out, succeeded in getting up in good time yesterday and got a smile not a scowl from the doorman.'

In a society where breadwinning was seen as a man's responsibility, the jobless men of Ireland didn't take kindly to this new operation which was virtually a women-only zone. The Dublin Unemployed (Able-bodied) Men's Association petitioned the Irish Hospitals Trust to open its doors to males. The Trust responded with a letter that was read out at a meeting of the Association. It was reported: 'The question of the possibility of employing a percentage of male labour from the Association has been fully investigated by the Minister [with responsibility for employment]. He apparently was satisfied with the explanation given by the Hospitals Trust that the work was unsuitable for men.'

The minister may have been satisfied that the work was unsuitable for men, but the men weren't. In June 1932 a newspaper reported the 'widespread rumour' that the Irish Hospitals Trust was about to bow to union pressure and take on some male clerical staff. It then dismissed such a development as 'extremely unlikely, as it is the duty of the committee to keep the running costs as low as possible'. In all occupations at the time, where men and women did comparable work, women were paid considerably less than men. The same story reported that the unions were unhappy with 'persistent rumours that many ladies whose husbands and parents were in comfortable circumstances are employed to the exclusion of many needy applicants from working class homes'. There was truth in this as the ex-IRA families from whom many of the women were drawn now made up a significant part of Ireland's new political and social upper crust.

As a fabulously successful 1932 drew to a close the danger arose that the debate over jobs with Hospitals Trust might become academic, as news emerged of plans to set up a new offshore sweepstake to benefit

British hospitals. Championed by Sir Charles Higham and supported by a cross-section of the British aristocracy who offered to sit on its committee, the new sweep would operate out of Monte Carlo. Tickets would be sold under the title Principality of Monaco Sweepstakes. Unveiling his plans in October 1932, Sir Charles announced that arrangements were already underway to stage the first draw on the Aintree Grand National the following March. The Prince of Monaco would oversee the grand occasion.

What most shocked Irish readers was that Spencer Freeman, dubbed in reports 'the man who made the Irish Sweep', was linked to this new rival which threatened to wipe out the Irish presence in the lucrative British market. Sir Charles Higham said that final details of the first Monte Carlo sweep would be released once he had secured the services of 'a well-known man' who would run the show. This speculation intensified when Freeman was spotted at Euston Station in London.

Freeman released a statement to the press. It said: 'In view of the statements contained in the newspapers today to the effect that Captain Spencer Freeman is organizing a sweepstake on the lines of the Irish "Sweep" in the Principality of Monaco, Captain Freeman, who has just returned from Ireland, wishes to state that he has no connection, directly or indirectly, with the proposed scheme.'

It emerged that Freeman had indeed quit the Irish Hospital Sweepstakes, but not to take up a job with the Monte Carlo project. Motivated by a sense of patriotic duty to his native land, he was in London trying to float his own British-based sweepstake to aid that country's hospitals. In parallel with Freeman's own statement disassociating himself from the Monte Carlo sweep, the president of the British Hospitals Association announced that Freeman's proposal was the only one with the support of the Association. At a meeting two days earlier the hospitals' body had adopted a resolution that it was prepared to benefit from funds raised by sweepstakes. Whether by accident or design, Freeman's pitch to the British Hospitals Association had dealt the rival Monte Carlo scheme a damaging blow. In the light of McGrath's proven expertise in sabotage, and a later escapade in Mexico, there are slight grounds to lean more towards design than accident.

Back in Dublin, Joe McGrath was forced to admit publicly that the Irish Sweeps had lost its technical director. McGrath explained that

Freeman had resigned and returned to the home he kept in Surrey. McGrath put on a brave face for the press, insisting that the future had never looked more rosy. He said: 'We regret the departure of Captain Freeman. Indeed, he left us against my advice, but we have parted the best of friends and if at any time he should feel disposed to return, I, for one, would have no objection.'

McGrath's surprisingly warmhearted invite to a potentially devastating friend-turned-rival appeared on the day the last draw of 1932 came to a close with the drawing of the consolation prizes for the holders of scratched horses. For the man from *The Irish Times* for whom the novelty of the occasion was wearing thin, it was a bit like watching the last stragglers trail over the finishing line in a marathon.

He wrote: 'The draw is over! At four o'clock yesterday afternoon the great drum disgorged the last of its secrets. Superintendent Broy, deputizing for his chief, General O'Duffy, gave the word of command for the last time, and for the last time six nurses plunged their bared arms into the portholes and drew out six tiny scraps of paper, the last six counterfoils to share in the flood of wealth which the Hospitals Trust, during the past four days, has passed out over all parts of the world.

'They distributed only £150,800 at the Plaza yesterday during the four hours or so in which the drum rolled monotonously on—1,508 prizes of £100 apiece. Quite a lot of money, of course, judged by ordinary standards, but one grows blasé after sitting day after day and watching wealth being flung to the winds as lightly as if it came from the pockets of a millionaire's spendthrift heir. It is a monotonous business, this climax to a great draw. Who cares to sit and watch paltry hundreds of pounds being given away when only last Friday we were speculating on the destination of thousands?

'The answer is that hundreds of people do. Throughout the whole of the day the Plaza was crowded, and many of those who arrived at the beginning of the proceedings were evidently prepared for a long stay. I saw there people who had evidently come to make a picnic of the affair, people with sandwiches and vacuum flasks. Men came with stocks of newspapers and women brought their knitting.'

The flamboyant master or ceremonies, Spencer Freeman, was conspicuous by his absence. By now, his showboating had become a central feature of each production. At the first draw of 1932 a reporter had noted how he had choreographed the mixing of the counterfoils with 'drilling that made it seem more like a theatrical *scène de ballet* than the very serious business that it was'. Freeman had 'presided over it all in a tennis scorer's high chair from which he called out drill orders and directions to some hundreds of girls dressed in long, white peg-top trousers seamed with a red stripe and finished with a blue waistband'. Now, for the last draw of the year his high chair in front of the stage was occupied by a member of the Hospitals Trust staff. The report concluded with a denial from Joe McGrath that other senior Sweeps personnel were about to follow Freeman out of the organisation and into a rival venture.

McGrath said: 'As far as our own Sweepstakes are concerned, I do not think, indeed I am certain, that we have no cause to fear any opposition that may spring up on the Continent. All the world knows that our Sweeps are conducted fairly and honestly. We have the confidence of the world, and confidence is the main thing upon which the success of an enterprise such as a sweepstake depends. We have never failed to account for every penny we have received, and the public appreciates the fact that everything is straightforward and above board. If there was any alteration in the law as far as sweepstakes in England are concerned, it might make a difference to the Irish Sweepstake. But there is still a vast number of people in America whom we have still to tap for subscriptions, so that I have no fear for the continued success of our Sweepstakes.'

Soon enough McGrath would face precisely the scenario he speculated on, but before that there were hurdles to be cleared at home. As he contemplated the possibility that Hospitals Trust would be forced to concentrate its efforts on North America, McGrath received the very welcome news from Spencer Freeman that the British Home Office was implacably opposed to a British sweepstake.

Before you could say 'Game, set and match', Freeman was back in his tennis scorer's high chair.

Chapter 12 ∾

A GOVERNMENT INQUIRY
WOULD BE UNJUSTIFIED

By the close of 1932 the snowballing success of the Irish Sweeps had reduced its Calcutta rival, once the world's biggest sweepstake, to an also ran. At home, the Irish Hospitals Trust had completed the process of squeezing out would-be rivals. The original six Dublin hospitals to benefit were initially augmented by ones in Cork. Then, prompted by the Dáil, the list of institutions was expanded to include many more hospitals, nursing bodies, and the Poor Law hospitals which had been the only ones in the State exclusively funded by the taxpayer. With the State now treating the Sweeps coffers as a direct source of cash, the latter came to look more than ever like an official arm of government.

The Irish hospital system was transformed almost overnight. Containing a big thank you to the Sweeps at the end of 1932, the annual report of the National Children's Hospital detailed how the institution had received a much-needed head-to-toe makeover. The leaking slate roof was being replaced with a modern copper one. A new storey was being added to provide dorms so that nurses could sleep on site. The unsanitary ancient toilets and bathrooms were being demolished and replaced with clean modern ones. Modern x-ray apparatus was being installed. The latest central heating system was being put in, along with a reliable supply of running water. The kitchens were to be completely overhauled with the addition for the first time of refrigerators.

All across the country improvements were being carried out on a similar scale. Indeed, the bountiful scale of some of the enhancements was of concern to some observers. Flush with funds beyond their wildest dreams, the boards of some hospitals went on spending binges, ordering in state-of-the-art equipment for which there was often no call. An arms race of sorts grew up, with managements in neighbouring locales engaging in high-stakes games of keeping up with the Joneses. Some had world-class operating theatres but no surgeon on their staff. Others installed machines which would have been the envy of the best hospitals in the United States, but which saw little use in sleepy corners of rural Ireland.

It has been pointed out that without the influx of Sweeps money, Ireland's network of small local hospitals would have been forced to rationalise and amalgamate in accordance with the basic laws of economics. By distorting this situation, one lasting legacy of the Sweeps is a jealous territoriality that has left Ireland with a sprawling patchwork of local hospitals unnecessary to service a population of four million people.

After nine years of relative stability under W. T. Cosgrave's Cumann na nGaedheal Party, the Free State had its first change of government in 1932 when Fianna Fáil came to power. Many in Fianna Fáil had fought a Civil War ten years earlier to kill the partitioned Free State at birth, and many viewed the new government with nervous suspicion. During the election campaign Cumann na nGaedheal had lost no opportunity to present Fianna Fáil as the party of the gunman. One Cumann na nGaedheal deputy claimed that if Fianna Fáil were ever allowed to hold the reins of power, the party would open the jails 'and let out the murderers'.

In the event, there was no mass release of convicted killers on to the streets, and Fianna Fáil got down to dealing with the humdrum issues of democratic rule. As 1933 dawned, the time was approaching when the temporary legislation legalising the Irish Hospitals Sweepstakes would elapse. During the debates before that legislation was enacted, Richard Duggan's old enemy Thomas Johnson had predicted that by the time the legislation elapsed 'vested interests will have grown up' and 'if you refuse permission to carry on the sweeps you will throw on the unemployment market 600 clerks'. In fact, at different stages of the sweeps cycle the number employed fluctuated between some 3,000 and 4,200.

New Taoiseach Éamon de Valera understood that to preserve existing jobs and keep the cash flowing into the health service, the Sweeps would have to be set on a permanent footing. He also understood that the operation relied on the payment of massive amounts in kickbacks to customs officials, to postal workers, to seamen and very possibly to policemen on both sides of the Atlantic. De Valera realised that if these corrupt 'expenses' were to be made public, it would drag both the Irish Hospitals Sweepstakes and the Free State government into international disrepute.

The result was Section 2 of the 1933 Public Hospitals Bill which effectively told Duggan, McGrath and Spencer: 'Don't tell us whose palms you are greasing. We don't want to know.' On the face of it, the new legislation stipulated that every member of the Oireachtas should be provided with a set of audited accounts for each sweep. In effect, Section 2 made a nonsense of this by allowing the promoters to keep their 'expenses' off the books.

As the bill passed through the Senate, Sir John Keane challenged this provision saying: 'These figures leave me uneasy.' The original temporary 1930 bill had contained the safeguard that 'no tickets shall be issued free except by way of reward to a seller of tickets'. For 'tickets', the word 'cash' could be safely substituted, since demand was such that each ticket could be readily converted into ten shillings of hard currency. Keane wanted to know why these key words from the original Act had been quietly dropped from the new legislation. A government senator replied that there was nothing to be read into it. It was 'purely a drafting change'.

Sir John again protested that 'it is wrong that there should be even this element of hidden, undisclosed expenses, which may be of any magnitude'. His was a lone voice crying in the wilderness. The bill passed with ease through both Houses of the Oireachtas, with a government senator lecturing Keane: 'Everyone knows the circumstances under which these sweepstakes have to be run. It is no secret that the overwhelming majority of the proceeds come from countries where sweepstakes are forbidden. That, in itself, is an explanation of the necessity for a certain amount of secrecy being observed in regard to certain aspects of their administration.'

Section 2 provided the Free State government with a fig-leaf to hide its complicity in worldwide bribery and corruption. At the same time it gave the owners of the Irish Hospitals Trust free rein to pull figures from the air for public consumption and enrich themselves to an even greater extent with impunity.

However, Fianna Fáil's ascent to power in 1932 was not all good news for the Sweeps promoters. During the first decade of the Free State's existence, the Cumann na nGaedheal government had smoothed out diplomatic relations with Britain. It was in the interests of the party of business and big farmers to keep the lines of trade open to what was essentially Ireland's only export market.

As the party of the small farmer and the urban worker, Fianna Fáil had a different agenda. Once in office, de Valera made good on his electoral promise to stop paying back the repayments on loans granted by Britain to Irish tenant farmers half a century earlier to enable them to buy their smallholdings from the hated landlords. The repayments were a legal obligation imposed on the Free State under the terms of the 1921 Anglo-Irish Treaty.

Britain retaliated by placing an embargo on Irish exports, bringing trade to a standstill in what would become known as the Economic War, which would last for six years. The hostility de Valera's policy aroused in Britain can be gauged from a 1933 editorial in the *Times* of London which accused Ireland's new leader of pursuing a dangerously insane experiment with 'autarchy', which it defined as a 'fantastic belief in self-sufficiency'. For the men behind the Irish Hospitals Trust, the hostility aroused within the British establishment by Ireland's action was a deeply worrying development. After two years paralysed by indecision, attitudes in the Westminster Parliament towards the Sweeps hardened. If the Irish refused to honour their lawful debts, every effort must be made to ensure they could no longer milk the hard-hit British economy for easy millions.

Having made his deal with the devil in the form of the 1933 Act, Éamon de Valera had to put up with the consequences of the Free State's close identification with the Sweeps. In addition to his role as Prime Minister, de Valera was Minister for External [Foreign] Affairs. Much to his annoyance, the Department of External Affairs was viewed in some quarters as the Leinster House office of the Irish Hospitals Sweepstakes. The department received a steady stream of letters from around the globe containing bank drafts, cash, counterfoils and enquiries. The number of memos repeatedly reminding officials not to pass these items on to the Irish Hospitals Trust, but to return to sender, reflects that it was common practice for officials to help the Sweeps mail on its way.

A letter sent from the Department of External Affairs in August 1933 told H. Gabbutt of Ontario, Canada, to stop using the department as a PO box. The department secretary wrote: 'Referring to my letter to you of the 14th instant instructing you to discontinue the practice of sending sweepstake ticket counterfoils and remittances to this Department for transmission to the Hospitals Trust Limited, Dublin, I am directed by the Minister for External Affairs to inform you that a further set of counterfoils and Money Order £5 (Bank of Montreal) were received from you today. In view of the fact that you had not received my letter of 14th of August at the time of despatch [*sic*] by you, they were duly transmitted to the Sweepstake authorities. I am, however, to ask you to note specially that any further Sweepstake ticket counterfoils or remittances received from you will, as already intimated to you, be returned to you in the post.'

In another letter, counterfoils and a cheque made out to 'The Secretary, Department of External Affairs', were sent by the department to the Irish Legation in Washington with a request that they be returned to Mr Dushan Sekulitch, a diplomat in the Royal Yugoslav Legation there. An internal memo on the volume of Sweeps mail arriving at the department noted: 'The letters were addressed either to "The Irish Free State Government" or "Secretary Department of External Affairs". They came from Canada, the United States, Scotland and Norway. The cheques etc were made payable in some cases to Irish Hospitals Trust Ltd, in others to the Irish Free State Government, the Secretary, Department of External Affairs or (in one case) the Minister for External Affairs.'

There were other ways in which the Sweeps were a nuisance to the government. At the beginning of 1935 a circular signed by Joe McGrath put further stress on the already strained Anglo-Irish relations. The three-page document, branded a 'promoter's impudent letter' in the British press, was posted to subscribers in Britain offering advice on how to flout new anti-sweepstake laws. It assured the Sweeps agents that Irish Hospitals Trust was doing its bit to protect their identity by adopting 'greater measures for privacy'. McGrath assured them: 'We shall endeavour not to post to you any compromising letters.'

Appended to the end of the letter was a reminder never to address correspondence directly to Sweeps HQ in Dublin. It instructed: 'All communications from Cross Channel or Overseas should be addressed through an intermediary in the Irish Free State, or according to our special advices. Alternatively, arrange with a Business House, Institution or Friend in the Irish Free State to transmit your communications to us, or deliver personally. A Directory (eg Kelly's Manufacturers And Shippers Of The World Vol 2, pages 1,724 to 1,752 in 1933 edition) which includes the Irish Free State, may be seen in most libraries.' Britain's *Morning Post* newspaper deplored this footnote as 'a statement showing where and how tickets may be obtained'.

Britain's Dominions Secretary summoned the Irish High Commissioner in London and registered a complaint about McGrath's circular. He reprimanded the Irish diplomat with a reminder that the Free State had an obligation under international postal conventions to keep its mail free of items that would thwart the laws of other lands. Back in Dublin, External Affairs sent a stern letter to Joe McGrath.

McGrath wrote back to the department, scapegoating 'an agent of ours named Mrs Chapman'. He assured the department: 'Definite instructions have been given that no circular will accompany our issues in future except those of a very harmless nature. The Chapman Circular is, as I told you, one issued by an Agent, and we have severely reprimanded her. We have also issued instructions to all Agents to refrain from issuing circulars of any kind in the future. I think you can rest assured that there will be no further cause for complaint, at least in this direction.' Printed on the headed Hospitals Trust notepaper used by McGrath was the same footnote which had appeared on the circular that had so annoyed the British. The note printed on to the bottom of the standard Hospitals Trust stationery was an instruction not to send Sweeps mail to the address printed at the top of the sheet.

Five months after External Affairs gave McGrath his warning, the Irish High Commissioner in London wrote home to say he had had a meeting with the British authorities and they 'greatly appreciated the prompt and effective action' taken by the Irish government to curb McGrath's activities. However, tickets were still in circulation and the British 'thought that since An Saorstat Government exercised some control over the Irish Hospitals Trust they might ask the Trust to refrain from giving any facilities of any kind which resulted in actions which were infringements of British law'. The Irish government was unable to oblige, taking the position that Hospitals Trust was a private limited company.

The best de Valera could do was to repeat his instructions to all government departments to put a clear distance between the offices of the State and the offices of the Sweeps. In late 1935 he circulated the members of his cabinet with a detailed memo. It began: 'Prior to each Sweepstake conducted by Hospitals Trust Ltd the President's private office receives communications regarding them from other countries, principally from the United States. These communications generally take the form of enquiries or requests for tickets, or for the transmission of counterfoils or money to the Trust. Having regard to the fact that participation in Sweepstakes is now illegal in many countries, it is felt that it is not right that a Department of State, whose status confers on its correspondence a high degree of immunity in transit, should permit itself to be used as an intermediary or cover for the conveyance of articles which, if sent through the ordinary post from any of those countries, would be liable to confiscation or other penal action.' The memo said that Ireland's diplomats in the United States and Britain had been ordered 'to avoid carefully any association with the Sweepstakes which might possibly be construed as a breach of the domestic laws of those countries'.

De Valera, through his memo, expressed unease that his officials could be compromised by handling Sweeps money. It said: 'There is no machinery in the Department to ensure the correct receipt or delivery of money or money's worth entrusted to it for dispatch to the Trust, and it is felt that nothing should be done which could be even construed as an acceptance of any such responsibility. There has already been one case of an alleged lost remittance which, if pressed, might conceivably have given rise to considerable trouble.'

The memo raised the potential damage to the Free State's international reputation through guilt by association, pointing out 'the risk of implied assumption of liability in matters of which it has no proper concern'. Every sweep brought new cases to Dublin's High Court where family, friends and neighbours of winning ticket-holders claimed part ownership. The memo stressed: 'A serious situation might arise if a disputed claim to ownership of a winning ticket were made by a person who claimed to have sent the money and counterfoil through the Department, and if in consequent litigation the Department was cited as a witness.'

The memo also noted in passing that the French representative in Dublin had made complaints to the Irish government about the activities of the Irish Sweeps in France. In 1932 France's Minister for the Interior had issued a warning that anyone promoting lotteries faced a heavy fine and imprisonment, but the French were no more immune to the spell of the Irish Sweeps than any other people.

The Irish Legation in Paris was treated as a customer service department for French subscribers to the Sweeps. One letter addressed to 'The Irish Consul, Paris' asked: 'Could you please let me have a ticket for the Irish Sweeps, and if you have not any could you kindly inform me where I could buy one as quick as possible.' One missive sent from the *Legation D'Irlande* to officials in Dublin said: 'The other day a letter was left in here from America enclosing an order for sweepstake tickets and enclosing a draft. This communication was in due course forwarded to the Department. Since my arrival here I have also had brought to my notice correspondence in regard to sweepstake matters i.e. complaints in regard to the draw etc. As this correspondence does not concern government service it would be helpful to have some general direction.'

The Department of External Affairs replied: 'I am directed by the Minister to inform you that you should transmit any of these communications to the Department where the necessary action will be taken.'

Some of the complaints received by the Paris Legation were accompanied by threats. Georges Levy of Strasbourg wrote stating that he was convinced that the tickets he had paid for had not been included in the draw for the 1935 Grand National. He delivered an ultimatum to the Irish Legation that unless he was issued with new tickets or a refund of his 150 francs, he would notify the French government that the Irish Hospitals Trust 'not only sell their tickets by fraudulent means, but refuse to listen to any claims'. The Trust wrote back to the diplomats in Paris to say that their auditors, Craig Gardiner & Co., would issue Levy with a 'certificate' to prove his tickets had gone into the draw.

In 1934 the Paris Legation received a letter from a Mr R. Harel who was hoping the Irish government would consider a scheme for the 'reciprocal recognition of the legality of Irish sweepstake tickets in France and French lottery tickets in Ireland'. There appeared to be two obvious drawbacks to this plan. One was that French tickets would be assured of tiny sales in the small and impoverished Irish market. The second was that the 'French' tickets Monsieur Harel proposed to sell in

Ireland apparently wouldn't be French at all. As he wrote in his letter to 'Mr. Minister' in Dublin: 'Luxembourg lottery has been authorized to organize sweeps on the principal French races in association with French schemes for the relief of disabled ex-servicemen.' Passing on Harel's proposal to External Affairs in Dublin, the diplomat in Paris stressed that he wasn't recommending it as Harel 'is merely a private individual and I fancy that he would encounter much greater difficulty in carrying his scheme into execution than he seems to anticipate'. The Irish government gave Harel's preposterous proposal the consideration it deserved.

In 1934, shortly before the so-called 'Chapman' circular brought down the wrath of the British on the Irish government, another document for which McGrath denied responsibility brought a protest from the French to External Affairs via the Irish Legation in Paris. Not only was McGrath's organisation distributing leaflets advertising illegal Irish sweep tickets, but his promotional material contained the line: '*L'Irish Sweepstake est etroitement surveille par le Gouvernement.*' (The Irish Sweepstake is strictly supervised by the government.) The French were deeply annoyed with this apparent official endorsement of criminal activity.

A scribbled note from External Affairs to the Irish officials in Paris said McGrath had been tackled on the issue and: 'He assured me that he would get the offending phrase taken out of the circular, if the circular was really issued by the Trust or their agents. He was quite unaware of the existence of the circular.'

A typed government memo said that McGrath had been warned that the line which had vexed the French was 'an infringement of the spirit, if not the letter' of the stipulation in the Sweeps legislation that 'no advertisement . . . shall contain any words indicating, or which could reasonably be construed as indicating, that such sweepstake is being held under the auspices or patronage of the Government of Saorstat Éireann or any Minister'.

It observed that the presence of the line in the publicity material put the Free State government in 'a dilemma'. That dilemma was this: 'If we deny the accuracy of this phrase we will be met with the reply "not only are tickets being advertised in France, but they are being sold on false pretences if not in actual violation of Art 7 (2) of the Irish Act". If we don't deny it, it can be used, as it is in the present French note, to support the argument "if the Sweep is *etroitement surveille* by the

Government, the Government can stop it violating French law".'

The official who drafted the memo proposed an Irish solution to an Irish problem: 'On the whole I think it would be better not to refer to the phrase at all in our reply [to the French].'

In 1935 the Department of External Affairs was dragged into a dispute which left little doubt that the Irish Hospitals Trust was engaged in what one complainant described as 'fraudulent collusion'. The government's decision was to turn a blind eye, as can be gleaned from a note from the Attorney General to the minister. It says: 'I enclose your letter received by me, together with draft reply thereto. The letter in question, you will observe, contains serious allegations against the members of the Hospitals Trust. The facts in connection with the matter are not set out with sufficient clearness to enable me to judge whether there has been sharp practice by the Directors of the Hospitals Trust or others. I gather that what is complained of is that some person connected with the bookmaking firm of Douglas Stuart in London approached the holder of Ticket No. E M 88791 which had drawn a horse in the Cambridgeshire, through their New York agent and purchased either the whole or half of the holder's interest in the ticket. The ticket drew either the winning or second horse in the race. The holder apparently repented of her bargain and endeavoured to hold up payment out of the moneys. The London firm, however, had satisfied the Hospitals Trust of their title to the money and received payment before an injunction could be obtained in the courts here. The allegations made are that there was fraudulent collusion between the Hospitals Trust directors and the purchasers of the ticket which enabled the payment out to be made so quickly.'

The Attorney General's best guess was that a scandal was unlikely to surface. While the New Yorker in dispute with the Hospitals Trust had the option of taking her case to court, she may already 'have been advised that this would be both expensive and unlikely to be successful'. Her letter alleging fraudulent collusion against the Trust would never be revealed to the public on the technical legal grounds that it would be 'held privileged'. He concluded: 'A Government inquiry would, in my opinion, be unjustified as it would be an intrusion into the sphere of the courts.'

Chapter 13 ∾

| THE IRISH SWOOP

In the 1920s and 1930s pilots of both sexes jousted to set new speed and distance records from continent to continent. In 1934 the Australian city of Melbourne celebrated the centenary of its foundation by a band of Tasmanian settlers. To mark the occasion, Melbourne's mayor proposed a marathon 11,300 mile air race from England to his city's Flemington Racecourse. The Australian confectionery tycoon Sir Macpherson Robertson put up the enormous prize of £10,000 on conditition that it be called the MacRobertson Trophy Air Race.

The Royal Aero Club of Britain was put in charge of running the event which had five compulsory stops along the route. The first stage took the flyers to Baghdad in Iraq, followed by Allahabad in the jungles of India and then on to storm-lashed Singapore along what was described as 'the worst air path in the world'. After Singapore there was a risky jaunt over the shark infested Bay of Bengal which had never been overflown before. After touching down in the northern Australian town of Darwin it was a further 1,400 miles to the final stopover in the desert outpost of Charleville, before flying the last 800 miles to Melbourne.

The route was roughly the same, except in reverse, as that taken by the renowned Scottish aviator Jim Mollison when he set the speed record from Australia to England in 1931. The following year Mollison became the first pilot to fly solo across the Atlantic from east to west when he flew from Portmarnock in north Dublin to Pennfield in Canada. That same year Mollison married the even more famous flyer Amy Johnson and they became the golden couple of the most glamorous adventure sport in the world. In 1930, after Johnson became the first woman to fly solo from Britain to Australia, an estimated one million people lined the streets of London to welcome her home. She was a celebrity of such stellar magnitude that one item of fan mail posted in the Australian city of Adelade arrived in the letterbox of her family home marked simply 'Amy. England.'

The Mollisons were the star attractions entered for the race to Melbourne. Not only would they be given the honour of starting first, but they would be personally entrusted by King George V and Queen Mary with a letter to pass on to their son, the Duke of Gloucester, who was already in Melbourne.

Ireland had its own world famous aviator, and he too was among the starting line-up for the grand race, representing both his country and the Irish Hospitals Sweepstakes. Dublin-born James Fitzmaurice was an old friend of Joe McGrath. In 1915, aged 17, he enlisted in the British Army and the following year survived the slaughter of the Battle of the Somme. He rose through the ranks of the RAF and returned to Ireland in 1922 to help set up the Irish Army Corps following the foundation of the new Free State. Within five years he was commander of the Irish Air Corps. He became an international celebrity in 1928 when, together with two Germans, he made the first transatlantic flight from east to west, travelling from Baldonnel Aerodrome in north Dublin to Greenly Island in Canada.

Dubbed the 'Three Musketeers', the trio were given a ticker-tape parade in New York city along a route ten miles long. Other cities in the United States and Canada repeated the honour, while in Washington DC President Calvin Coolidge presented them with the Distinguished Flying Cross. The following year, 1929, Fitzmaurice was invited back to New York State for the dedication of the Fitzmaurice Flying Field, a new aerodrome named after him serving the town of Oyster Bay. A crowd of some 100,000 people came out to catch a glimpse of the famous flyer at the dedication. On a visit to Germany in 1933, some months before the Melbourne race was announced, Fitzmaurice was invited by one of his greatest admirers to drop in for a chat. He took up the invite and was given a warm welcome by Germany's newly installed Chancellor Adolf Hitler.

In April 1934, six months before the great race to Melbourne was due to start, the Irish High Commissioner to Britain held a luncheon at London's Savoy Hotel to officially unveil James Fitzmaurice as Ireland's contestant and the Irish Sweeps as his sponsors. Spencer Freeman and other Sweeps personnel attended. The toast, to 'The Flight', was proposed by Senator Oliver St John Gogarty, winner of the Bronze Medal for poetry at the 1924 Olympic Games and the inspiration for stately, plump Buck Mulligan in James Joyce's *Ulysses*. Gogarty told the gathering that air travel was now the great 'federaliser' of the world and that in sponsoring James Fitzmaurice, Joe McGrath and his associates had done more for Ireland aerially than the Irish government. He raised a chuckle saying that the government had put their hands in their pockets, only to find that they were insubstantial 'air pockets' and very little came out.

A letter was read out from Joe McGrath apologising for the fact that he was unable to attend because of pressure of work in Ireland. Revealing 'a little secret' to the diners, he wrote that for more than a year, the Hospitals Trust had been planning an international air race under the Irish Sweeps banner and with an identical first prize of £10,000. McGrath's missive continued: 'Then, suddenly, this project of the London to Melbourne air race appeared. I could see, apart from other considerations, that the two schemes might clash, and this would be hurtful to both of them, and I thereupon decided that the sporting thing to do would be to lay aside our own scheme and enter a machine in the MacRobertson race.' He added that it was 'time that we in Ireland did something to put Ireland on the nation map of the world'.

McGrath's letter pointed out that since Ireland was 'very much behind the times in aerial development', an aircraft for the race would have to be sourced abroad. For this Fitzmaurice had a blank cheque from the Sweeps and a free hand to choose his own machine. McGrath's lone stipulation was that he picked the aircraft with the best chance of winning. Ensuring the launch luncheon would get a favourable splash in the British press, McGrath concluded: 'I make this promise. Should Colonel Fitzmaurice select an all-British machine, and win the race with it, we will give the £10,000 prize money to British hospital charities. Should he, on the other hand, decide that the machine of some other country is more suitable for this purpose, and with that machine win the race, we will give £5,000 of the prize money to the charities of the country manufacturing the machine and the other £5,000 to British charities.'

In the event, Fitzmaurice went shopping for his race plane in the United States. After checking out available models, he approached the celebrated designer Giuseppe Bellanca who agreed to custom build a new aircraft for the Irishman. The one-and-only Bellanca 28-70 was christened the Irish Swoop and shipped to Europe by ocean liner.

Throughout the day of 19 October 1934 huge crowds descended on the Royal Air Force base at Mildenhall in East Anglia to watch the race aircraft assemble and go through their final test flights. Over 60,000 people would return at dawn the following morning to watch the Mollisons lead off the field in their Comet Black Magic. Frenetic preparations were also the order of the day in Dublin, where the marathon draw for the Cambridgeshire sweep was to get underway on the 24th. The theme of the pageant was flight and a large model of the Irish Swoop took pride of place at the Plaza Ballroom which had been transformed into the Hospitals Sweepstakes Airport for the occasion. It was expected that the winning time to Melbourne would be three to four days, meaning that if everything went perfectly to plan, news of the Irish Swoop's victory would arrive in Ireland just as the mixing of the counterfoils was kicking off.

The race halfway across the globe generated huge interest worldwide. *Time* magazine described the scene at the starting point for American readers. 'The great doors of the Royal Air Force hangars opened wide at 3 am. One sleek machine after another was wheeled out. The deep-throated roar of their engines being tuned up fairly shook the field. Since midnight they had been converging on the new RAF airdrome at Mildenhall, 60 miles from London. Over the field and its floodlights hung pitch-black night. Motors warmed, the twenty planes were lined up in two rows for the start of the greatest air race in aviation history. Chattering in little groups were flyers, mechanics, officials, men in dungarees, women in evening dress from London. At 6.30 am Sir Alfred Bower, Acting Lord Mayor of London, gave the starting signal.

'First away were Jim and Amy (Johnson) Mollison, 12-to-1 favorites in their De Havilland Comet. Two minutes later Roscoe Turner and Clyde Pangborn took off in their big Boeing, just as an orange-red sun edged over the horizon. One by one the rest took the air and headed south. Last off, 16 minutes after the Mollisons, was Captain T Neville Stack, carrying a complete motion picture of the start.

'On the sidelines "Tony" Fokker looked up from the technical journal he had been reading in time to see Stack's plane disappear over the horizon. Finish of the race: Melbourne, Australia, 11,323 miles away. Month on long month of intensive preparations by the aviation industry throughout the world had preceded the race's start. Represented by each entry were countless technicalities, endless research, details, delays, many a heartbreak. Of the 64 original entries, more than two-thirds had withdrawn. The night before the start Colonel James C Fitzmaurice, Irish transatlantic flyer, had been disqualified when his US-built Bellanca special, Irish Swoop, proved overweight.'

James Fitzmaurice and Joe McGrath's great race was run before it had even started. The officials of the Royal Aero Club ruled that the Irish Swoop was in breach of its design specifications and was carrying far more than the 400 gallons of fuel for which it was certified. Fitzmaurice and his co-pilot Eric Bonar were told they wouldn't be allowed to compete unless they drastically cut their fuel load to 120 gallons. Reluctantly, Fitzmaurice withdrew the Irish Swoop just hours before the dawn start.

McGrath's letter to the London luncheon seven months earlier had said: 'Aerial racing and aerial contests promise to be the great sport of the world in the near future. It will really be an international sport freed of the difficulties besetting other forms of international contests.' If only. Now, in Nazi Germany the Minister of Public Enlightenment and Propaganda, Joseph Goebbels, accused the Royal Aero Club of an act of bad sportsmanship by nobbling the Irish entry.

Goebbels doubled as editor of the Nazi newspaper *Der Angriff* (The Attack) and he used that organ to accuse the British of forcing Fitzmaurice out of the race because they thought him 'too dangerous an opponent'. The paper stated: 'No expense was spared for the greatest sporting event of the British Empire. Neither was any effort spared to see that an English flyer and an English aeroplane won the race.'

In Britain the Communist Party's newspaper, *The Daily Worker*, made common cause with the despised Nazis, running a report headlined 'Trickery that Only Just Succeeded'. The paper stated that the Irish Swoop was the race favourite 'but at the last moment a very strict interpretation of the airworthiness rules was enforced. The machine was reckoned too heavy with full fuel tanks, so it had either to fly with half-empty tanks and waste time refuelling en route, or be disqualified.'

Fitzmaurice and Bonar announced they would shortly take off to fly the route to Melbourne, although not as competitors, confidently predicting that they would set a new speed record. In the event, their attempt would take them no further than Belgium before technical problems forced them to retire. In Dublin, meanwhile, the great draw staged around the Irish Swoop turned into a performance of Hamlet without the prince, as news reached Ireland on the first day of the mixing that a British team had arrived first in Melbourne.

The weather in Dublin was a washout, but the lashing rain didn't keep the large crowds away from the pageant. One report said: 'Nearly everything it is possible to think of concerned with flight and the sky is depicted by the costumes of the mixing teams. The loaders represent the sun, moon, Mars and flight, while the carriers—the girls who take the counterfoils from the track to the mixing machines—were dressed as Mercury, classical Venus, speed and parachutes. The track operators, whose duty it is to push the trucks containing the counterfoils around the tracks, represented Saturn, modern Venus, war and aeroplanes. Some of the girls wore the uniforms of an air force and others had white flying costumes and helmets. After the usual delays for the photographers and cinematograph men the mixing began, and, until lunchtime, the Civic Guard Depot Band played selections. The work continued throughout the day until the first mixing of the counterfoils had been completed and a test analysis made by the auditors. Several times queues formed in the rain outside the building to await their turn to see the mixing operations. Mr Seán Keating, who painted the setting and the panels depicting the history of flight around the walls, spent most of the morning and afternoon critically inspecting his work now that it is in position.'

Just over a year after the disappointment of the Swoop débâcle, the Irish Sweeps ran an advertising campaign for the Derby sweep picturing a jolly cartoon character dressed in a pilot's blazer and standing by a large aircraft. The copy-line was: 'He started drawing plans for building a home-made Flying Flea—but then he drew a horse!' The Flying Flea was a popular do-it-yourself miniature aircraft with a reputation for crashing. The Sweeps winner pictured in the advert could clearly afford something bigger and grander.

One Sweeps winner who splashed part of his prize money on a Flying Flea should have gone for a larger, safer model. Scotsman James Goodall was badly injured after his aircraft plunged into a ditch outside

Aberdeen. It was reported: 'He made light of his injuries and was taken to Aberdeen Royal Infirmary where he died a few hours later. Goodall is stated to have won a large sum in the Irish hospitals sweepstake several years ago.'

Chapter 14

THE GREAT BRITISH BLACKOUT

Throughout the early 1930s the Irish Sweeps were a source of endless column inches in the British press. Each draw was covered in lavish detail by a Fleet Street landing party, while tales of Sweeps-related sharp practice were lapped up by the British public. Human interest, tragic and oddball stories from Ireland were reported in Britain and vice versa.

One story from the latter category from 1932 was headlined 'Thought He Had Won Sweep'. It told of a middle-aged Dublin man, Christopher Farrell, who appeared in court charged with failing to pay a £2-0-9 taxi fare after taking a four-hour cab ride, calling at a number of banks. 'Farrell was also charged with being a dangerous lunatic', stated the report. The delusional defendant was under the false impression that he had won a £30,000 fortune on the Sweeps. He just didn't know which bank it was in. 'He made rambling statements about his expected fortune and said he wanted a revolver and the service of two detectives to look after him and his money.'

The *Daily Telegraph* told of the case where Dublin man Patrick Byrne was charged with taking £30 from his brother-in-law in Middlesex to purchase tickets. He spent £3 on six tickets and forged receipts for the rest. Byrne then went on a spending spree that aroused suspicions, and he was rumbled when a police search of his dustbin turned up evidence of his forgery scam. A shipbroker's clerk stole £25 and splashed out on Sweeps tickets. He got four months in jail after the counterfoils were found in his pockets when he carelessly got himself arrested for being drunk and disorderly.

Under the headline 'Swindler's Shocking Fate' the *Sunday Independent* picked up an English report recording a coroner's verdict of suicide while of unsound mind following the death of Fred Mynott, a commercial traveller from Ramsgate. Mynott's body was found at the foot of cliffs. Shopkeeper Charles Moody told the inquest that he had given money for Sweeps tickets to the dead man on behalf of himself and several customers. On the day of his disappearance Mynott had called in to Moody claiming he had no receipts for the tickets because his son had accidentally burned them. Moody knew Mynott was lying because the indiscreet salesman had confessed to another shopkeeper that he had never posted the cash to Dublin.

Moody testified: 'I got very wild and angry and told Mynott he was a liar, swindler and robber of poor people's money. I pushed him about and told him to clear out of my shop as he had done a dirty action. After Mynott's departure his wallet was found in a dark corner of the room where we quarrelled and looking inside it I found £30 worth of Irish Derby sweep tickets with the names, *noms-de-plume* and addresses of the counterfoils which had not been sent in.' Despite his monetary loss, the shopkeeper said he was 'grieved and shocked' to hear of Mynott's death leap.

Balancing out the tales of swindlers and suicides, there were plenty of lighter stories. One headlined 'Fled From Marriage Proposals' reported: 'Private life has almost ceased to exist for Mr Sidney Lane, once of Jamshedpur. He has been driven from India by good fortune.' Since Lane had won £30,000 'he has had to struggle desperately to avoid the attentions of women of every age and kind who want to marry him'. In contrast, after the Irish papers reported the second Sweeps win of Dubliner P. J. Kearney, he had them insert a clarification notice correcting the statement that he was married. 'He is still single', said the notice.

The simmering hostility between the British government and de Valera's Fianna Fáil administration was paralleled by a general wave of anti-Irish feeling at a time when the Economic War was fuelling a fresh migration of Irish job-seekers to Britain where jobs were already in short supply. Britain was struggling to pay off its war loans to the United States, which meant cutbacks on imports of raw materials for the factories and less food on the shop shelves. Noting the vast sums of money leaving Britain for Ireland, some British hospitals even sought financial aid from the Free State. The Royal Eye Hospital in London, for instance, requested £30,000 on the grounds that: 'This hospital serves that part of London in which the majority of Irish people reside and nearly 25 per cent of our patients attending here are Irish or of Irish descent.' The request was turned down with the explanation that the Sweeps legislation stipulated that only Irish hospitals could benefit.

In an attempt to grapple with the Irish Sweeps, and to tidy up the existing laws which were outdated and widely disobeyed, the British government established a Royal Commission on Lotteries and Betting. It was tasked with investigating the current state of affairs and drawing up 'desirable and practicable' recommendations. Chaired by a judge, the commission sat for 14 months between 1932 and 1933. As it wound up its deliberations John Stewart-Murray, the Scots Gaelic-speaking Duke of Atholl, was setting in motion a one-man campaign to kill off the Irish Sweeps operation in Britain. Atholl set up his own illegal, but patriotic, lottery and became embroiled in an angry war of words with his fellow ex-British Army officer, Captain Spencer Freeman. The Tory MP attacked the Irish Sweeps and branded Freeman a traitorous British subject profiting from the underhand flight of money from the land of his birth. The Duke further charged that he and one of his associates had been threatened by unidentified persons who were in the pay of the Irish Sweeps.

Freeman issued a statement repudiating the allegations. He said: 'No such threats have been made on behalf of the Irish Sweepstake authorities and, as an Englishman, I deplore this unbecoming and theatrical outburst. I challenge the Duke of Atholl to produce conclusive evidence of these threats and will pay £1,000 to any British charity if these charges are substantiated.'

Brushing off Atholl's accusations of disloyalty to Britain, Freeman pointed out that a year previously he had offered to conduct 'a perfectly supervised sweepstake in aid of the British hospitals', but this had been shot down by the Home Office. He continued: 'My conscience, therefore, is quite clear so far as my loyalty to England is concerned and it is only fair that it should be known that my effort was made with the goodwill of all connected with the Irish Sweepstake.'

Freeman then made the cavalier claim that Britain 'loses no money' through the Irish Sweep. Estimating that £17 million had so far migrated across the Irish Sea he elaborated: 'To suggest that this amount remains in the Irish Free State is contrary to the facts because in addition to the amount returned to Great Britain in prizes, which is

£12,000,000, at least another £5,000,000 has found its way back to England in such expenditure as building materials and equipment for Irish hospitals; money originating from salaries and Sweep expenses which is spent on British merchandise, British provided entertainment and British holidays. In addition a large percentage of foreign and Empire-won prize money is spent by the winners on British merchandise and left in British banks.'

Spencer went on to show yet more brass neck, insisting that the Irish operation was 'the only sweepstake of all time in which mystery and secrets are non-existent'. He chided: 'If the Duke is so anxious for a legalised sweepstake in England, I would say that his present scheme, the conditions of which omit proper safeguards to the public of control and supervision, is one the effect of which is most likely to prejudice the British authorities and people against the sweepstakes the Duke so strongly advocates.'

The dispute rumbled on, and some weeks later the Duke launched another attack on the Irish Sweeps. This time Freeman rolled out a different line of defence, saying: 'If it were not for the Irish Sweepstake, Great Britain would be inundated with invitations to subscribe to the dozens of Continental lotteries, and of the amount of money which would inevitably leave this country for those Continental lotteries next to nothing would return, except the bare prize money.'

Dubbed a 'disguised lottery' by the press, the Duke's venture raised some £60,000 for British charities and earned him a trip to court and a £25 fine. When the royal commission issued its report in June 1933 it deplored the financial drain of foreign lotteries and pointed out the opportunities for fraud created by the black market in Irish Sweeps tickets. The commission advised that the government had two options. It could legalise a rival superlottery or superlotteries to the Irish Sweeps, or it could draft and enforce tighter laws to suppress the Irish operation in Britain. The Tory dominated coalition government opted for the latter, and the Betting and Lotteries Act became law on the first day of 1935.

The Act permitted the holding of small lotteries on a village fête scale where the prize fund didn't exceed £10. Specifically aimed at the Irish Sweeps was a range of strict new laws making it a criminal offence to print lottery tickets, to sell them or advertise their sale, to post money out of the country for tickets, or to encourage another person to do any of the above. The new Act imposed a complete publicity blackout on the media. No adverts could be published. The long lists of winners which took up pages of newspapers and boosted their circulations were banned. The blanket coverage of the elaborate Dublin draws could no longer be carried if the authorities judged that it was 'calculated to act as an inducement' to participate in any lottery.

The penalties specified under the new Act meant the days of judges handing down paltry £1 and £5 fines were gone. On summary conviction, the fine allowable for a first offence was £100. For a second summary conviction the maximum penalty rose to £200 and three months in jail. If the defendant insisted on his or her right to a jury trial, and lost, the punishment for a first conviction went up to £500, and for a second shot to £750 and a year behind bars. Any cash seized in connection with a conviction was now to be confiscated.

The publicity blackout applied to the silver screen too. An early casualty was the Hollywood comedy *The Winning Ticket* which revolved around an Irish Sweeps win by a humble Italian barber clearly inspired by Emilio Scala. When the ticket goes missing the baby of the household becomes the prime suspect. After a series of japes the ticket is found and the family are showered with riches. The British censor took a dim view of a scene portraying the draw in Dublin and took his scissors to it.

As the new legislation was debated at Westminster the MP Isaac Foot, father of future Labour Party leader Michael, quipped: 'I do not want to see the Irish Sweep abolished until I win it twice.' However, as a general principle he approved of the publicity blackout. He elaborated: 'We are not going to have the publicity which sets out all the wins and says nothing about the losses. It took two pages of *The Times* newspaper to give the names of the winners in one of the big sweepstakes. If we had had the names of the losers they would have occupied 24 pages of *The Times* for one hundred successive issues. We get a publication intended to whet the appetite and the cupidity of people, of the fact that some unemployed man has won a big prize, but what about the unemployed who have contributed to that prize and upon whose homes the loss falls? Ask those who are in the front line of social activity, who are right up against poverty and distress in the big towns, and they will tell you where the burden of the loss falls.'

Captain F. F. A. Heiligers employed an altogether more hostile tone for his contribution, stating: 'I not only hate the idea of the Irish Sweepstake but I hate sending so much money to de Valera by which he is able to make up his balance in trade by the invisible exports we are sending him as a result of the Sweep. But I hate still more the fact, I regard it indeed as an insult, that these Sweepstakes are based on the results of races in this country instead of on Irish races.'

Ten weeks before the new anti-Sweeps Act was to become law, a *Time* magazine reporter suggested that the British public were embarked on a frenzied spending spree to buy tickets for the last Irish sweep before the draconian crackdown. In fact, the distribution of prizes when that last draw was made suggested that many in Britain were bowing to the spirit of the new law in advance of its enactment. Usually some 70 per cent of prizes went to Britain, but for the last one before the ban British winners made up less than half the total.

But that fall-off couldn't have been known to the *Time* writer who began his report: 'In Bristol the Conservatives were holding their annual conference, marked as usual by factional differences over India (which was demanding its independence from British rule). What interested Britons, however, was not India but the action of the Conservative conferees regarding lotteries.'

The report stated that even though the strict new Act had been passed by both Houses of Parliament, there were still those among the governing Conservatives who protested that the reinforced law was still an ass. The *Time* reporter cited as proof, although wrongly since the Act was not yet law, that: 'Last week Britons were technically violating it by the hundred thousand to subscribe to this year's Irish Sweepstakes. In the closing hours of last week's conference of the Conservative Party, up rose Sir William Henry Davison, a fellow member with Atholl of the swank Carlton Club. "Ordinary citizens," he cried, "resent the government's attempts to prevent them having a flutter."' Davison's protest raised a cheer from the ranks of his fellow Tories, but when his rogue motion to establish a national lottery was put before them, they slipped obediently back into line.

While the new legislation didn't entirely stem the flow of large sums from Britain to Ireland, it may have halved the revenue making the journey across the Irish Sea into the Hospitals Trust's coffers. The Free State's High Commissioner in London calculated that ticket sales in Britain had 'dwindled to a tremendous extent' after the Act became law.

Denied exposure in the newspapers and cinemas, the Irish Sweeps promoters set their minds to opening other channels of communication to the British public. The best plan they came up with was to broadcast radio signals into Britain. From the outset, the Sweeps had sponsored a light entertainment programme on Radio Athlone which would become Radio Éireann in 1937. The national station was particular about whose money it took. For the first two decades after its opening in 1926, the advertising of women's cosmetics was rejected lest it should stir immoral thoughts in listeners, while no adverts were aired on the Church festivals of St Patrick's Day, Ash Wednesday, Holy Thursday, Good Friday and Christmas Day.

When the Free State government denied the Sweeps promoters permission to set up their own broadcasting service to target Britain, the Trust suggested that Radio Athlone in the dead centre of the country could be relocated 70 miles to the east to achieve maximum coverage in Wales and the west of England. This was rejected out of hand, but the government did agree to boost the signal from Athlone in return for a boost in the fee paid for the sponsored show.

While broadcasts from Ireland covering the west of Britain were a source of annoyance to the authorities there, a far greater source of irritation to the Downing Street government was a subversive broadcaster on its eastern flank. In 1933 Radio Luxembourg began broadcasting an English language service using the most powerful transmitter in the world. It quickly captured large audiences in Britain and Ireland with a menu of popular tunes that made the state broadcasters of both islands sound as crushingly dull, staid and starchy as they actually were.

A deeply hostile British government condemned the new broadcaster as a pirate station, in the sense that it was pirating several wavelengths the BBC was testing for its own use. The new station continued to broadcast adverts into Britain, where the lone legal station was a commercial-free zone. Like the Irish Sweeps organisation in Ireland, Radio Luxembourg was a shameless pirate raiding plunder from other countries while remaining a perfectly legal entity in its home base of the Grand Duchy. The Irish Sweeps quickly became the station's biggest advertiser, taking daily slots and sponsoring the 30-minute Sunday show, 'Golden Hour of Music', described in a 1935 edition of *Radio Pictorial* as 'the Irish Concert recorded programme'.

Over two decades later, in December 1956, the Sweeps were behind the 75-minute Thursday night show 'Irish Requests'.

In the same year, 1956, the Rolling Stones guitar legend Keith Richards was 12 years old and in the first throes of his love affair with R&B and rock 'n' roll. These fresh sounds from America were hard to find, but one night in 1956 he found two which would rock his world and change the direction of his life. Many years later he recalled: 'You were lucky if you heard it [American rock 'n' roll] on Radio Luxembourg. I remember when they played 'Long Tall Sally' and 'Heartbreak Hotel', and I can still remember the ad for the Irish Sweepstakes that followed. I was 12, 13, and I was supposed to be in bed and not listening to the radio. Electrifying night for me.'

But while the broadcasts from Athlone and Luxembourg helped maintain a profile in Britain, the penalties and press blackout had done their damage. As the 1930s pushed on, Britain became a land of diminishing returns. But as one door closed, the entrance to the richest territory in the world was swinging invitingly open.

Chapter 15

HE UPSET THE POUND-DOLLAR EXCHANGE RATE FOR THE DAY

By the close of 1934, with the tough new British laws about to come into force on the first day of 1935, the Irish Hospitals Trust was expanding its operations in North America. With US Postmaster James Farley giving newspapers the go-ahead to print good news stories about the poor chambermaid and the unemployed miner who hit the jackpot, the tap of free publicity had been turned on again.

In the run-up to the final sweep of 1934 there was extensive coverage of a ritual that was now in its third year. Sidney Freeman Jnr, son of Spencer's older brother Sidney, was holding court in New York's five-star Ritz-Carlton Hotel. There, quite openly, he was engaging in the practice of 'plucking the chickens'. The chickens queuing to be willingly plucked were the holders of tickets on short-odds horses.

One observer described the scene: 'They sat on the edges of their chairs, teetering, twisting. Their clothes and manners showed that few of them were at ease amid the splendours of Manhattan's swank Ritz-Carlton Hotel. But it was less their surroundings than the fateful decision that each and every one of them was about to make that caused them to squirm nervously.

'Out of a huge drum in Dublin their numbers had been drawn for horses entered in the Cambridgeshire Stakes at Newmarket, England, a race which decides one of the three great annual lotteries of the Irish Hospitals Sweepstakes committee. That meant a sure $2,000 return on each one's $2.50 investment. It also meant a chance to win $150,000, $75,000 or $50,000 for tickets on the horses which took first, second or third places. But there were 37 horses entered in the race. And at the

Ritz-Carlton last week sat a big, bland, dapper, young Briton ready to pay from $3,500 to $16,800 cash for tickets on a large number of likely winners. He was Sidney Freeman Junior, sole US representative of "Dougie".

'A syndicate and not a person, "Dougie" is London's Douglas Stuart Limited, the world's biggest firm of racetrack bookmakers. For years this British syndicate has been sending Sidney Freeman Senior, one of the directors, to the US to buy up Sweepstakes tickets from persons who prefer a small sure thing to a large chance.

'Last summer Sidney Freeman Junior went along, watched his father trade $100,000 cash for Epsom Derby lottery tickets which won some $225,000. After that lesson Sidney Senior decided that Sidney Junior was ready to try his luck alone. One day last week Mr Freeman installed himself at the Ritz-Carlton with a telephone and a great stack of US currency at his elbow. Cables streamed in from London with instructions, betting odds. One after another ticket-holders shambled into his office, nervous, undecided, wanting to haggle. Mr Freeman remained cool, crisp, firm as ever his father had been. "Take it or leave it. That's the price now and we may not be buying tickets on that horse later." By one o'clock in the morning Sidney Freeman had traded without a break for 24 hours, had paid out some $300,000 for 73 tickets and upset the pound-dollar exchange rate for the day.'

The report went on to note that the result of the big race had reached the US east coast around ten the morning after Freeman's late night of horse-trading in the Ritz-Carlton. Wychwood Abbot had pipped Commander III at the post with Highlander third. Of the $16 million the promoters claimed they had taken in, some $3,750,000 had been sent to Ireland from the United States, the greatest amount to date. Around $2,600,000 would return to the United States in the form of prizes. Although the Irish Sweepstakes was outlawed in the States, by a crafty act of double-think the US government classified winnings as income and therefore subject to income tax. It was calculated that $400,000 would be deducted in total from the winners of the final sweep of 1934. The heavy concentration of American ticket sales in New York can be gauged from the fact that the three US citizens holding tickets on the winning horses were all from the Big Apple.

Plucking the chickens at the Ritz-Carlton for the previous sweep, the elder Sidney had received a visit from the police. The law officer in question had accepted $6,500 for a half-share of his ticket which had drawn Windsor Lad in the Epsom Derby. Windsor Lad won the race and Sidney Snr was up $70,500 on the deal. A half-share in the second-placed horse, Easton, gave him a $37,700 profit on his $7,500 outlay.

During one of his sojourns in New York, the elder Sidney invited *Life* magazine to send over a reporter and photographer. The readers were informed: 'The dapper, grey-haired gentleman wearing the striped bathrobe and the lounging slippers is Sidney Freeman, the world's most powerful gambler. From behind a barricade of detectives and lawyers, he was securely ensconced in a six-room suite at New York's Ritz-Carlton Hotel.'

The writer described how 'a strange collection of truck-drivers, sandhogs and bartenders' made their way through the lobby to sell Freeman part or all of their ticket. Freeman reportedly had ready access to a cool million bucks in folding money, and would keep up to $75,000 in the suite. 'Usually it is hidden in the leg of a chair or under a mattress', said the writer.

The article explained: 'His business is mathematically sound. He cannot lose money. He simply buys four tickets on each horse in the race [and] pays less for all those tickets than the total amount the winning tickets will bring him.' The magazine estimated that Freeman could always expect to make a profit of some $100,000 on one single visit.

Sidney Freeman, fawned the writer, was a gentleman gambler in the English tradition. Soft-spoken, pleasant and 'invariably honest' in his soft wool turtleneck sweater, he plied members of the press with champagne while puffing away on Egyptian cigarettes. A photo-spread to accompany the feature showed Freeman in his pyjamas and dressing gown going through a list of race odds which had just been cabled through from Dublin. A shot of a sidekick named Cruise, a former music hall comedian, showed him puffing out his cheeks while wearing an oversized fake moustache. Photographed at a number of tables in the suite, a small group of men and women checked ticket stubs. Other assistants studied a large map of North America which, readers were told, was divided up into 14 districts. They were informed: 'Freeman has a representative in each district who buys tickets [and] keeps in touch with Freeman by wire.'

A well-worn small cuddly toy was identified as 'Piggy', Sidney Freeman's lucky mascot of 15 years. Readers were told: 'Like all gamblers, Freeman is highly superstitious, but he never lets sentiment interfere with business.' His secretary, Miss Claire Frankel, was snapped counting a wad of banknotes.

The *Life* feature concluded with a piece of Jesuitical reasoning put forward by Sidney Freeman. It said: 'Nobody seems to be quite certain whether Freeman's business is legal. In the US the sale of lottery tickets is forbidden, but Freeman argues that what he buys is not a receipt from a lottery, but a security with a minimum value. He buys merely for a possible rise in that value . . . Until now, at least, no US authorities have tried to interfere.'

What Sidney Freeman did not reveal to *Life* magazine was that the result of the draw in Dublin was sent to him in code, so that he knew the names of the holders of tickets on fancied runners before anyone else. This meant that Freeman had the names and addresses of the chickens to be plucked before they had been given the news themselves, giving him a head start on rivals who were also trying to buy shares in short-odds tickets.

There was another minor piece of deception practised in the States. Sidney Freeman Jnr was not, in fact, named Sidney at all. Just as his father had dreamed up the name Dougie Stuart as a more folksy alternative to Spencer & Benson Bookmakers, it was decided to retain the name Sidney Freeman when the son named Abraham took over his chicken-plucking duties in the States. Indeed, a *New Yorker* magazine profile described the entity known as Sidney Freeman as 'a kind of American trade name for a syndicate of British bookmakers who are in the business of buying up Sweepstake tickets'. Sadly, Abraham's stint masquerading as Sidney was to be a very short-lived arrangement. One month after the youngster upset the pound-dollar exchange rate for a day, *Time* magazine carried the following death notice: 'Died. Abraham Spencer Freeman, 24, son of Sidney Freeman of London's famed betting commissioners "Dougie's" (Douglas Stuart Ltd.); in a motor accident; in London. Acting for his father, he bought up $300,000 worth of Irish Hospital Sweepstakes tickets in Manhattan.' Three years later in 1937 the individual conducting business at the Ritz under the name of Sidney Freeman was, in fact, Edward Benson, son of Freeman's partner in Douglas Stuart Limited, Martin Benson.

Benson explained to the *New Yorker*: 'It's one and the same thing. Since Sid is the one who established the goodwill here, we fear that

Americans might not have confidence in another name.'

By 1938, Sidney Freeman had run into trouble with the British tax authorities for the non-payment of taxes on his Sweepstakes winnings and skimmings. Although Freeman was notoriously modest in calculating his profits, it is believed he offered the British Revenue the vast sum of £250,000 if they would waive all claims. They accepted. Immediately after Freeman was nailed by Britain's taxman, the Irish Revenue authorities sought and got an order for the discovery of documents against Hospitals Trust Limited. But apart from a published notice of this, the subject of their inquiry was never made public. Sometime later the ex-chairman of the Revenue Commissioners was to receive commissions from Hospitals Trust. Sidney Freeman's share-buying was not his only activity in New York. He also visited those who actually won prizes and told the winners it would take several months before they would get paid from Dublin. Without giving any reason for the delay in prize distribution, or mentioning that his brother was in charge of it, he told the winners that he had funds available immediately if they were prepared to pay him a commission of five per cent. Many accepted the offer and the plucking of the chickens went right down to the last downy feather.

In the mid-1930s the United States appointed a new representative in Ireland with the official title of Minister to the Free State. Described as a tall, bald, big-handed man with a wart on his nose, William Wallace McDowell docked at Cobh in April 1934. The copper magnate said that most of his miners were of Irish stock and that the town of Butte was known locally as Little Ireland. The train assigned to carry him from Cork to Dublin was draped in flags bearing the Stars and Stripes and the Irish tricolour. The driver set out to break the record time for the journey and succeeded. One of McDowell's first acts as Washington's Minister to the Free State was to attend the Dublin draw for the sweep on the Grand National.

The following spring Richard Duggan's favourite pet politician, Dublin's Lord Mayor Alfie Byrne, crossed the Atlantic in the reverse direction as a goodwill ambassador for the Irish Sweeps. Byrne was the guest of honour at New York's St Patrick's Day parade, presenting Mayor Fiorello La Guardia with shamrocks supposedly gathered from the enchanted shores of the lakes of Killarney. The presentation was made at City Hall where Byrne, bedecked in his mayoral chain, told those present that the Irish Sweepstakes were a harmless bit of fun. He was warmly received by an administration which just months earlier had rounded up thousands of illegal slot machines and dumped them off a barge, with La Guardia swinging a sledgehammer at several one-armed bandits for the cameras.

Meanwhile, Postmaster General James Farley was finding that his gospel of tolerance towards the Irish Sweeps was falling on deaf ears in his own legal department, which, drawing down its independent powers, made a public declaration that the anti-gaming laws would be enforced to the letter.

From late 1934 US customs and police were claiming they were winning the war on illegal lottery tickets, not just from Ireland, but from France, Cuba, Mexico, Italy and even Canada, where there was a legal draw to benefit the army and navy. Twenty-four postal exchange stations were designated as clearing houses for all mail leaving for Ireland, Canada, Cuba, France and Luxembourg. A blacklist was circulated to these postal depots of names and addresses abroad. US postal staff were forbidden to issue postal orders in favour of anyone on the blacklist. Cash sent to be translated into postal orders would be returned to the sender by registered mail, but to accept the returned cash would be to risk prosecution, so the authorities found themselves with a nice profit. Tickets intercepted coming into the United States or seized in raids were taken to the Dead Letter Office in Washington and shovelled into a giant furnace in the basement of the building.

One raid on a beauty parlour resulted in the seizure of 250 books of Irish Sweeps tickets and the arrest of 70-year-old Oscar Stevenson and his 39-year-old son. Police claimed the pair were distributing tickets to some 3,000 'lesser agents' whose names appeared on lists captured from the two men. The raiding party also found printed cards identical to ones accompanying Sweeps tickets in the mail. The message on the cards read: 'Under separate cover am sending you a box of assorted cosmetics. As soon as you return the numbered tags with $25 per dozen jars, I will send you as many as you can dispose of. Single jars, $2.60 each.' Charles Murphy, Assistant US Attorney, told the media that the word 'box' was code for book, 'jar' stood for ticket, 'cosmetics' meant sweepstakes and 'tag' stood for counterfoil. Two young women posing as manicurists who were processing tickets at the time of the raid were also arrested.

Two women were among the ten people arrested in synchronised raids which netted more than a million genuine Sweeps tickets and long lists of agents across the United States. One swoop was on 'an ostensible jewellery' store on Manhattan's Amsterdam Avenue carried out by detectives of the Bomb and Forgery Squad. According to one press report: 'There they took four prisoners and a huge supply of sweepstakes foils, steel cabinets containing the files of agents all over the country, addressograph machines and other elaborate mailing equipment.' The triumphant detectives said they had suspected for some time that the jewellery store was 'merely a blind' for 'widespread operations' and they had had it under surveillance for three months. Several members of a Kelly family were arrested, as was 33-year-old Michael Hayes who said he was over on an innocent visit from his native Dublin.

Even the seizure of one million counterfoils was not all bad news for the Sweeps promoters. The police stressed that they were all genuine, and the press passed on the spin that the seizure of one million genuine tickets reflected well on the sound running of the Irish Sweeps in a period when a Frenchman was arrested with 100,000 forged French lottery tickets as he stepped off the liner *Ile de France*. The Cubans were also held up as far less trustworthy than the loveable rogues behind the charitable Irish enterprise. It was widely reported that 3 million tickets for a Cuban lottery had been sold in the United States, but that only 100,000 went into the drum for the draw.

In August 1935, against the Postmaster General's wishes, his legal department clamped down hard on the Irish Sweeps and other illegal lotteries. Thousands of letters and packages suspected of containing Sweeps tickets were confiscated. Worse was a new blanket ban on any coverage of Sweeps-related activity in newspapers carried in the mail. The ban was good news for an evening paper called the *New York Journal-American* which bypassed the postal service in favour of newsstand only distribution. The *Journal-American* was now able to boost its circulation by publishing the winners' lists its bigger rivals no longer could.

The blanket ban on publicity was not an unqualified success for the legal eagles of the us Mail, as many editors continued to poke about for loopholes by publishing human interest stories with a Sweeps theme. Some months after the latest clampdown, for instance, the *New Yorker* carried the following: 'About two years ago we were wondering what would happen to winners in the Irish Sweepstakes—among them a postman in Long Island City. Now comes a letter from a Long Island City lady informing us that this fellow is her postman, and that he seems to be tramping resolutely around, just as before. He takes a day off now and then. And one day he left a note attached to a letter which the lady received from the Fiji Islands, asking if he could please have the stamp. Apparently he took his Sweepstakes winnings and bought a stamp collection.'

There was widespread coverage of the story of how a newsreel reporter got his break into Hollywood movies by improvising a comic character who bought a losing ticket in the Irish Sweeps. The story went that David Oliver was 'bored to desperation by the routine of filming 1936 Irish Sweepstakes winners', so he 'donned a silly little hat, went before his own camera and created a burlesque character John Q Dohp (dope)'. The reporter turned comic was such a hit that he expanded his skits to poke gentle fun at the Easter Parade and the Kentucky Derby. Oliver got his break in movies playing opposite Bela Lugosi in *The Postal Inspector*. His many screen roles as a bit-part actor included characters named Butch, Dutch, Flash, Spud and Salty.

The routine condemnations of the Irish Sweepstakes continued unabated. One in 1936 came from the Baptist Church in Jersey City, which warned the faithful that each ticket purchased was going into the pockets of racketeers. Some senior politicians believed that money leaving the United States for Ireland should be diverted into an American lottery to fund the pensions of World War 1 veterans and other worthy causes, just as the Italian dictator Mussolini was using lottery revenues to fund his beloved navy. One Congressman, Edward Kenney, made a detailed historical study showing that in the colonial past Congress had used lottery money to fund the building of roads, schools and prisons, while many congregations had staged lotteries to build new churches. The Lottery Bill which bore Kenney's name and which would have legalised gambling was debated by the Ways and Means Committee in Washington, but Congress ultimately rejected it.

I WISH WE'D NEVER WON THE MONEY

The Irish Sweepstakes were such a huge instant success that they inevitably spawned imitators. In 1931 a London-based body calling itself Hospitals' Trust Limited launched a sweepstake which the promoters claimed would generate funds for a number of English hospitals. A circular sent out with the tickets stated: 'Owing to the existing law in this country, a huge amount of money is being diverted to the Irish hospitals. This is an appalling state of affairs, as our own British hospitals (which are the finest institutions in the world) are so urgently in need of funds. In consequence of this, Hospitals' Trust Limited have now put the necessary machinery into motion to circumvent similar loss to British hospitals.' The hospitals named in the circular rushed to make clear that they had no involvement with the illegal project. This was followed by a statement from the *doppelganger* Hospitals' Trust Limited saying that the project was being abandoned 'due to unfavourable comments in the press'.

In 1933 *John Bull* magazine ran a report headlined 'Shun Them!' warning readers to steer clear of a sweep to be run on that year's Aintree Grand National. Under a second headline saying 'Queer Facts', the organ told of a body calling itself the British International Association which had its registered headquarters in the town of Zoppot in the Baltic Free State of Danzig. The *John Bull* reporter wrote: 'Its directors, I understand, are two New Zealanders, an Australian and two Germans or Danzigians. It is in part heir of the ill fated Brooms Syndicate whose former sweepstakes venture was such a disaster.' The Brooms Syndicate was an Australian gaming cabal which persuaded the government of tiny tax-free Andorra to grant it a concession to operate a sweepstake from there, targeted at the British market. The British protested to the government of France, which exerted a great deal of power over Andorra, and the Andorrans withdrew the concession. Nothing more was heard of the Danzig-based sweep.

The mid-1930s were arguably the high summer of the Irish Hospitals Sweepstakes. There were still condemnations. One Northern Ireland clergyman said the sweeps 'rallied the drinkers of intoxicating liquor, the crooks, the card sharpers, the pickpockets, all the parasites that fattened on the stupid simplicities of the public'. A columnist with the *Evening Herald* by-lined as Macura took a diametrically opposite view. A decade earlier, in the mid-1920s, he was stopped on the German border and taken for a British national. He wrote: 'Perhaps [the border guard] was not to be blamed for that was ten years ago before the Irish publicity thrust commenced. It would be hard today to find a frontier or a country where the name Ireland does not signify something big— Napoleonic in design and execution. They all know Ireland now.'

The Sweeps, he argued, conjured up 'the irresistible glamour of success. What a feather in the cap of our race, placed there by bold ideas and bold steps taken by a small group of virile-minded men. You must go abroad to appreciate it fully. It may not get you through the customs—in fact it won't in most places—but you'll no longer be mixed up with nondescript nationalities of doubtful character and pursuits.' The writer concluded: 'Charity has become its own reward.'

There were plenty of good news stories in circulation, stressing the rewards being generated for Ireland's hospitals. Sir Joseph Glynn, the chairman of the National Health Insurance Scheme, boasted that the fully refurbished all-electric National Maternity Hospital on Dublin's Hollis Street was so state-of-the-art that medics from all over the world had written seeking postgraduate courses there. The fame of the spruced up maternity hospital had indeed spread far and wide. One letter arrived simply addressed to: 'The all-electric hospital, Dublin.' The Electricity Supply Board showcased the hospital's newly electrified kitchens in adverts. In 1935, just half a decade after Ireland's voluntary hospitals were sinking in a morass of debt, Ireland signalled its ambition to become a world leader in the field of medical science with the foundation of the Medical Research Council, funded by an endowment from Hospitals Trust Limited.

As the 1930s wore on, the pageantry surrounding the big Dublin draws became ever more elaborate. One procession featured two live elephants while the dray cart carrying the boxes of counterfoils was modelled in the form of a giant elephant. According to one report: 'It was tempting fate to have elephants in the procession. They are usually associated with hot climates and fine weather—and of course jungle romances in which men are men—so to parade them through the streets of Dublin naturally led to a perversity on the part of the weather, and down came the rain. Nevertheless, the "Indian bridal couple" who accompanied the procession should have been glad that the sweepstake people chose elephants as the dominant feature because they were able to shelter from the rain under the model elephant.'

The elephants' keepers, who spoke only German, fed the animals sugar as they paraded, with one writer estimating a consumption rate by the animals of two pounds per mile each. The young women mixing the counterfoils were dressed in the wedding costumes of brides and bridegrooms around the world. Spencer Freeman's chosen theme for the draw was 'If dreams came true', on the assumption that many young people buying sweep tickets would have marriage on their minds. Wedding dreams were the theme of another draw which featured a fleet of ribboned cars, a giant model wedding cake and huge model castles.

Another draw was themed around speed. One reporter wrote: 'The first of the decorated cars was an exaggerated pigeon with a wire-netted body in which a number of racing pigeons were caged. Then came a car bearing a replica of Sir Malcolm Campbell's famous racing car Blue Bird, but without the Union Jack that Sir Malcolm's car carries on its tail. The next was decidedly futuristic, depicting a rocket to the moon—the rocket was taking a first prize of £30,000 with it. In the rear was speed *in excelsis*—a woman at a telephone spreading the news to all her friends.'

Most of the girls doing the mixing were dressed in the same costumes as for the previous draw. According to Spencer Freeman this was not Hospitals Trust's latest penny-pinching scheme, but was due to the fact that it was raining heavily on the previous occasion and as the girls were wrapped up in raincoats the thousands who lined the streets had been unable to see their costumes. He added that there were a small number of new costumes on view too, depicting 'birds of beauty and birds of speed'. Scores of racing pigeons were released for the cameras.

On another occasion the stores of Dawson Street were fitted with false fronts in imitation of the skyscrapers of New York's fast-rising

Michael Collins (*second from left*) at a 1922 pro-Treaty rally. Joe McGrath and W. T. Cosgrave sit at the right of the picture. (*Getty Images*)

The Sweeps pageant brought a touch of the Rio street carnival to drab Dublin during the Great Depression of the 1930s. Here, two specially imported elephants were fed sugar by their German keepers as they paraded through the drenching rain. (*National Library of Ireland*)

The dray cart carried millions of ticket counterfoils, an 'Indian bridal couple' and a giant elephant. (*National Library of Ireland*)

Young sweethearts saving for marriage were wooed with draws themed on dream weddings. (*National Library of Ireland*)

Crowds filed in and out of the Plaza for three days, many bringing a packed lunch. (*National Library of Ireland*)

The women mixing the counterfoils were costumed as brides and bridegrooms around the world. (*National Library of Ireland*)

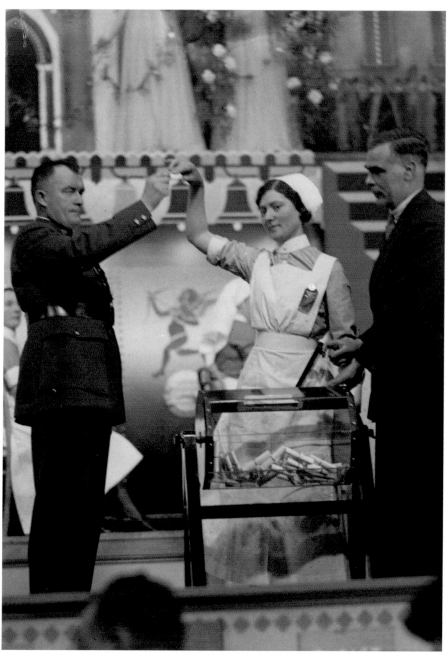

Eamon 'Ned' Broy, former spy under Collins and McGrath, now Garda Commissioner, vouchsafes one of the 1935 draws. (*National Library of Ireland*)

Ice-cream man Emilio Scala, the first and biggest Sweeps superstar, celebrates with family members. (*The Irish Times*)

The drum for the first draw was too small, so countless tickets never got in. This new drum was much bigger. (*Getty Images*)

Blind children were replaced by nurses with bare arms to show they had nothing up their sleeves. (*The Irish Times*)

The 6 pm deadline for entries often ran hours late, with many arriving on the mailboat from Britain. (*Getty Images*)

The first Sweep was a wild success. The second was a sensation, and Dublin was deluged with tickets and banknotes. (*Getty Images*)

The chests of tickets are carried in procession to an early draw. Later pageants became more lavish. (*TopFoto*)

Thousands of women processed the paperwork during the Great Depression. Jobless men protested. (*TopFoto*)

The workers were almost exclusively female. One reason was that women could be paid far less than men. (*TopFoto*)

Artist Seán Keating finishes an image for the ill-fated Irish Swoop gala at the Plaza in March 1934. (*The Irish Times*)

A speed-themed draw featured a giant racing pigeon, a moon rocket, and a woman on the telephone. (*The Irish Times*)

The Irish Swoop draws a crowd at the start of the 1934 London to Melbourne race. It was disqualified. (*TopFoto*)

Pilots James Fitzmaurice and Eric Bonar prepare to fly. Their disqualification upset top Nazi Joseph Goebbels. (*TopFoto*)

Ireland's Great Humanitarian and Sporting Gesture—

The SWEEPSTAKE ON THE RED CROSS CHASE

DRAW JAN. 15. RUN AT LEOPARDSTOWN JAN. 20.

The greatest Steeplechase ever held in Ireland. **STAKES OVER £3,000**

A race in which the most famous Irish and English horses will compete.

To raise funds for the Red Cross Society whose primary objects are:

To furnish volunteer aid to the sick and wounded of armies in time of war.

To furnish relief to prisoners of war.

In time of peace or war to carry on and assist in work for the improvement of health, the prevention of disease and the mitigation of suffering throughout the world.

There is an Irish Red Cross Society

Already it has been called on to succour survivors landed on our shores. It needs funds to be prepared for further acts of charity and human kindness.

If you take a ticket in this sweepstake you can assist Ireland to give a helping hand to any unfortunate person, civilian or combatant, afflicted by the war.

Ticket holders may allocate the benefit to the Red Cross Society of any country they favour.

Every Irishman should assist energetically in the prosecution of this noble work. As an example, this Sweepstake is being conducted and financed by Hospitals' Trust Ltd., without any remuneration whatever.

You can get tickets from all Hotels and Shopkeepers.

PRIZE LIST

Prizes for every £30,000 sent

Winning Horse	£9,000
Second Horse	£4,500
Third Horse	£3,000
Drawers of other Horses as specified in the scheme divide	£5,000
100 £25 Prizes	£2,500
600 £10 Prizes	£6,000
	£30,000

THOUSANDS OF PRIZES

5/- TICKETS
—take two!

CLOSING DATE DECEMBER 29th

Send us the name and address of your grocer or other local shopkeeper if you are unable to get tickets conveniently.

USE THE COUPON BELOW

Hospitals' Trust Ltd.,
Ballsbridge, Dublin.

If you send tickets to_____

It would enable me to obtain my requirements conveniently.

NAME_____

ADDRESS_____

Help Ireland to help the helpless —and help Yourself!

By subscribing early you help to keep thousands in employment. Do it NOW!

HOSPITALS' TRUST LTD., BALLSBRIDGE, DUBLIN

This advertisement for the first Red Cross Sweep covered the front page of *The Irish Times* early in World War II. (*The Irish Times*)

The front of the Sweeps building displayed announcements in French, English, Irish and German. (*Getty Images*)

(*Left to right*) Red Skelton, Lucille Ball and Gene Kelly star in the Sweeps-themed movie *Du Barry Was A Lady*. (*Rex Features/SNAP*)

Ginger Rogers stars in *Lucky Partners*, where a halved ticket brings romance with Ronald Colman. (*Corbis/Bettmann*)

"Why does your Uncle Flanagan in Dublin have to send a telegram about his visit THIS week..?"

By the time of this *Vancouver Sun* cartoon in 1965, Canada was becoming the main market. (*Simon Fraser University*)

"Evidence has just come to light, men, that some person or persons unknown are pushing, peddling and passing illegal lottery tickets..."

Vancouver Sun 1969. Bribing the authorities was part of the marketing strategy. (*Simon Fraser University*)

Publicity mastermind Spencer Freeman (*right*) presents two gold trophies to top trainer Paddy Prendergast for the 1965 Irish Sweeps Derby. (*TopFoto*)

Jacqueline Kennedy at the 1967 Irish Sweeps Derby escorted by Taoiseach Jack Lynch (*left*). (*TopFoto*)

skyline. A cast of 24 Hollywood lookalikes included doubles of Jeanette MacDonald, Katharine Hepburn, Claudette Colbert, Marlene Dietrich and Maureen O'Sullivan, each of them costumed in the style of their most famous role. Genuine stars passing through Europe such as Rosco Ates (*The Champ*, *Freaks*) and Red Skelton would occasionally bring a sprinkle of Hollywood stardust to the proceedings.

In April 1935 the Plaza ballroom where the draws were staged was destroyed by fire. Joe McGrath rushed out a statement assuring those holding tickets for the coming draw for the Epsom Derby that no counterfoils had been destroyed in the blaze as these were stored with the auditors. Equally speedily, Dublin's Lord Mayor Alfie Byrne offered Hospitals Trust the use of his official residence, the Mansion House, which had staged the first three draws. One month after the Plaza fire, the Mansion House was the setting for the Phoenix draw to symbolise the Sweepstakes rising from the ashes. The centrepiece of the parade was a giant phoenix emerging from fake flames, described by one commentator as 'a bit obvious'. The draw at the Mansion House was a cramped affair. It was also a stationary affair, with no indoor railway to move the millions of counterfoils. The track at the Plaza had been destroyed in the fire.

Despite the British publicity ban and the on-off American censorship, Sweeps-related news reports were published around the globe. In 1936 a number of journalists were wined and dined by Hospitals Trust Limited at Dublin's Dolphin Hotel, with pride of place given to George Clarke, assistant editor of New York's *Daily Mirror*. Lord Mayor Alfie Byrne hosted the dinner in the absence of Joe McGrath, telling his guests that the new research fund provided by the Sweeps would benefit humanity throughout the world. Clarke suggested, perhaps in jest, that the Blarney Stone should be taken on a six week tour of the United States sponsored by Irish Hospitals Trust or the Irish Tourist Board in association with his newspaper.

Hard luck stories concerning the Sweeps had an equal or greater appeal than feelgood ones. One report claimed that the biggest winner of them all, Emilio Scala, had lost the bulk of his vast fortune and had gone back to earning a living 'selling ice-cream cornets to London urchins'. He was quoted as saying: 'I still have a few pounds left but now all the worry of that amount of money is over my wife and I have come back to this life and work that we understand. I still have to work at something like this to be really happy. I had to do something because all my relatives—I once counted 49 of them—seem to have spent the money I gave them unwisely. Now they have nothing. I have opened this shop mostly for their benefit. I do not want any profits for myself.'

Emilio Scala would pop up in the newspapers several times over the next two decades and it would transpire that he had kept his fortune largely intact. His main motivation for going back to work was boredom with his life as a member of the idle rich.

If Emilio Scala was disappointed with his leeching relatives, other reports brought tales of much deeper family rifts. In 1935 the Paris edition of the *Daily Mail* ran a story under the headline 'Sweeps Trail of Misfortune Revealed by Will'. A building foreman from Cheshire, George Cuffin, died in October 1934 at the age of 58, just over two years after winning the huge sum of £30,000. His will showed that his fortune had dwindled to £2,015. The *Mail* said: 'Behind these bare facts lies yet another tragic story of misfortune and calamity that has beset successful sweepstakes winners. What is the secret doom that has overtaken so many of these unfortunates?'

The not-so-secret doom of George Cuffin was that he used his winnings to drink himself into an early grave. Cuffin quit his job as a foreman to become a farmer. Three months later his wife took him to court for neglecting to maintain herself and her three daughters from a previous marriage. She also applied to the Chester magistrate for a separation order. She told the court: 'I wish we'd never won the money. There was more comfort without the money than with it.' Her lawyer added: 'Since winning the Irish Sweepstakes he has been drinking heavily and has frequently ill-treated his wife who complains that he has been associating with another woman. On June 22nd Cuffin assaulted his wife threatening to shoot her and break her neck. As a consequence his wife and three children had to leave the house.'

Mrs Cuffin told the court that her husband had given her a lump sum of £200 to invest, but that he had made no contribution to the upkeep of the household since the night he drunkenly assaulted her. Asked what she had done with the £200, she said: 'I have spent it on clothes that he has damaged.' Sometime after fleeing the home, the wife went to see her estranged husband at a new farmhouse he was building with his Sweeps money, taking along one of her grown-up daughters. Cuffin ordered them off the property, throwing the daughter's bicycle out of his field.

Mrs Cuffin denied saying to her husband: 'I'm not going to work. I am going to be a lady.'

Asked to explain why he had tried to cut off his wife from his winnings, Cuffin replied: 'Because she had a house full of daughters and they would not work.' Asked if the others expected him to keep them, he replied 'yes'.

Other newspaper reports carried variations on the same theme. An Essex housewife secured a court order compelling her husband to maintain her. The husband, who had won £1,400, immediately embarked on a campaign of heavy drinking and lost his job. Manchester shopkeeper Ellen Edmundson died shortly after she won £600. Neighbours blamed her Sweeps win for worrying her to death, insisting 'she was a changed woman, so afraid was she that her money would be stolen'. Londoner Leonard Mayes won £1,250 and gave up work, but he found no happiness. Shortly after his win he killed himself by jumping into the River Lea.

The Irish Sweeps generated plenty of business for the legal profession in Ireland and elsewhere, as endless disputes arose over the ownership of winning tickets. The Irish Hospitals Trust Limited issued a warning against the practice of parents putting the names of their children on the counterfoils, as judges would often order that prize money be placed in a trust until the child reached adulthood, with the parent or guardian drawing the interest.

In one case Mrs Signe Peterson of Chicago took her 15-year-old daughter Gloria to court in an attempt to free up a £10,000 prize won on the Grand National. The counterfoil bore the name Gloria Peterson and the prize had been lodged in a trust by court order because the girl was under age. Signe Peterson testified that she and her husband had bought a ticket each from a woman in Chicago. She instructed the woman to put the name Gloria Peterson on the counterfoil, but, she claimed somewhat improbably, this did not refer to her daughter but to herself. She insisted: 'Gloria was a pet name used for me by my mother. Owing to the fact that when I was a little girl my mother and I used often go to the pictures and we had a great admiration for our compatriot Gloria Swanson, and I used to dress up and imitate her and my mother would call me Little Gloria. Afterwards, when my daughter was born, I called her Gloria after the famous film actress, but I positively swear that in using the name Gloria on the counterfoil I had no thought of benefiting my daughter.' The judge gave her the benefit of the doubt and the prize was split three ways between parents and daughter.

A judge in Dublin heard an appeal by an Indian father of a 5-year-old girl to have a prize of £456 paid to him 'for her maintenance during her minority'. He had put her name on the counterfoil. In an affidavit he pleaded that the little girl's entire future was at stake, claiming: 'The best dowry can only be given by me to my daughter Darshani if I get the amount of her prize . . . In India, among Hindus, a daughter has no share in the property of her father. All that she gets is the dowry at the time of her marriage, which solely depends on the choice of the parents. The choice depends generally on the financial position of the father, especially in the cash that he possesses.'

Mr Justice Johnston made an order declaring that the money belonged to the little girl, and directed that the winnings be invested in Irish State bonds, and that the annual dividends should be paid to her father until she was old enough to take possession of her prize.

In 1935 the Irish Sweeps founder Richard Duggan was diagnosed with terminal cancer. He settled his estate, selling his racehorses to his fellow turf enthusiast Joe McGrath. One account of his funeral says the capital's flags flew at half-mast, work ceased in parts of the city and thousands lined the route to the cemetery, while cabinet ministers and other powerful individuals followed the hearse on foot. Originally hostile to the Irish Sweep, *The Irish Times* now conceded that Duggan had 'given to posterity far beyond anything the promoters conceived'. In his will he left the vast sum of £77,604, naming his son Patrick to take his place on the board of Irish Hospitals Trust Limited.

While ticket sales in Britain were hit by the publicity blackout and tough new penalties introduced on the first day of 1935, smuggling carried on. One backdoor route into Britain was to use Northern Ireland as a staging post, concealing the books of Sweeps tickets in crates of foodstuffs and machinery. While most were intended for consumption in Britain, some were mailed on to other destinations. Packages with British stamps were less likely to attract the attention of watchful customs officers than those from Ireland.

One probably fanciful method of smuggling which has entered Sweeps lore was said to involve aircraft from Ireland dropping large bundles of tickets under cover of darkness to cronies on the ground.

The sea lanes were a far more reliable route for the bulk smugglers, although that reliability could not be guaranteed. In 1937 Liverpool police raided a garage and seized up to 40 suitcases which were found to contain receipts for tickets addressed to all corners of the globe. The receipts covered ticket sales of £500,000. Three policemen were among the 18 people brought to trial. The judge said the defendants were members of 'a very clever and complete' smuggling network which landed tickets in bulk at the Liverpool docks and distributed them in the north of England and beyond. A local convent provided laundry services to the ferries, and one of their vans was used by the smugglers without the nuns' knowledge. A keen-eyed observer twigged that far more suitcases of supposed dirty laundry were going into the back of the van than should be the case. The driver was stopped by harbour police, but after fielding a couple of questions he was allowed go on his way.

Sometime later he was stopped again and he blew the whistle on the whole scam, claiming he had been busted because he hadn't bribed the policeman manning the gate of the docks. In his police statement he complained: 'There's a right racket going on down at Princess Dock with your fellows. There are thousands of pounds worth of Irish Sweep tickets being brought across from Dublin daily in suitcases and your fellows are being paid to allow them through the dock gates.'

The van driver revealed that he sometimes transported 60 suitcases of tickets from the dock each week, receiving ten shillings for each. In addition to the three policemen demanding bribes, he named well-heeled 'businessmen' deeply involved in the conspiracy. A seaman implicated in the scheme told the court he had been sucked in by a Dublin man called Thompson who was representing the Irish Hospitals Trust. He agreed to smuggle tickets. He explained: 'The tickets were sent on board ship in suitcases. I'd bring them over in my cabin. I'd usually bring cases over in batches of two, three or four. I generally arranged to get cases out of the dock by secreting them among cargo in different wagons going out. At other times I'd take them out myself. Sometimes I have taken suitcases to the garage in my car.'

The days of judges handing down token fines of a few pounds were over. The scale of the operation was so large and the scandal of the corrupt policemen considered so grave, that stiff sentences were passed.

Ten of the 18 were convicted, including two of the accused policemen. The pair were each sentenced to nine months behind bars, while others were fined and also jailed.

A conviction of far more concern to the British authorities was the one held by their intelligence service that the Sweeps smuggling network was being used both to generate funding for IRA activity in Britain, and potentially as a channel for illegally importing weapons. Security files released from Britain's National Archives in 2009 show that the secret service kept a wary eye on London-based Doctor Moira Connolly, a daughter of James Connolly who was executed for his part in the 1916 Rising. Moira Connolly was a ticket agent for the organisation run by her father's old comrade Joe McGrath.

The British secret service discovered her sideline while investigating her husband, Richard Clyde Beech, a zealous communist and admirer of the Soviet Union. The Metropolitan Police's Special Branch informed the secret service that Connolly was the trustee of a slush fund for communists and IRA members on the run from Ireland. Another trustee was said to be Tomas O'Sullivan. The file says: 'Any communist who is on the run from Ireland must prove his *bona fides* to Doctor Connolly, while IRA members must be able to satisfy Tomas O'Sullivan of their genuineness by producing a letter from their [commanding officer].'

British intelligence suspected that because of her links to republicans, Connolly was funnelling the proceeds from the sale of Sweepstake tickets to the IRA. However, the recently released files show that the authorities never established conclusive proof.

According to British intelligence files, Connolly's husband worked in London for Russian Oil Products, which also had an office in Dublin. It sold Russian oil products internationally and was believed to be a front for Soviet intelligence. Beech also ran the London operation of the Progressive Bookshop, which shared an office with Tass, the Soviet news agency.

Britain's secret service discovered that Beech was having Sweeps tickets delivered in books from the Irish branch of the bookshop. A note on his file said: 'Beech has had connections with the Soviet espionage organisation here. In 1925 he married a daughter of the late James Connolly and has since been in touch with Irish extremists in London. He is secretary of the James Connolly Club.'

The British authorities had good reason to fear that the cash machine that was the Irish Sweeps could aid terrorist activity. Joseph McGarrity, who held great sway with the body in the United States, remained an implacable foe of England up to the time of his death in 1940. In a letter he penned in 1934, McGarrity proposed 'demolition' operations in Britain 'with a view to demoralization of the enemy'. Two years later in 1936 he issued a circular to all Clan na Gael district bodies in the States. It urged: 'As an organization we must come alive out of what each of our members will agree has been the long sleep of the last few years.'

In June 1936 the Fianna Fáil government outlawed the IRA. The organisation's Chief of Staff, Maurice (Moss) Twomey, was quickly packed off to serve three years' imprisonment at the Curragh military camp. During those three years Twomey's family survived on cash sent to them by Joseph McGarrity. McGarrity was hell-bent on starting his 'demolition' job in Britain with Twomey's help, but after travelling over to inspect the group's units there, Twomey concluded that the IRA was in no position to launch an effective campaign. Taking himself off the active list, he instead opened a shop selling newspapers and sweets.

The campaign went ahead without the former Chief of Staff. The IRA's Army Council declared itself the rightful government of the notional Irish Republic, drawing a distinction with the 26 County administration of the Free State. As the government of the Republic, it issued Britain with an ultimatum on 12 January 1939 demanding a complete withdrawal from the island of Ireland and from Irish affairs. Three days later and nine months before World War II ignited Europe, a proclamation was posted across Ireland declaring war on Britain. The proclamation was written by Joseph McGarrity.

A document known as the S-Plan or Sabotage Plan set out precise tactics aimed at paralysing Britain by destroying civic, military and industrial targets. Direct military actions against troops and armament factories were only to be carried out if there was some chance they wouldn't become suicide missions. Public utilities including railways, water supplies and gasworks were targeted. Businesses and industrial plants were on the hit list, as were the big newspapers.

One day after the IRA's declaration of war, five bombs exploded. Three targeted power stations, causing little damage, with the other two bringing terror to the little market towns of Coleshill and Alnwick. The following day there were more explosions. Police guards were assigned to all gasworks, power stations and telephone exchanges, while security was stepped up at the BBC's most powerful transmission base. All ships from Ireland arriving at Hollyhead, Liverpool and Fishguard were subjected to a rigorous inspection.

Fourteen men in Manchester and London were arrested and charged under the Explosive Substances Act. A bomb exploded at a Tralee hotel where Francis Chamberlain, son of the British prime minister was staying on a shooting holiday. The Army Council said it had no part in the Kerry blast, claiming it was the work of local freelancers. The Irish government rushed through the Treason Act and the Offences Against the State Act arming itself with draconian powers against the IRA. After three weeks of the campaign, *The Times* of London attempted to play down the threat to life and limb. It assured readers: 'The signatories of the ridiculous ultimatum to Great Britain are men of no account. Nobody in this country would have taken them seriously, but for the recent outrages in Great Britain. As a political force in Éire, the IRA simply does not count.' In April, an IRA communiqué was read out to those attending an Easter Rising commemoration at Dublin's Glasnevin Cemetery. It stated that the 'operation groups' in Britain were under strict orders to avoid inflicting casualties.

There were casualties though. In July a bomb planted in the left-luggage area of King's Cross railway station severely injured three people, one of them fatally. Five were badly wounded the same day in an explosion at Victoria Station. The most notorious outrage of the campaign took place in Coventry, where a bomb went off in a crowded shopping district, killing five and wounding over 50. Two Irishmen found guilty of the Coventry bombing were speedily hanged. By February 1940 the number of Irish deported under new legislation was 119.

Another individual to attract the avid attention of British Intelligence in this period was John Andrews with an address in the Dublin suburb of Clontarf. Documents declassified in 2010 show that in 1939 Andrews made contact with a British customs official offering to sell a list of 12,000 Irish Sweeps agents operating in the United States. Andrews claimed that German operatives in Dublin were anxious to get their hands on his list with the intention of recruiting a pro-Nazi

Fifth Column in the United States.

Andrews wrote to the Customs man: 'I was employed by Hospitals Trust for six years. For four years I had charge of all monies from its Foreign Department handling about £20 million for two years. I was supervisor of foreign agents' correspondence. In June 1936 I went to the US. I obtained a greater knowledge of the working of the Hospitals Trust's organization in the US. I found that a small clique controlled the organization there.

'One of the men [Joe McGarrity of Philadelphia], most of whom have extremist opinions on Irish politics, [was among] the prime movers in the Clan na Gael organizations that supplied funds for the bomb outrages in England. I have a complete list of names, 12,000 or so. I was approached by someone in Dublin who wants to buy it. I suspect that it came from someone in touch with Nazi Germany. The potentialities of the list for obtaining information are enormous. I refused to have anything to do with the proposal. The USA authorities are anxious to get the information.'

British Intelligence officials discussed the matter in an exchange of memos. One wrote: 'Wire our man in New York and tell him of Andrews' offer. [FBI chief] Mr Edgar Hoover might like to know, and in particular the allegation that the Germans are looking for the same list. The significance of this is, I think, that the list might be regarded as representing anti-British extremists in all parts of the US who would form good potential enemy agents.'

Later, in November 1941, a senior MI5 officer expressed the belief that Andrews' real purpose in hawking his list to several contacts was to extort money from the Hospitals Trust in return for sitting on his list of names. Later in the war, Andrews, who had fallen on hard times, sought permission to work for a US contractor building military bases in Scotland. The Irish Department of External Affairs warned the British authorities that Andrews was 'undesirable'. In a letter to the head of Britain's passport control office, the same MI5 officer speculated that the Irish government feared that Andrews would use the military job to make his way back to the US where he would attempt to damage the Sweeps operation there.

The 'demolition' campaign dreamed up by Joseph McGarrity had fizzled out by the spring of 1940. By then a large number of IRA suspects were detained in Irish and British jails and internment camps, and with

Allied warships and Nazi U-boats prowling the seaways the smuggling of arms had become virtually impossible. The Irish Sweeps, which relied on smuggling as its life-blood, seemed to have reached the end of the line.

Chapter 17 ∾

| NO MORE EASY MONEY

A t the beginning of 1936 a housewife from the Canadian town of Midland, Ontario, made international headlines when she tore up an Irish Sweeps ticket worth $4,950. Described as 'a pious Protestant churchgoer' Mrs Charles Fenton had destroyed the ticket bought for her by her husband on the grounds that gambling was plain wrong. One report said: 'Mr Fenton, gloomily agreeing, spent some of his own hard-earned money cabling the Irish Sweepstakes to keep the $4,950.'

A Toronto reporter asked clerics of the Protestant, Jewish and Catholic faiths what they thought of Mrs Fenton's act of denial. The Protestant reverend said: 'She is quite right.' The Jewish rabbi took a less hardline view, remarking: 'She did not have to tear up the ticket, but if she felt it was proper she was certainly right.' The Catholic monsignor clearly indicated he felt the woman had been most reckless, arguing: 'Life suffers more from monotony than from adventure. Risk is only censurable when it is too big for the one who undertakes it. The lady in question failed to draw the line between a legitimate risk and a foolhardy plunge.'

The *Time* magazine report was headlined 'Three Faiths' and was one of many which framed attitudes to the Irish Sweeps in terms of religious rivalries. At a time when the dominant culture of the United States was still overwhelmingly WASP (White Anglo-Saxon Protestant), the issue of gaming was often, although not always, used to contrast puritanical Protestant piety with Catholic moral laxity.

The coverage of Mrs Mildrid Small did not specify her religion, but her plans for spending her Sweeps winnings would not have met with the approval of those who had been dismayed by the recent repeal of Prohibition, the 14 year ban on alcohol spearheaded by the Methodists.

Mrs Small was a Harlem laundress who won $150,000. Asked how she would spend her windfall, she announced she would drink beer and dance the Lindy Hop with her gentleman friend, Frank Oxley. The *New Yorker* magazine gave Mildrid's priority list its ringing endorsement, saying: 'After the virtuous (and lugubrious) plans expressed by other winners, we are grateful to Mrs Small for this simple vision of her heart's desire. May the beer flow strong and friendly; may the shoes fit easy on her dancing feet.'

The divide between Catholics and Protestants regarding tolerance of gambling was stressed in reports of a row between 'Protestant Episcopal Bishop William T Manning of Manhattan' and 'Catholic Postmaster General Farley'. Against his wishes, Farley's legal department had slapped a ban on any mail addressed to the Grand National Treasure Hunt. The treasure hunt was a 'contest' organised by a lobby group called the Association for Legalizing American Lotteries. The association argued that the millions of dollars leaving the country for each Irish sweep could and should be kept in the United States by creating legal lotteries to benefit good causes. Participants in the treasure hunt could enter a draw for big prizes by sending off one dollar to purchase an 'application for membership' of the association. The Post Office declared the scheme an ill-disguised form of gambling and barred it from the post.

The man credited with spurring the Post Office to action was Bishop Manning, who weeks earlier had delivered a widely reported sermon about the evil of lotteries and specifically of the Irish Sweeps. The bishop didn't deliver the sermon from the pulpit of his own cathedral. Instead, he made the trip downtown to St Bartholomew's on swanky Park Avenue, described as having a 'socialite' congregation. His choice of location was a pointed one. One of New York's most elevated socialites, Mrs Grace Harriman, was a parishioner of St Bartholomew's. She was also the campaigning president of the National Conference on Legalizing Lotteries.

One report said: 'A large, determined, forthright lady, Mrs Harriman thinks it is a shame that millions of US dollars are exported for the Irish Hospitals Sweepstakes and other foreign lotteries when they might be kept at home. People who agree with her to the extent of paying $1 to join her Conference automatically become eligible to enter a "Selection Sweepstakes". Here they are called upon to display their skill and judgment by arranging, in order of desirability, a list of sixteen ways the Government could spend the money it might raise by legalizing lotteries. For best arrangement: $20,000. Other prizes total $40,000.' The politicised categories to be put in order included child welfare, tax reduction, hospitals and old age pensions. In a previous contest those paying one dollar for membership could win big prizes by choosing the best name for a painting by the famous artist Howard Chandler Christy. The painting illustrated the virtue of charity.

Unfortunately for the bishop, Mrs Harriman was not in church that morning to receive her verbal belt of the crozier. Mrs Harriman told reporters: 'I'm glad I wasn't at the service. I might have got up and answered him then and there. I have deep respect for Bishop Manning, but I would like to call his attention to the fact that the first Episcopal church, near Cheshire, Connecticut, was built by a lottery.' Another Protestant bishop added his voice to the debate, denouncing all forms of gambling as 'a habit forming drug' that destroyed an individual's moral character.

Grace Harriman's pro-gambling crusade led to her being hauled before the Post Office solicitor to explain her breach of the department's prohibition on posted material promoting the chance to win prizes 'dependent in whole or in part on lot or chance'. She faced stiff penalties. The sanction for a first offence was two years in jail, and for a second, five years. She argued that, despite the word 'Sweepstakes' in the title of the competition, the prizes were awarded on merit by a panel of judges, and that there was no drawing of tickets. A woman of some importance, she escaped punishment.

One account of Mrs Harriman's legal wrangling with the Post Office solicitor featured a large photo of the latest Irish Sweeps draw, with the girls mixing the counterfoils dressed as gauchos of the South American pampas. The report began: 'Ardent supporters of legalising lotteries had a hearing at the Post Office Department in Washington. Countrywide interest in the proceedings was heightened by the memory, only a few days old, of the excitement occasioned by the drawings in one of the world's largest lotteries—the Irish Hospitals Sweepstakes.'

It continued: 'Unquestionably, the advent of the Irish Sweepstakes about six years ago, with its attendant fanfare and ballyhoo, gave the lottery industry a tremendous impetus. The last Sweepstakes drawing was said to have taken about $5,000,000 out of the country of which less than $3,000,000 came back.' By implication, the Irish Sweep continued to be widely endorsed in the American press as a better bet than rival schemes. One report, for instance, informed readers: 'Police say that an Italian lottery, based on weekly publication in Rome of tax disbursement figures, extorts a "staggering" sum from Italian colonists in America and yields very little except thrills in return.'

Mrs George Hammond of Detroit was a big winner on the Irish Sweeps in 1936, collecting a cool $75,000. The *Detroit News* cheekily described this as the woman's second piece of financial good luck in a short time, the first being the death of her husband which entitled her to one-third of his considerable estate. George Hammond had started out as a small-time butcher before inventing the refrigerated railroad car which revolutionised the transport of meat. He became such a celebrated tycoon that the city of Hammond, Indiana, is named after him. Hammond had millions but was so tight-fisted that his wife filed for divorce in 1924 citing his 'stinginess'. As determined to keep his spouse as his cash, George fought his wife's action and the Michigan Supreme Court denied her the divorce. With a share of her late husband's fortune and her $75,000 from Ireland, Mrs Hammond had the wherewithal to spend lots of quality time hanging out with her good friend Wallis Simpson, the woman for whom Edward VIII gave up the English throne.

As was the practice, many newspapers carried reports of Mrs Hammond's big win in editions which went straight to the news-stands, while omitting the story from editions distributed in the mail. Early in 1937 the Office of the Third Assistant Postmaster General announced that he was considering a postal ban on publications which published Sweeps stories in news-stand editions. Members of Congress expressed surprise at the mooted move, with some arguing that it would be illegal. Postmaster General Farley made no comment, but off the record some of his officials fed reporters the pro-Sweeps line that the proposed ban would certainly be declared unlawful.

Grace Harriman suggested that the law was an ass, as it failed to prevent some $9 million of illicit tickets travelling through the US mail each year. She contended: 'The Federal ruling against printing news of lotteries will, I am sure, be unpopular with the public for the tremendous human nature interest in lotteries, and the stories of sudden wealth to poverty-stricken families, carries an irresistible appeal to readers. However, it is the law and should be enforced, and if it cannot be enforced then it should be repealed and lotteries legalized for the benefit of hospitals and charitable institutions.'

Another advocate of legalised lotteries predicted: 'The ruling of the [Third Assistant's Office of the] Postmaster General will, if enforced, deal a death blow to the Irish Sweepstakes in this country. It is no secret that their principal market is in this country. More than 50% of the winners in the last drawings were American. The sale of Irish Sweepstakes tickets in this country reached a new high this year of 73%. Strict enforcement of the new Federal ruling, as well as of the Penal Law of this State, would undoubtedly cripple the Irish Sweepstakes in this country. It would be interesting, however, to observe the public reaction to Federal and State enforcement of the law. American contributions of over $25,000,000 yearly to the Irish Sweepstakes for the support of Irish hospitals constitute a self-indictment of our lottery policy. The trend is definitely towards legalization.' Congressman Edward Kenney, whose bill to legalise American lotteries for public projects had been voted down in the House, said the Post Office would stray 'beyond its authority' if it went ahead with the second-hand ban.

The issue of the postal ban on Irish Sweepstakes even made it into the definitive American guidebook on how to run a newspaper. Written by the editor of the *New York Times* and published in 1940, *Without Fear or Favour* stated that the responsibilities of a newspaper editor included deciding whether to run separate editions with and without Irish Sweeps news.

By 1938 the widely syndicated columnist Drew Pearson was arguably the most powerful political commentator in the United States. His writings and wireless broadcasts never gave the faintest hint of his five years as a highly paid secret agent of Hospitals Trust, but in one column of that year he put in a good word for the Irish Sweeps, contending that they did make some contribution to the public purse of the US.

He wrote: 'The famous Irish Sweepstakes will perhaps bring riches to a handful of American citizens on March 25th, but there is one sure-shot winner, Mister Uncle Sam. Under the anti-lottery law the Post Office Department is required to exert every effort to prevent the sale of Irish Sweeps tickets. Postal agents vigorously press the hunt and from time to time confiscate large batches of tickets. But once the race is run, another branch of the Government, the Internal Revenue

Department, steps forward and demands from the lucky winners a large cut in the form of taxes. Under the tax laws, winnings of any kind are classed as income, and Irish Sweepstakes prizes are no exception. The holder of a ticket on the winning horse must give the Treasury $59,000 in surtaxes and $6,000 in normal taxes, making a total dent of $65,000 in his $150,000 plum.'

Pearson went on to point out a popular strategy for avoiding the full payment of tax. He told readers: 'These payments are reduced materially if there is more than one owner of a winning ticket, since the more a prize is split up the less the surtax charge to each individual winner. Example, five holders of a $50,000 ticket would pay only $300 each in surtaxes as compared to the $7,700 sock to a single owner. But it must be proved to the Internal Revenue sleuths that the split ownership is a *bona fide* division and not merely a device to dodge taxes! A number of winners have claimed divided ownership, but relatively few have gotten away with it. For Uncle Sam may be down on lotteries as a matter of public morals, but when it comes to collecting taxes on the "take" he passes up no bets.'

One of Pearson's rival syndicated columnists was the equally hard-hitting Westbrook Pegler. In his 1936 'Fair Enough' column he lashed out at the Irish Sweep for being neither fair to its participants, nor for providing Ireland's hospitals with anything like enough of a cut. He wrote: 'There are not quite 3,000,000 souls in the Irish Free State and, unless the majority of the population has been enjoying very poor health, the dividends from the great international gamble should have been sufficient to relieve the sick of every ill money can cure.'

This was clearly not the case, said Pegler, claiming that he had checked with relatives in the west of Ireland and learned that the healthcare system there was a shambles. He contrasted the continuing plight of the sick in the west of Ireland with the high life enjoyed by the personnel of the Hospitals Trust and the many powerful guests they wined and dined at great expense. He pointed out that there was 'plenty of money for advertising and salaries and for the wine that can reduce to a state of coma the journalists of the wide world who can be induced to accept free transportation to Ireland to ballyhoo the promotion'.

The Irish Sweepstakes were likewise lacerated, along with other forms of gambling, in Eric Bender's widely read polemic of 1938 entitled *Tickets To Fortune*. The book was marketed as a self-help manual for those tempted to have a flutter, by exposing with hard facts what one critic described as 'the fake and bunk and futility of trying the get-rich-quick rackets'.

The following year the reputation of the Irish Sweeps as above board and incorruptible took another pasting as an elaborate swindle grabbed the front page headlines.

One report began: 'The theft of between $1,500,000 and $4,500,000 from the Irish Sweepstakes ticket-buying public of the United States was disclosed here tonight when District Attorney Walter A Ferris announced the arrest of three alleged members of a gang that in the last three years is believed to have pocketed payments for Sweepstakes tickets and supplied victims with forged tickets. One of the key figures, the police said, was the manager of a New Rochelle bus terminal in whose modest home was found a costly cellar playroom, a vault which the police were unable to open, and what was described as one of the best-stocked private bars in Westchester County. In the man's car, Mr Ferris said, were 204,000 receipts valued at $510,000 for tickets on the Irish Hospitals Sweepstakes Grand National.'

The report went on to say that a year-long investigation into the scam had uncovered a fraud ring involving 'countless' others, and encompassing New York, Chicago, Philadelphia, Baltimore, New Jersey and Connecticut. The high-living bus terminal manager was 43-year-old Philip Griffin while his two arrested accomplices gave their occupation as printers. Griffin had been under surveillance for some time before his arrest. The police sprang when they saw him load up his car with packages from a printing factory. When the car was stopped and searched, officers found 17,000 books of forged receipts, each containing 12 fakes, for the upcoming Grand National.

The report continued: 'The receipts, the prosecutor said, were excellent forgeries, even bearing the watermark which the purchaser is cautioned to look for. Mr Ferris said that if the $510,000 in receipts for the coming Sweepstake was an example of the the gang's operations for one race, in the last three years the "take" would be close to $4,500,000. Whether real tickets on the Sweepstakes were sold or whether even the tickets were fraudulent was not known. At any rate, Mr Ferris said, the gang pocketed the sales money and supplied forged receipts.'

At the beginning of September 1939 Nazi stormtroopers steamrolled over Poland, bringing Britain and France into what would escalate into World War II. As the Germans mopped up in Eastern Europe, the next seven months on the Western Front settled into an uneasy calm-before-the-storm, described by the British as the Phoney War or Bore War, by the Germans as the Sitting War and by the French as the Joke War. There were skirmishes on the French-German front and full blooded clashes in Norway, but on flights over Germany, RAF aircraft were dropping propaganda leaflets rather than bombs.

One theatre of war where full-blown hostilities did begin from the off was the North Atlantic, where most of Germany's warships and U-boats had already taken up position when war was declared. There was a strong popular feeling in the United States that there should be no involvement in Europe's war, although the US was neutral on the side of the Allies, supplying cut price armaments and other goods. For the Irish Sweeps, the war in the Atlantic was a disaster, virtually cutting off the smuggling routes to by far its biggest market. By the end of 1939 only a relative trickle of tickets had arrived in North America for the following spring's Grand National. When newspapers speculated that this would be the last draw until the war's end, or perhaps forever, Joe McGrath issued a statement insisting that the operation would carry on regardless.

His fighting words were taken with a pinch of salt, and throughout February 1940 a rash of closure stories appeared across the international press. One typical headline said 'No More Easy Money'. When the outcome of the sweep on the 1940 Grand National came through, the *Newark Star Ledger* of New Jersey ran the headline 'Sweeps Cash Goes to Only Six in State', noting that this 'yielded an all-time American low'.

In April 1940, with the Germans building up troop numbers to bring blitzkrieg to France and bombing to Britain, McGrath issued another statement which suggested that the Irish Hospitals Trust was on the brink of surrender. He announced that the company was to be liquidated because of the war. A new Irish Hospitals Trust (1940) Limited was to be established in its place. The new company would incorporate the Irish Sweeps into a broadened portfolio of gaming activities 'if it is decided to continue under the existing conditions'.

One syndicated columnist in the United States declared himself delighted to bid goodbye to bad rubbish. Of the money that would no longer be leaving the economy, he wrote: 'Many [tickets] were bought, few were chosen.' He rejoiced: 'Americans have not been pestered lately by peddlers of . . . the Irish Sweepstakes.'

Chapter 18 ∾

HELP THE HELPLESS AND
HELP YOURSELF

The final Sweeps draw of 1939 took place six weeks after Britain and France declared war on Germany. It was a sombre affair, with none of the usual razzmatazz. The recycled costumes worn by the girls mixing the counterfoils had been in mothballs for the past two years. Members of the public were invited inside the Mansion House for the draw itself, but were excluded from the preliminary three days of mixing.

At the draw the chairman of the Hospitals Committee, Lord Powerscourt, told the audience: 'Now that the supreme tragedy of war has descended on many of our subscribers, who must be now in a state of supreme anxiety, not to say actual misery, it would be very thoughtless to continue to follow the custom of opening these draws with the glamour and joy and gaiety to which we are accustomed. It has therefore been decided to dispense with all the pageantry and speech making for the duration of the war.'

Even if it had been deemed appropriate, the usual motorised pageant would have been a non-starter. Petrol rationing had been introduced and the roads were virtually empty of cars. Although hostilities had not properly commenced in Western Europe, the October sweep on the Cesarewitch was an early casualty of the war. The race scheduled for 25 October was shifted to 2 November with a changed field of starters. The Sweeps promoters announced that since this was 'an entirely different race' they would abandon the two-tier sweepstake and hold a straightforward lottery, advertised as the 'All-Cash Draw', in the Mansion House with each of the 95 tickets drawn winning a straight £947.

Joe McGrath and Spencer Freeman, both high-ranking soldiers in a former life, had seen this day coming from a long way off. As the clouds of war gathered in the early part of the year, fearful uncertainty stalked the minds of millions in Britain and Europe. In the circumstances, many preferred to keep their money in their pockets rather than send it off for a wager on a race that might never take place. Few Americans suspected that the United States would get dragged into a European war, but many who might normally have had a flutter on the sweep thought the better of sending their hard-earned dollars into some No-Man's Land thousands of miles away. The upshot was that the prize fund for the 1939 Epsom Derby sweep was the smallest since the very first in 1930.

At the draw in May the vice-chairman of the Hospitals Committee, Sir Joseph Glynn, put the paltry prize money down in part to the 'difficulty of the international crisis'. The theme of that May draw was: 'Siotchain—Peace'. According to the London-based News Review the scaled-down ornamentation featured 'an enormous Angel of Peace standing over a pile of broken weapons as flags of all nations [the swastika included] bowed homage'.

There were other early portents of the hardships that lay ahead for the Irish Sweeps. In July 1939 a meeting of the Mayo Board of Health was told that the Minister for Local Government was refusing to reimburse the board the £80 it had spent to have plaques put up at several hospitals in the county in memory of the late Richard Duggan. One board member said it was 'very mean' of the minister, as without Duggan the hospitals would not have been built or upgraded.

The sharp dip in ticket sales for the May 1939 sweep on the Derby suggested that the writing was on the wall for the thrice-yearly event. The closing date for entries to the October draw on the Cesarewitch had been set months in advance for 29 September. Precisely four weeks before this closing date the Germans invaded Poland. Remarkably, instead of stopping the sweep in its tracks, the outbreak of war sparked a spate of panic buying.

Covering the October draw, the Dundalk Examiner noted: 'The large audience in the Mansion House literally gasped with amazement when the auditors' statement disclosed the fact that, in spite of the outbreak of this terrible war, nearly £1.5 million has once more been collected.' According to the Hospitals Trust auditors, £400,000 had been taken prior to the outbreak of war. This evaporated to a trickle in the week that followed the invasion of Poland. But in the following three weeks leading up to the deadline the trickle raged to a deluge amounting to some £1 million. A representative of the Hospitals Committee attempted no explanation of this extraordinary development, but stated: 'We are going on with the confidence that they will be a complete success in the troubled months or years ahead.'

While he wasn't saying so, Joe McGrath knew much better than that, and for weeks he had been furiously working behind the scenes to cobble together a Plan B which smacked of equal parts audacity and desperation.

On 3 September 1939 Britain and France declared war on Germany. Within hours a U-boat sank the passenger liner *Athena* off the west coast of Ireland. Over one hundred were killed, including some 50 Britons and 30 Americans. Rescue vessels landed hundreds of survivors at Galway and Glasgow. Even as the survivors were disembarking, the Germans were rushing to claim complete innocence of the deed. Feigning high dudgeon, one Nazi newspaper griped: 'The American press is already making use of this catastrophe in favour of Britain.'

With 30 Americans killed, the US press was indeed on the warpath. It reported in detail the angry reaction of the recently appointed United States Ambassador to Britain, the Irish-American ex-Prohibition bootlegger Joseph P. Kennedy. An appeaser who had sought personal meetings with Hitler in order to reason with the Fuhrer, Joe Kennedy dispatched his young son, John F. Kennedy, to help out the US survivors in Glasgow. Meanwhile, Kennedy Snr sent £1,000 to Ireland to aid those stranded in Galway.

The Fianna Fáil government, meanwhile, was making a start-up bequest of £1,000 to a new organisation holding its inaugural meeting just as the *Athena* survivors were supping hot drinks and slipping on dry clothes in Galway. The senior Fianna Fáil figure Frank Aiken told the founders of the newborn Irish Red Cross that the government urged them to establish first aid societies and to collect voluntary contributions in every town in the land. The new body had been established by an Act of the Oireachtas on 1 August. Another speaker stated that had it had more time to organise, its members would right now be handling the 'reception and sustenance' of the 450 *Athena* survivors in Galway.

The advent of the Irish Red Cross set Joe McGrath beavering away on a scheme to keep his Sweepstake operation ticking over for the duration of the war. He drew up a memo for a new sweep attached to the Irish Red Cross and its international counterparts. Eleven days after the Irish Red Cross came into existence, the secretary of the Department of External Affairs wrote to Taoiseach de Valera informing him of McGrath's scheme. He pointed out McGrath's contention that a Red Cross Sweepstake would improve Ireland's tarnished image with the British people, 'especially by taking charge of some of the permanently disabled' casualties of war. Ireland's decision to stay out of the war was widely deplored by the British authorities and the general population as a stab in the back.

Nine years earlier, opposing the legalisation of the Irish Hospitals Sweepstakes in the Seanad, the Labour Party's Thomas Johnson predicted with unerring accuracy that Joe McGrath and his partners would be able to exert a powerful blackmail over future governments by threatening heavy job losses in a feeble economy. The original legislation had only granted the Sweeps a four-year lifespan. Johnson said that no government could countenance the loss of hundreds of jobs, and the Sweep would be put on a permanent footing. Now, as he had done in the past and would again in the future, McGrath played his unemployment trump card.

Two weeks after External Affairs put the Taoiseach on alert about McGrath's Red Cross lobbying, the Department of Justice wrote to External Affairs: 'Mr McGrath of Hospitals Sweeps has approached several Ministers on the subject of running a sweep in connection with a special race, on St Stephen's day next, proceeds to go to the Red Cross here and the Red Cross in other countries in which tickets are bought. The main idea is apparently to keep the Sweep staff in employment: there is apparently a serious danger—almost a certainty—that if something like this is not done, three or four thousand girls will lose their employment within a few months.'

A year earlier the scholarly Douglas Hyde had been appointed the first President of Ireland without a vote of the people, chosen as the best man for the job by the leaders of both Fianna Fáil and Fine Gael. He had also accepted the post of first president of the Irish Red Cross, marking his accession by making a £500 personal donation. McGrath sought out his endorsement for his Red Cross Sweeps. Hyde's presidential office wrote to the Taoiseach's Department, saying: 'It has been proposed to the President, as President of the Irish Red Cross Society, that he should purchase the first ticket of the sweepstake to be promoted for the benefit of that Society and that a simple ceremony, framed of course with due regard to the dignity of the Presidential office, should be associated with the event and filmed. The President sees no objection but would like to have the views of the Taoiseach before committing himself.'

De Valera poured scorn on McGrath's latest attempt to hijack an office of the State for his own ends. The Taoiseach's department told McGrath bluntly that for the President of Ireland to appear promoting gambling on newsreels screened around the world was 'scarcely in keeping with the dignity of the Presidential post'.

McGrath did not confine his recruiting drive to Ireland. External Affairs files from late 1939 reveal that he went after the endorsement of the International Red Cross in Geneva, offering a cut of the takings in return. The departmental secretary J. P. Walsh, who had been kept busy monitoring McGrath's multi-stranded lobbying campaign, noted: 'In view of the rather discouraging reply from the International Red Cross, Mr Joe McGrath, the promoter of the scheme, has decided to abandon that particular project.' A telegram in the same departmental file shows that McGrath had been comprehensively rebuffed by the International Red Cross which stressed that it would not 'accept any responsibility, particularly technical or financial, nor extend any patronage for such a scheme'.

While de Valera ruled out any figurehead role for President Hyde as undignified, he could not ignore McGrath's ace in the hole, the 2,000 or so jobs which would be lost at a time of national emergency if the sweep was to go to the wall. McGrath's lobbying in the corridors of power was matched by the planting of stories in the newspapers in praise of his new project. The directors of Hospitals Trust held huge sway over the media, wining and dining favoured writers and editors, and wielding the clout that large advertisers can and often do.

Before September was out, the following teaser appeared in the *Tipperary Star*. 'Important discussions are in progress about the future of the Sweepstakes. The war has dealt them a severe blow and if postal restrictions are not relaxed abroad, future draws will be very tame affairs indeed and the employment of thousands of girls who have been brought to Dublin, as well as those from the capital itself, will be jeopardized. If every letter to this country is opened by the censors abroad the transmission of money through the post will not be an easy task. I am not surprised therefore, to hear that new plans are being considered.

'If the Sweepstakes were held in aid of some international charity, it is contended that foreign governments might be disposed to relax some of their restrictions on them. There have therefore been hints that future Sweepstakes might be held in aid of the International Red Cross.'

The piece went on to suggest that the promoters could persuade the Dáil to rush through enabling legislation by the application of 'considerable political pressure from various parts of the House' to preserve 'the employment of thousands of women, even at small pay'.

Members of the Irish Red Cross committee canvassed by the newspapers gave the plan their eager endorsement. Sir John Lumsden described it as 'admirable' while Viscountess Powerscourt gushed: 'It was very kind of the Hospitals Trust people to suggest it to us.'

Once again the country's political establishment bowed to the will of Joe McGrath. A bill was rushed into law on 18 October 1939, and the very next day the staff of Irish Hospitals Trust were hard at work preparing for the first Red Cross Sweepstake to be held in the near future. In contrast to the original Sweeps legislation, the enabling legislation for the Red Cross spin-off allowed for a portion of the cash raised to aid causes outside the State. Senator Robert Rowlette, who was involved with the committees of both the hospitals and the Red Cross, welcomed the passing of the Act, stating that the Hospitals Committee 'does not look upon it with any jealousy because it will enable a good deal of the employment given by the Hospitals Trust to go on uninterrupted during the coming months'.

Labour's James Everett, who had previously criticised working conditions in the Hospitals Trust, wanted the government to extract a quid pro quo from the promoters in return for granting them their Red Cross Sweepstake. Two weeks earlier McGrath had stated that some job losses were inevitable, and that some branch offices would be forced to close for the duration of the war. Everett urged the Minister for Justice to ensure that employees working for 'pin money' would be let go by the Trust before those 'in receipt of small wages'. Everett described those working for pin money as the wives of highly paid civil servants and other well-heeled women who valued their jobs as a means of getting out of the house, rather than for the income they brought in. He thought it would be a scandal if many of these were kept on, while many who desperately needed the small wages paid by the Trust were laid off.

The minister paid no heed to Everett's suggestion, while a columnist in the *Irish Independent* dismissed it with open contempt, insisting that those on a small wage whom Everett was seeking to protect should have had something put away for a rainy day. Preaching the virtue of frugality, especially at a time of war, the writer contended: 'The girl who can succeed in looking fashionable by her own ingenuity while helping to keep her family, or members of it, is a person to be respected. On the other hand, the girl who has been making good money for years and spending it as it comes, without putting away something to put her over a possible period of sickness or unemployment, has only herself to blame, and her parents who gave her no better training.'

The *Mayo News* also gave a rebuff to Everett's call, spinning the McGrath line that even though some 900 staff might still have to face the axe because of the wartime downturn, the advent of the Red Cross Sweepstake had been welcomed with great relief by the Hospitals Trust's employees. It added: 'Every effort is being made by the directors to see that people who are not wholly dependent on their earnings should be first to go.'

As the Irish Hospitals Trust was annexing the newly established Irish Red Cross for its own branding purposes, the Roman Catholic Church was embarked on a campaign to keep the organisation out of the clutches of Protestants. The *Catholic Standard* went big with a story headlined 'Catholics Fear Bid to "Capture" Red Cross'. In smaller blocks it added 'Hand-Picked Committee Had Two Catholics, Ten Non-Catholics'.

Readers were informed: 'There is growing concern amongst Catholics at the covert attempt now being made to secure control of the Irish Red Cross by what may be called non-Catholic Ascendancy elements. It is felt that these efforts are directed to creating here—not an Irish organization for charitable and humanitarian effort for national and even wider benefit—but a camouflaged branch of the British Red Cross Society.'

The Red Cross branch which had elected ten non-Catholics to its committee was in Galway, where Bishop Michael Browne and Mayor

Joe Costello led the protests. Allegedly at stake were the very souls of the children of Ireland. According to the *Catholic Standard*: 'A further cause of uneasiness is found in the suggestion that the Red Cross Society may be given control of child welfare organization. To so place the influence and direction of work among the poor children of Ireland ... would be to court obvious dangers.' There were further calls to have a Catholic Red Cross for a Catholic people some weeks later after newspapers claimed that a group of Catholics had been thrown out of a British Red Cross dance held at Ballyculter Orange Hall, Co. Down.

At the close of November 1939 the Hospitals Trust announced details of the first Red Cross Sweepstake, buying up the entire front page of *The Irish Times* to draw attention to 'Ireland's Great Humanitarian and Sporting Gesture'. The closing date for entries was 29 December. The draw was set for 15 January and the race, featuring the biggest ever prize pot for an Irish chase, would take place at Leopardstown Racecourse on the 20th. The slogans directed at the Irish public included: 'Every Irishman should assist energetically in the prosecution of this noble work', 'Help Ireland to help the helpless and help yourself!' and 'By subscribing early you help to keep thousands in employment'.

Delayed for a week for adjustments to the Leopardstown course, the first Red Cross Sweepstake attracted a big field and raised a respectable £61,000 to be distributed by the Red Cross at home and abroad. As feared, however, it did not prevent the axing of 900 jobs from a workforce of 2,200. The accusations once again flew that needy workers were being let go while the well connected and well heeled were kept on. The Hospitals Trust responded by insisting that the 900 lay-offs had been fairly decided on a 'last in, first out' basis. The jobs crisis in Ireland's flagship employer kept the letters editors of the national newspapers busy. One correspondent signing him/herself 'Justice' attacked the Hospitals Trust for letting go those in need while keeping on 'farmers' daughters and country gentlemen's daughters'.

A recently dismissed Sweeps employee wrote to complain bitterly that, while she had been kept on when 900 of her colleagues were sacked, she had only kept her job by agreeing to a 40 per cent slash in her wages. She said that the wage cut was accepted by staff who were 'under the impression' that it would mean their jobs were safe. She felt betrayed by the Trust.

But that was only the beginning. The draw for the regular sweep on the English Grand National, which had been relocated from Aintree to Gatwick, took place on the last day of March 1940. The prize fund of £224,000 was, for understandable reasons, the lowest ever. There was no pageant, no bunting and no bands. Gramophone music was piped into the street outside the Mansion House. Within hours of the draw it was announced that there would be no Irish Sweepstake on the summer Derby and the remaining 1,300 Hospitals Trust staff were put on notice of dismissal. Sir Joseph Glynn of the Hospitals Committee told the press that jobs could be saved if the government passed legislation which would indemnify the Trust and the Committee against any losses made.

This was the second such request in a year for the State to shore up Hospitals Trust's solvency. In 1939 the Dáil had passed legislation which effectively ensured that if the promoters ran up an operating loss on any race, they could claw back the shortfall from the money which was earmarked for the hospitals. This is precisely what happened with the sweep on the 1940 Grand National, where the hospitals were denied more than half the money they were due. This was never the intention of a piece of legislation cobbled together in haste, and the government closed the loophole. Now, with 1,300 jobs on the line, the government again tweaked the legislation at the Trust's behest. Labour's James Everett was an isolated voice pointing out that the net effect of the latest concession to Joe McGrath was to cut the amount of each sweep going to aid the hospitals, while increasing the amount the promoters could claim as expenses.

At the same time as McGrath was engineering a way to increase his income at the expense of the hospitals, Dublin's medics were protesting that the distribution of the existing funds was warped, with hospital beds sitting empty throughout parts of rural Ireland while patients were being turned away in the capital for want of an empty berth. In the Dáil, Fine Gael's James Dillon raised these concerns with the Minister for Health's stand-in. Dillon asked: 'Is he aware that, after the Sweepstakes have been in existence for ten years, there are still people dying in the tenement houses of this city for the want of accommodation in hospitals, individuals whose lives could be saved if there was room in the city hospitals to look after them?'

The government insisted that the state of the capital's hospitals was much improved since the funding from the Sweeps had begun to flow ten years earlier, stating that 775 new beds had been opened in the city's main hospitals, including special hospitals caring for 'the deaf, dumb and mental defectives'.

Dillon wanted to know how many of these additional beds were private and how many were 'available for non-paying persons'. The Hospitals Trust had been given its licence in 1930 specifically to aid charitable hospitals caring for the poor. The minister's stand-in couldn't answer that one, but he disputed Dillon's claim that the poor of Dublin were dying in their tenements for a lack of hospital beds. He did concede, however, that after ten years of Sweeps money flowing into the system: 'There is no doubt that the hospital accommodation in Dublin City is far from sufficient at the present time, and we hope to make more spectacular progress within the next two years than we have in the past.'

Unimpressed, Dillon countered: 'If the Parliamentary Secretary has no such information as I suggest is available, might I suggest to him that he should consult any reputable hospital consultant in this city and ask him that question, as to whether in his opinion persons are not dying in tenement houses in this city for want of hospital bed accommodation wherein they might be adequately treated. I think he will find that the answer will be in the affirmative. That is a shocking state of affairs after ten years.'

There was no Irish Sweep on the 1940 Derby, but the promoters were back on track by the end of the year with their own race, the Irish Cesarewitch. From then until the end of the war, they would stage Hospital and Red Cross Sweeps on races held in Ireland. During these years, the amount of cash reaching the hospitals dried up to a dribble, but the promoters and their champions on the Hospitals Committee continued to talk up the Trust's crucial value to the health system.

In 1941 committee member Robert Rowlette declared that great gratitude was due to the Sweeps for preventing a scaling back of health services at a time when the wartime price of medical commodities was soaring and the demand for hospital treatment was higher than ever before. The following year the committee's president, Viscount Powerscourt, said the Irish Hospitals Trust should be thanked for the fact that all the hospitals in the State were still open. He pointed out: 'There are new hospitals, large and small, equipped with every modern invention for curative treatment. These are fully staffed, and in some cases employ a third more than they did before. The accommodation has increased by almost 50 per cent.'

This, according to critics, was precisely what was wrong with the system. When the Sweeps money had flowed, it had been used to build hospitals where they were not needed, fitted with state-of-the-art equipment sitting idle, giving employment to underworked staff, while the sickly poor of Dublin were being turned away. Powerscourt seemed to tacitly acknowledge this unjust state of affairs when he closed his speech: 'When sufficient money has been collected [by future Sweeps] the problem of Dublin's greater hospitals will be dealt with.'

The most high-profile individual laid off as the Hospitals Trust pared back its operations to see out the war was a Scottish Shakespearean actor named Ian Priestly-Mitchell who had hosted the Sweepstakes' sponsored programme on Radio Éireann for the past five years. In early 1940 Priestly-Mitchell told listeners the show was being 'temporarily discontinued'. This was music to the ears of the super-patriotic Labour deputy Patrick Hogan, who had complained bitterly that the 'advertising of foreign culture' on the Sweeps programme was 'not at all desirable'. Particularly undesirable to Hogan was the choice of host.

Shortly after the Scotsman's appointment in 1937, Hogan took it up with the Minister for Posts & Telegraphs in the Dáil. He cavilled: 'I do not tune in to the sponsored programme very often, but the other night—quite accidentally—I found myself listening to what I thought was an English programme. Even the voices were decidedly and distinctly English. I want to know what became of those people whose voices were Irish and who were conducting and announcing the sponsored programme for some months. Has it been necessary to go across to England to find people to run the sponsored programme? Has the Minister any responsibility for this programme? Is the Minister responsible for having persons with decidedly English accents running the sponsored programme when there are plenty of people in this country who would be in a position to act as announcers and conduct that programme?'

Hogan was asked if he was in favour of 'expelling any English person earning his living in this country'. He said he didn't regard that question as relevant.

The loss of the half-hour Sweeps shows from the schedule was a considerable blow to Radio Éireann's finances, reportedly amounting to roughly £40,000 annually. One report to mark the programme's passing noted: 'It was the only sponsored programme where the scripts were written and produced by the same people. In this connection a special recording machine, the finest available, played an important part. On this machine interviews, pieces of music and any interesting items were recorded and then played as records on the radio. Because the sponsored programmes have ended for the time being, ten thousand gramophone records will have to be filed away.'

Also filed away was a court case which was adding embarrassment to the financial injury being suffered by the Hospitals Trust. Chicago-based Michael O'Kiersey had been a major distributor for Sweeps tickets in the US Midwest. As Joe McGarrity had expanded his stranglehold on the States, he and his sidekicks had squeezed others out of the lucrative trade, including O'Kiersey. The Chicago man attempted to exact revenge by suing the Hospitals Trust. He alleged that in 1934 he had made a verbal agreement with the Trust to manage the sale and distribution of tickets throughout the Midwest for a fee of $50 a week plus expenses. He asked the judge to force the Trust to open their books to reveal the true sums owed to him and 'expenditure by him on the Trust's behalf'. Happily for the Hospitals Trust, the judge threw out the case on the technicality that O'Kiersey had failed to lodge £75 with the court as security on his costs.

Another individual who felt ill-served by the law was the Irish Sweeps' first and biggest superstar, Emilio Scala. In June 1940, as the Phoney War was rapidly escalating into the real thing, the Italian ice-cream man was woken from his sleep early one morning and hauled away to be interned as a potential fifth columnist. His friends and family protested that he was by now virtually a pillar of the British establishment, and that two years earlier his son's wedding had taken place in the hallowed surrounds of St George's Cathederal in London.

The Irish Hospitals Trust company which saw out 1940 was a different entity from the one which had started the year. Immediately after the March draw for the Grand National, the original Trust laid off its remaining 1,300 staff. It followed this with the announcement that the company was to be liquidated and reconstituted as Hospitals Trust (1940) Limited. Directors Joe McGrath and Spencer Freeman were joined on the board by Richard Duggan's sons Richard and Patrick, with McGrath the kingpin. The mission statement of the new company was to expand on the activities of the old one. Its objectives were 'to carry on the business of publicity agents, printers and publishers, and of organizers or promoters of sports meetings, horse race meetings, greyhound race meetings, football matches, and of sweepstakes or drawing for prizes'.

As 1940 closed the Irish Hospitals Sweepstakes teetered on the brink of extinction. As 1941 opened an outbreak of foot and mouth disease brought that prospect closer to reality.

Chapter 19 ❧

FROM HOLLYWOOD TO HAPPY DAYS

In 1930 the Irish Sweepstakes had made a dazzling entrance on to the world stage, glowing through the gloom of the Great Depression as a focus for the fantasies of untold millions. In 1940, with the Sweeps all but dead and buried and untold millions staring death in the face, the craving for escape grew much greater, fuelling a nostalgia for the tickets that had vanished together with many other precious tokens of peacetime.

In the year that Hospitals Trust Limited laid off its workforce and went into voluntary liquidation, a movie opened starring Hollywood hot tickets Ginger Rogers and Ronald Colman which used the Irish Sweeps as the vehicle to bring the pair together. The plotline of *Lucky Partners* begins with Rogers accosting Colman on the street with a hare-brained scheme for winning a bundle. She explains that on the previous occasion they had crossed paths he had wished her 'good morning', and that same day she had received an elegant new dress as a gift from a secret admirer. She takes this as cast-iron proof that Colman is her lucky mascot and persuades him to go halves on a ticket.

The plot that starts out daft swiftly turns preposterous. Rogers explains that she needs the Sweeps win to finance her honeymoon. Colman has romantic designs on her and persuades her to persuade her fiancé to let her go on a platonic dry run of the honeymoon route with him, Colman. Incredibly, the fiancé agrees and the pair set off. The horse doesn't win, but it transpires that Colman has sold half of his half-ticket for the handsome sum of $6,000. The prize money then provides the dynamic for a frenetic conclusion that leads Colman and Rogers first to the criminal court and, inevitably, to the altar.

In that same doom-laden year of 1940 a groundbreaking new musical opened on Broadway which also used an Irish Sweeps ticket as its central prop. Penned by whites who assembled an all-black cast, *Cabin In The Sky* starred Dooley Wilson (ivory tinkling Sam from *Casablanca*) as a married warehouseman with a roving eye who is assaulted over gambling debts. As he lies seemingly on his deathbed, his loving wife prays for him with such faith and forgiveness that he is granted a six month reprieve to prove he is worthy of going to heaven. Unconscious, Wilson's character dreams that the Lord and the devil are locked in a tug-of-war for his immortal soul and that they agree to give him a six month reprieve to decide whether he is deserving of heaven or destined for hell.

Lucifer turns for help to a diabolical advertising agency whose ideas department decide the stricken husband should win a fortune in the Irish Sweepstakes. Showered with sudden riches, the question that would decide his fate was whether he would stick with his loving wife Petunia, or fall into the arms of steamy temptress Sweet Georgia Brown. Wilson's character does the right thing and saves his soul. In 1943, with the United States now in the war, the feelgood *Cabin In The Sky* was transferred to the big screen with an all-star cast that included Louis Armstrong and Duke Ellington.

A second Irish Sweeps-themed movie of 1943 also showcased a line-up that positively glittered. Gene Kelly, Lucille Ball, Virginia O'Brien, Red Skelton, Zero Mostel and band leader Tommy Dorsey all featured in MGM's first Technicolor musical, the visually lavish *DuBarry Was A Lady*. The Cole Porter songs included the classics 'Friendship' and 'Well, Did You Evah'.

Adapted from Porter's hit 1939 Broadway musical of the same name, *DuBarry* tells the story of Louis Blore (Red Skelton), a hat-check boy at a nightclub who is in love with the resident singing star May Daly (Lucille Ball). Inconveniently for Louis, May has her heart set on marrying someone with money. In spite of herself, she has already fallen in love with hoofer Alex Barton (Gene Kelly), who is so poor he can't even afford matching shoelaces. However, the strong-willed May forces her head to overrule her heart, reasoning: 'I can't afford to marry for love.'

A blue uniformed postman arrives into the nightclub with a telegram for Louis. It reads: 'This is to inform you that you have won

$150,000 on the Irish Grand National Sweepstake.' Louis faints. The next day he is on the front of all the newspapers. We next see him lording it in a car showroom, surrounded by a scrum of flashing photographers, as he buys a gleaming new car. The automobile itself costs $2,000 while the tyres are so super-dooper they come to an additional $5,000. A radio reporter thrusts a microphone in his face and asks: 'Would you say a few words for your millions of new friends?'

Taking a minute out of his wild spending spree, Louis announces to the press pack that he is going to marry May. Alex confronts May, who insists it's her intention to marry Louis. She then tells Louis that she will marry him, but purely for his money. Louis is happy enough with this arrangement, cocksure that she will grow to love him.

Louis throws a lavish party at the nightclub. Alex is there, still protesting against the wedding plans. To shut him up, the new hat-check boy slips Alex a Mickey Finn spiked drink. Instead, Louis knocks it back, passes out and dreams that he is King Louis xv of France, that May is his mistress and Alex is a notorious rebel called the Black Arrow. When Louis awakes, he realises that his Irish Sweeps fortune won't buy him May's heart and he should encourage her to submit to her true love for Alex.

Louis takes comfort in the fact that he still has $80,000 of his winnings left, but there is a twist in this morality tale as the Revenue inspector who had made a brief appearance earlier returns to relieve Louis of his $80,000 to cover government duties.

From early on, the life-changing properties of the Irish Sweeps had provided a dramatic device that could be adapted to the most heavyweight or frivolous of purposes. Written in 1933, Somerset Maugham's final play, *Sheppey*, revolved around a Sweeps win, as did the 1932 Fox cartoon short simply entitled 'Irish Sweepstakes'. Down the decades the Irish Sweeps proved a popular source of mishap and mischief in the world of animation. A 1938 instalment of the series *Captain And The Kids* required the kids in question to outfox the scheming John Silver as he tried to get his hook into their winning ticket. In a 1941 episode of *Popeye The Sailor Man* entitled 'Olive's $weep$take', the ever excitable Olive Oyl got into a tizzy when she mislaid her winning ticket. In an early episode of *The Flintstones* entitled 'The Sweepstake Ticket', Fred and Barney tried to keep their black market purchase from their wives, while Wilma and Betty tried to keep their husbands in the dark about their own secret flutter.

The first major Hollywood movie to focus on what the *New York Times* described as 'the Sweepstakes madness' was 1935's *The Winning Ticket* from MGM in which a Brooklyn barber called Joe is pressured into buying a ticket which he promptly misplaces. According to Drew Pearson's biographer, Oliver Pilat, *The Winning Ticket* was 'Pearson's greatest coup as a gambling underboss'. The suggestion in Pilat's book, which mentions a 'provided script', is that Pearson was somehow instrumental in getting the film made as a promotion for the Irish Sweeps. Pilat writes: 'After all arrangements had been made, Drew hired a former *Washington Post* reporter, later on *Time*, to go to Hollywood at $250 a week to watch that the provided script—including one scene showing Irish cops selling the illicit lottery tickets—was not changed at the studio.'

The film critic of the *New York Times* was not overly impressed with *The Winning Ticket*, saying its 'brewmeisters' at MGM were 'not inspired'. He wrote: '*The Winning Ticket* gallops about with appropriate desperation, managing, in its lightweight and rather predictable way, to be good enough fun. Thank the actors for that. There is Leo Carrillo as the barber, who says "sweepups" when he means "sweepstakes" and generally massacres King George's English. There is Ted Healy, a really droll fellow, as the shiftless brother-in-law who sells Joe the ticket. There is the apoplectic Luis Alberni as the frantic friend and attorney who invents mad schemes for tracking down the lost ticket. Comedians all, and good for a laugh any time. Add Louise Fazenda as the barber's Irish wife; the cooing infant who was last seen with the precious ticket; the pair of frustrated juveniles, and sufficient business to keep the plot boiling for seventy-five minutes. Pretty thin, to be sure, for a feature-length comedy, but it passes the time pleasantly. Do they finally locate the ticket? They do. The lady in the seat behind this patient reporter averred that she hadn't laughed so hard in weeks. The customer is always right.'

Another 1935 movie, *Sweepstakes Annie*, was a cautionary tale about how the winner of a $150,000 prize finds herself swiftly swamped by hangers-on, charlatans and relatives who have crawled out of the woodwork. The heroine who filled the title role in 1941's *Sweepstakes Winner* was made of sterner stuff, resolving to use her $150,000 windfall to wreak an elaborate revenge on an old enemy.

Nearly four decades later, in 1979, a package of Irish Sweeps tickets was raising laughs in an instalment of the popular American sitcom *Happy Days* entitled 'Joanie Busts Out'. Ron Howard was the teen star of *Happy Days*. Ronald Howard, no relation, played the lead role in the first Sherlock Holmes series made for television. Aired in 1954, the drama was set in the 1890s, four decades before the creation of the Irish Sweeps, but that fact was not let get in the way of a good story.

A man breaks into the apartment of Holmes and Watson, and falls asleep in a chair while waiting for them. When they discover the sleeping intruder, Watson asks: 'Who is he?' Holmes answers without hesitation: 'An Irishman by the colour of his shirt and the shamrock in his buttonhole.'

The Irishman, Brian O'Casey, explains that he is owed £8,000 as his third share of a winning Irish Sweeps ticket. He needs the money to put an end to his terrible homesickness which had become 'worse and worse until I couldn't look at anything that didn't remind me of my home in County Killarney [*sic*]'. He had bought one-third of a ticket with Englishman Albert Snow and Belle, a girl who ran a cake stall until she and Snow had disappeared following the Sweeps win. The three had cut up the ticket, with each keeping a third. The deadline for claiming their prize was fast approaching and O'Casey was at his wits' end.

The cake girl finally shows up with the terrible news that Snow is dead and his third of the ticket is nowhere to be found. She explains that the two remaining parts are worthless. She takes out her third and apparently throws it on the fire. She then asks O'Casey for his so she can do the same to put a final end to this unhappy chapter. Holmes and Watson materialise and Holmes tells her to go ahead and burn the Irishman's third, knowing that she is attempting to pull a fast one on O'Casey and steal the final third of the winning ticket. She bursts into tears and admits that Snow faked his own death and the pair had plotted to cheat O'Casey out of his share.

But how did Holmes rumble the plot? He explains that when he inspected her abandoned stock of cakes, the only one missing was a wedding cake, from which he deduced that she and Snow had intended to wed on the strength of their ill-gotten gains.

Chapter 20

WE BROKE ALL THE LAWS
OF GOD AND MAN

With a world war raging, shortages were the order of the day. Fine Gael's Senator Michael Hayes attacked the Fianna Fáil government's Department of Supplies, which he said had 'given the people a fuel muddle, a tea muddle, a sugar muddle, a petrol muddle, a potato muddle and a situation in which supplies are plentiful only for the rich on the black market'.

With petrol rationed and scarce, it became increasingly unfeasible to stage horse race meetings as neither the public nor the horses had a reliable means of getting there. The number of meetings plunged, causing further headaches for the promoters of the downsized Irish Sweeps and their minor league Red Cross siblings. Things got worse for the on-course bookies in 1943 when the Minister of Supplies ordered new clothing restrictions.

The bookies, together with cattle dealers, were dismayed with regulations imposing the so-called 'austerity suit' on Irish men, which by law must have no more than seven pockets. These two special needs professions appealed to the Minister of Supplies for extra pockets to accommodate the large amount of walking-around money they needed to carry. Their request was turned down. The only derogation granted was to Catholic priests who were allowed an extra inside breast pocket on their waistcoat for carrying sacramental Communion wafers.

For the church-going Joe McGrath and his fellow promoters there was no sign of divine intervention to revive the fortunes of the Irish Sweeps. The entire prize fund for the Cesarewitch in October 1941 was £28,410, representing a small fraction of the £354,724 won on Emilio Scala's single ticket ten years earlier. The prize pot on the 1942 Derby was similarly sparse. In both cases there was a single first prize of

£10,000, with £3,000 for second and £1,000 for third. The Irish sweep ticket was originally designed to closely resemble a banknote, to the point where the Hospitals Trust came under international pressure to make it look less so. During the war the crushing devaluation of this Confederate currency was underlined when a national newspaper offered a top prize of £10 and 50 Irish Sweeps tickets for the winner of its crossword competition.

In the course of the war years ten Sweeps were held in aid of the Irish Red Cross, but the charity received a paltry £218,000 in total after its share of the takings was cut from 25 per cent to 20 per cent following the first race, when Hospitals Trust claimed an inability to pay any more. Both of McGrath's Sweeps brands received a small but welcome shot in the arm once United States troops began to land in Northern Ireland and Britain in preparation for the D-Day landings. The soldiers reopened channels for tickets to once again circulate in Britain and the US, albeit in negligible numbers compared to the pre-war years.

For Captain Spencer Freeman, the war clouds hanging over the Irish Sweeps were as nothing compared to the task in hand of making sure that the next landing on the beaches of France would bear no relation to the last, which had ended in the mass evacuation from Dunkirk.

Aged 53 when World War II was declared, the captain lost no time in writing away to the British authorities offering his services. His distinguished record in the Great War, combined with his key organisational role with the Irish Sweeps, ensured a speedy invitation to meet with Peter Bennett MP, head of an Emergency Services division whose portfolio would include dealing with the expected bombing blitz on London. Freeman left the interview unsure as to whether he had got the job as Bennett's second-in-command. He soon found out that he had, once the British Secret Service had done a final background check on this Welshman who had spent the past ten years as a leader of a most troublesome Irish organisation.

Bennett gave Freeman a baptism of fire, seconding him to a senior civil servant charged with replacing the untold tons of tanks, heavy artillery and other equipment abandoned by the retreating British Expeditionary Force at Dunkirk. After a crash course learning the logistical ropes, Freeman was given an office in Bennett's HQ and told to do whatever was required to keep the lines of production and supply running. Bennett recalled in later life: 'We broke all the laws of God and man, but we did the job.'

Spencer Freeman did a short apprenticeship on the night shift, receiving and correlating reports of factories and utilities bombed in the early onslaughts of the Blitz. It wasn't long, however, before he was given greater freedom to begin breaking all the laws of God and man. Freeman is credited with coming up with an audacious brainwave that played a part in the ultimate victory of the Allies. In an early Nazi air raid a key aircraft assembly plant was hit. The building was shattered but the plant machinery survived with hardly a scratch. Knowing that the exposed machinery was vulnerable to the elements, Freeman, acting on his own initiative, bought up an entire factory's stock of tarpaulins for a huge sum of taxpayers' money. While his maverick action shocked the Exchequer, its value to the war effort was quickly recognised and the tarpaulin became the standard sticking plaster remedy applied across the landscape of war-scarred Britain.

Freeman is also credited by an admiring biographer with making another significant contribution to the war effort by employing the expertise he had gained as mastermind of the Irish Sweeps' striking publicity campaigns. After a carelessly dropped cigarette in an air hangar led to the reckless destruction of 20 vital bombers, Freeman handled the public information campaign to prevent such a needless disaster happening again. He asked the distinguished painter Dame Laura Knight to paint a poster for him. Pointing out that serious artists did not do posters, she refused at first, but after he took her to see the wreckage of so many desperately needed aircraft, she relented. Freeman rushed out her dramatic poster featuring a blazing grounded bomber and the slogan: 'Victory Delayed.' It was the beginning of a multimedia campaign which reportedly led to the volume of accidental fire losses being cut in half.

After the German surrender of May 1945 Spencer Freeman, now honoured with a CBE from Buckingham Palace, took a few months to tidy up some loose ends before announcing his intention to return to Dublin. He arrived to revive an organisation which was a shadow of its former self, but which was already boasting of how the takings for the first post-war Irish Sweep had 'quite smashed the best Sweep of the Emergency'.

In reality it was the Sweep itself which was quite smashed, and the challenge of restarting it as a going global concern would be tougher than starting it up in the first place, when it had had the advantages of surprise, dithering governments, gaping legal loopholes and a free run of the media.

In 1945 all of these were gone.

Chapter 21 ∾

THE EX-IRA MAN AND
THE NEXT QUEEN OF
ENGLAND

As the fog of war cleared, Joe McGrath and his partners faced a different set of challenges in reviving the Irish Sweep to the ones they had faced starting from scratch in 1930. Loopholes in the laws of Britain, the United States and elsewhere had been closed off. Some countries had put strict publicity bans in place backed up by stiff penalties. Millions of people had been killed and millions more scattered to the four winds, with the result that the old distribution networks built up over the course of a decade had been destroyed or severely disrupted.

But the promoters of the Irish Sweeps had built a global empire from scratch on silence, exiles and cunning, and they wasted no time in setting out to do it all over again. Irish construction workers and nurses streamed into Britain to help with the reconstruction of buildings and bodies. Shortly after the return to peace the British authorities uncovered 'a heavy traffic' of tickets in the post, which led them to suspect there was probably an equally busy suitcase traffic. The *Dublin Evening Mail* did more than suspect a swift return to something like business as usual. Its coverage of the first post-war draw in late 1945 included a piece headlined 'Tons of Money' and the line, 'One of the most striking things about today's draw is the preponderance of cross-channel winners.'

Joe McGrath was quick to step into the spotlight to frame the return of the Irish Sweeps in the context of a general return to normality. Late in 1945 he sat down at his new Ballsbridge HQ with Randolph Churchill, the black sheep son of Winston who had recently returned to journalism after losing his Tory Westminster seat in the Labour landslide of July 1945. Churchill concocted a fawning pen-portrait of the Sweeps chief for syndication around the globe. Readers learned that McGrath was 'a sterling millionaire and the richest self-made man in Ireland', and that 'after de Valera, Joe McGrath is probably the most powerful man in Southern Ireland'.

Churchill gushed: 'McGrath is a genial, middle-aged man with a double dose of Irish charm. He is rated one of the best poker players in Dublin. He has many other financial interests apart from the Sweepstakes and has recently become a big purchaser of Irish livestock. He no longer plays a public part in Irish politics but he is believed to be backing the career of ex-President Cosgrave's 28-year-old son who was recently elected to the Dáil.'

W. T. Cosgrave's son, Liam, would one day become leader of Fine Gael and Taoiseach of Ireland, and the McGrath family would seek his support, and that of his party, as the political and commercial tides began to turn against the Irish Sweep.

McGrath announced to Churchill that in 1946 he expected to employ 'even more' than the 4,000 workers on his books before the war. He then went on to construct an argument as to why any large state trying to take him on at his own game would suffer the consequences. It is an argument so far-fetched and self-serving that it is worth repeating.

Churchill wrote: 'McGrath explained to me that a sweepstake is only economically profitable to a small country. There are two reasons for this. If a sweep were organised in a large country, such as Britain or the United States, probably only 15% or 20% of the receipts could be drawn from abroad. In addition, the hospitals in a rich country would not profit to the same extent, since a successful sweepstake by which hospitals profit invariably leads to an immense falling off of voluntary subscriptions. This happened in Ireland. Some people who normally subscribe to hospitals are shocked that they should profit from organised gambling. Others feel that the hospitals are getting so much money from the sweepstakes that there is no need for private charity. This did not matter in Ireland where voluntary contributions were not very large and were greatly exceeded by the rake-off from the Sweeps. But in countries like Britain and the United States, where voluntary contributions are enormous, the hospitals would almost certainly lose more than they would gain if they tried to set up a rival business to Joe McGrath.'

But even as McGrath was giving Randolph Churchill a guided tour of his purpose-built new venue with its ten acres of rolling grounds, he was trying to place an each-way bet with the Irish government. With the outbreak of war imminent in 1939, McGrath orchestrated a lobbying campaign to allow his Hospitals Trust to run additional sweeps under the auspices of the Irish Red Cross. He got his way, although the legislation stipulated that the arrangement was strictly limited to the duration of the war. But McGrath had been there before and had made light of it. The Irish Hospitals Sweeps had originally only been authorised to last four years.

Shortly after the war's end, the Irish Red Cross wrote to the government seeking an extension of the legislation allowing Hospitals Trust to keep running sweepstakes under its banner. The request was turned down on the grounds that the legislation explicitly limited the licence 'to the duration of the European war'.

Since its establishment, Hospitals Trust Limited had consistently run rings around the country's legislators, repeatedly treating state agencies as branches of its own business, repeatedly playing the employment card to have legislation passed, and repeatedly flouting rules and regulations. The war had cut the Trust down to size, and some in government felt the timing was perfect to bring the organisation under tighter State control, or even stamp it out entirely. In late 1945 the Department of Justice noted: 'If the Sweeps are given time to increase to anything like their pre-war proportions it will be more difficult to abolish or restrict them than it would be at the present time.'

The abolition option was quickly ruled out on the usual grounds of employment and revenue to the State, but there was a belief within Justice that something must be done to extinguish the culture of smuggling which had brought Ireland into disrepute abroad before the war, and was now starting up again. The situation was particularly exasperating for the Justice department itself, since it was the Justice minister who had to rubber stamp each Sweep on behalf of the State. A memo from Justice noted: 'It seems questionable whether it is proper for the Minister to sanction a scheme which contains provisions designed to promote the sale of tickets in countries in which their sale is unlawful.'

Having followed the money trail in so far as that was possible, officials in the Justice department concluded that McGrath and his fellow directors, in addition to their handsome on-the-books incomes, were raking in piles of cash under the counter. One wrote: 'It is possible that some of the shareholders have made big additional profits by way of commissions on the sales of tickets, profits on purchase of winning tickets, etc.' The minister felt that if the promoters had less funny money to throw around to shady middle-men, there might be less funny business surrounding the Sweeps. He argued that if the Sweep was to be allowed to rebuild, 'the rate of profit of the promoters should be cut drastically'. Such a move might have diverted some extra revenue into the State coffers, but with so much undeclared cash swilling around it would have been wildly optimistic to think it could change a business model formulated on the greasing of palms. The minister's proposal went straight to the dead letter office.

With business picking up steadily, the Trust's greatest ambassador was once again wheeled out to remind the world of how making the choice to buy an Irish Sweeps ticket could be a life-transforming act. Shortly before the war, the international media carried shock-horror reports that the biggest winner of them all, Emilio Scala, had squandered his vast fortune and gone back to selling ice-creams for a living. He was even quoted as saying: 'I still have a few pounds left but now all the worry of that amount of money is over.'

Now, however, Scala was being recast to show himself and the Sweeps in the most flattering light. It now emerged that he was not the fool who had been soon parted from his money, as enemies of the Sweep had portrayed him. On the contrary, he had proven himself the sort of shrewd and frugal manager of his good fortune that all big winners could and should be.

Scala met the reporter from the Manchester *Sun Chronicle* in his 'nickel coated ice cream bar' in Fulham. He was immaculately dressed in smart blue serge. Parked outside was the impressive Lancia roadster he had bought for the enormous sum of £1,285 in 1934. 'It's a decent car,' he said. 'Why should I buy a new one?'

Far from being penniless, he was still living in the sumptuous hilltop mansion he had bought for £10,000 shortly after his win. Its features included 'a quarter-acre of rose and fruit trees, an electric piano, a radiogram, and all the popular Verdi operas twice over, on record and piano rolls'.

He explained how he had kept hold of his money while showing generosity to family and friends. He had sold three-quarters of his ticket for £10,500 so his real take-home pay-off was some £100,000. The legal wrangle which brought him to a Dublin court to establish his ownership of the ticket had set him back £20,000. Once he had settled some cash on his seven siblings he was left with around £70,000 which he invested in rubber, steel, tobacco, breweries and Woolworth's. One year he was up £12,000 and the next year down that amount, but he was earning a steady £2,000 a year from his investments and financially he was in the same place he had been 15 years back, meaning he still had his £70,000 fortune.

Following his widely reported arrest at the start of the Blitz for the crime of being Italian, he had spent 11 months in a civilian internment camp on the Isle of Man. He harboured no hard feelings towards his jailers. That was just the way of war. His ice-cream bar and factory had been wrecked by a German flying bomb, but he had rebuilt them and was back in business. He was still making his famous ice-cream 'mix' using substandard war rations, and he dreamt of the day he would be back making cassata with real walnuts, cherries and strawberries. It was true he sometimes served at his bar, but that was because he liked to work and certainly not because he needed to.

The work ethic underpinned his sage advice to a new generation of Irish Sweeps ticket-buyers from a winner who had kept his feet firmly on the ground to live the dream. 'Keep calm. Don't drown yourself in beer, whiskey or vino blanco. Go to a bank manager. Invest in securities. Don't squander. A poor man who finds himself rolling in money, then poor again, is worse off than he was to begin with. You'll get letters by the sackful offering to sell you goldmines. Forget them. Above all, go on working. Work keeps you lively and cheerful. Don't sit down and die just because you've been lucky.'

The Irish Sweeps wireless show made a quick return to Radio Éireann after the war's end with its much-loved signature tune 'When You Wish Upon A Star', first in a daytime slot before moving to the preferred night-time position on the schedule. The atmospherics after dark meant that the signal from Ireland penetrated further and sharper into Britain. In time, the show would develop a set format revolving around popular music, the latest racing results and hot tips for the next day's meetings.

Hospitals Trust Limited complained incessantly to the Department of Posts & Telegraphs that the Radio Éireann signal into Britain was too weak, and that the national broadcaster was failing to keep its side of its sponsorship deal with the Sweep. Again, Spencer Freeman lobbied to have the point of broadcast shifted from Athlone in the centre of the country to a location on the east coast where the signal to Britain would be stronger. Freeman tried a carrot and stick approach, threatening to cancel the lucrative sponsorship deal with Radio Éireann, while asserting that a stronger presence in Britain for Ireland's national station would boost tourism and remind the large Irish community there that they hadn't been abandoned by their homeland. The Department of Posts & Telegraphs made some half-hearted gestures of appeasement, but the more the Hospitals Trust tried to browbeat the officials, the more the promoters aroused simmering hostility.

There was hostility too from the Reverend T. F. Blennerhasset who, in October 1946, told the committee of the Temperance & Social Welfare Society that the amount the Irish were spending on drink had shot up from £13 million in 1941 to £21 million in 1945. The Reverend asserted: 'Thousands of pounds are paid in betting taxes, which means that thousands of foolish people are throwing away millions of pounds to feather the nests of bookmakers . . . Night after night from Radio Éireann they hear insidious propaganda sponsored by the Irish Hospitals Sweepstakes to try to throw the veneer of Christian charity over the desire to gamble. This country, the island of saints and scholars, is known the world over for two things—good horse flesh and gambling.'

Other pot-shots were pinged in from different angles. Shortly after the cessation of hostilities in Europe, the United Nations sent a delegation to Dublin to recruit doctors and nurses for aid work on the Continent. Such was the rush to join up that the Red Cross officials helping with the recruitment were overwhelmed. The chief reason for the huge response was that the UN proposed to pay the nurses annual salaries of £300 to £600, which was far more than they were receiving in the Sweeps-funded hospitals. Many nurses had already deserted Ireland for Britain, where the radical new National Health Service was being established to provide universal healthcare.

At a time when the Hospitals Trust was predicting a return to the cash bonanzas of yore, home-based critics were increasingly asking why parts of the Irish hospital system were still so feeble after so many millions had been raised in its name. One commentator wrote: 'It may be nothing more than a coincidence that several Dublin hospitals which share in the Hospitals Sweepstake money have been advertising for nurses recently. The scarcity of nurses is so great that in some Dublin hospitals, in order to allow nurses to have their holidays and still keep the institutions at the peak of efficiency, women who volunteer to do the ninety days course of training are being encouraged to take the course during the summer. It is strange when you look at it that way.'

Some of the Irish Sweeps' harshest critics were high-ranking medics such as Professor Henry Moore who, in 1941, explained to an audience how the Sweeps had brought the free-wheeling baronies of the Irish hospital network into State enslavement. The Irish Sweeps, he said, had started life in a simple one-to-one relationship with the voluntary hospitals, but they quickly became 'an industry of national importance'. He continued: 'Not only were many private fortunes built up through their agency, but they provided a vast amount of employment. Incidentally, they gave the country an advertisement abroad which might be considered by some as of dubious value. As a consequence of State supervision, government departments soon began to control the distribution of money to the hospitals, and consequently worked themselves into a position where they could attempt to dictate hospital policy.'

One way in which the State attempted to dictate to the hospitals was through the establishment of the Dublin Hospitals Bureau, better known as the Bed Bureau. With the capital's hospital system still a shambles, despite all the Sweeps money pouring in, the Bed Bureau was set up to allocate patients to beds on a rational city-wide basis. When they were funded entirely on charitable donations, each of the voluntary hospitals was an independent republic. With the State acting as middle-man between the Sweep and the hospitals, and taking its cut in the form of stamp duty, the hospitals were coming under State control. By law, the hospitals had to inform the Bed Bureau on a rolling basis of how many beds were available for urgent admissions. Bed Bureau officials quickly realised that the hospitals were understating the numbers of vacant beds to obstruct the agency's work, which was resented as the meddling of intruders.

Just as Joe McGrath had predicted in late 1945, the Irish Sweeps did begin to make a rapid recovery. In June the following year the total proceeds for the Derby Sweep shot up to £1,313,445 from £802,741 for the previous one. The promise of a return to the good old days amplified calls for the Hospitals Trust to strike a fairer deal with the hospitals. When the government announced that a part of the local authority rates would be diverted to subsidise hospitals, the secretary of the Irish Ratepayers & Taxpayers Association, J. T. Maloney, complained: 'It has come as a shock to the already overburdened citizens of Dublin, and to every person in the 26 Counties, to be told that the upkeep of the necessitous poor in the hospitals—towards which the charitable people of the world have subscribed—is now to be borne by the impoverished ratepayers, for whose relief the Irish Hospital Sweepstakes were established.'

He somewhat naively urged that Hospitals Trust Limited must pressurise the government into reversing its decision, so that 'Irish people throughout the world are not made to blush with shame through the actions of those who are always talking about "national dignity", and at election times profess to be the servants of the people'.

Maloney did not make any concrete suggestions as to where extra funding might be found which would eliminate the need to pick the ratepayers' pockets. Four years later the English Churches' Committee on Gambling did offer a ready solution, which chimed precisely with that offered by the Irish Justice Minister in 1945—let the Hospitals Trust have less and the hospitals more. The secretary of the Churches' Committee, Reverend Clark Gibson, was so bold as to suggest that it was a sham for the Irish Sweeps to include the word 'Hospitals' in its promotional material.

Lord Powerscourt, chairman of the Associated Hospitals Sweepstakes Committee, dashed off an indignant rebuttal to the British newspapers. 'I emphatically refute the suggestion that the Irish hospitals do not benefit adequately from the Sweepstakes. The total so far received by them from the Sweepstakes exceeds £18,000,000, a sum which, in my opinion, has fully justified the description "Irish Hospitals Sweepstakes".'

Powerscourt stated that the only way the amount going to the hospitals could be increased would be by reducing the proportion of the take going into the prize pot. This was a non-starter, he insisted, because the Irish hospitals were far too grateful to their subscribers, the ticket-buyers, to deprive them of the maximum possible wins.

The Viscount continued: 'Far from feeling that the use of the word "Hospitals" in connection with the Irish Sweepstakes is unjustified, I am exceedingly proud of the association. By reason of their charitable purpose, the Sweepstakes have a virtue and character which distinguishes them from gambling on football pools, dog racing and horse racing, from which hospitals receive no direct benefit.'

Joe McGrath and his partners at the Hospitals Trust were well insulated from all such criticism within the sturdy walls of their monumental new headquarters in Ballsbridge, a mile or so from Dublin's city centre. The Sweeps' publicity blurb described the premises as 'one of the largest office buildings in the world', but this was gently dismissed by one American visitor in the 1950s who allowed that 'it may easily become that in time, by having additional storeys erected'.

The visitor did, however, declare himself impressed with the new centre of operations which was now home to the thrice yearly mixing and drawing of the counterfoils. He wrote: 'The counting of the money is accomplished in enormous, well-lighted rooms. The ceilings and walls are sound-absorbent, but even if they weren't it would be a quiet place, like a cathedral.' He observed: 'There appears to be something about the looking at and handling of vast sums of money not belonging to them that makes clerical personnel in such a place speak in the hushed tones one ordinarily associates with reverence.'

Joe McGrath's personal holdings were every bit as impressive as his Ballsbridge showhouse. In 1933 he had purchased a south Dublin mansion, Cabinteely House. In 1940 he had augmented his lands with the purchase of the neighbouring Brennanstown demesne. Over the following years he would continue to buy up land in the south of the capital, becoming one of the biggest landowners in the country. Richard Duggan had sold McGrath his string of racehorses shortly before his death in 1935, and McGrath had gone on to build up a bloodstock empire with stud farms in Dublin, Meath and Kildare and some 200 horses stabled in Ireland and Britain. In the years spanning 1942 to 1946 McGrath was the champion owner in Ireland.

Joe McGrath's finest hour as an owner came in 1951 when his horse Arctic Prince romped home as a 28/1 outsider to win the Epsom Derby. The man once regarded by the British establishment as a notorious terrorist was now invited into the royal box to receive the congratulations of Queen Mary and the young princess who would shortly be crowned Queen Elizabeth II.

In the post-war years McGrath invested in a range of businesses, becoming one of the most powerful industrialists in the country. In 1932, together with Richard Duggan, he had bought the Irish Glass Bottle Company (IGB) and turned it into the biggest producer of milk bottles and glass jars in Ireland. In the 1950s the Glass Bottle Company took control of Waterford Glass, establishing the brand internationally as a byword for quality crystal.

McGrath's acquisition of Waterford Crystal involved the employment of what some at the time felt smacked of sharp practice. In the late 1940s Waterford's hallowed tradition of glass-making was revived by immigrants Charles Bacik and Miroslav Havel, in partnership with Irish jeweller Bernard Fitzpatrick. Glass manufacture was a forgotten craft in the south-east, so 80 cutters and blowers were recruited from Czechoslovakia, Belgium and Italy. In 1950 Bacik approached Joe McGrath hoping to secure a cash injection into Waterford Glass. McGrath ran an eye over the company and decided he wanted it for himself. According to Brian Havel's 2005 book *Maestro of Crystal*, McGrath forced the sale by damaging Waterford's business. He did this by undercutting Waterford Crystal's prices for beer glasses by importing cheap merchandise from Europe. He also bullied IGB clients into a boycott of Waterford Crystal. Havel writes: 'One prominent Limerick publican and beer franchise . . . had invested some money in the Bacik operation and was repeatedly warned by IGB that if he continued doing business with Waterford Glass he would be cut off as an IGB customer.' McGrath got his prize.

Joe McGrath's stroke of genius in relation to Waterford Glass was to transform it into a niche producer of high-end crystal expertly targeted at the American market. One of his chief Sweeps agents in the United States, Connie Neenan, was given the additional task of marketing Waterford Glass. The prestige and profile of the brand received a boost when several US sports bodies commissioned Waterford Glass trophies.

McGrath subsequently added Donegal Carpets to his expanding portfolio of industrial interests, again targeting the prestige end of the market. Elaborate carpets were custom-made for the presidential residence, Áras an Uachtaráin, the Irish Embassy in London, the White

House in Washington, City Hall in Belfast, 10 Downing Street and the Houses of Parliament in London, and other government buildings around the world. Spencer Freeman, one of the directors of Donegal Carpets, turned the manufacture of one order into a widely reported news story. A luxury hotel in the South African city of Durban wanted a special carpet made to contain two million hand-tufted knots, and it wanted it delivered within weeks. Donegal Carpets won the tender and the tufters worked around the clock in shifts for three weeks to make the deadline, with Freeman sending photographs of the 'prodigious effort' to newspapers around the world.

Paddy McGrath, who later took over the running of his father's business empire, explained: 'Business is a funny thing. First thing you have got to do is establish what is probably known as a track record. After that, doors are open to you and everything else like that and you can go ahead from there. Credit is available to you. You can finance other businesses. That's where the Sweep came into the whole business. The success of the Sweep financed all our other industries, in other words enabled the finance for the other industries to be set up.'

Industrial relations at Sweepstakes headquarters in Ballsbridge became fraught at the end of the 1940s when the Workers' Union of Ireland (wui) began to agitate for better conditions for the 1,400 staff there. The union organised in January 1949 at the request of workers who complained of 'excessive overtime'. Hospitals Trust management refused to negotiate with the union and instead, in February 1949, set up a rival House Association which staff were encouraged to join. Most did, with the result that the House Association quickly had a membership of roughly 1,000 workers, as against some 380 in the union. Some trades union officials with long memories linked the Association back to the bogus unions McGrath had formed to thwart attempts at organising labour on the Ardnacrusha electrification project in the 1920s.

The wui took its case to the recently established Labour Court which rejected its claim that the Hospitals Trust was denying its workers the right to organise by refusing to negotiate with the union. *The Irish Times* reported: 'The management of the Hospitals Trust certainly appeared to have let it be known that it would prefer the employees to be members of the association rather than the union. But, even allowing for the difficulty of securing definite proof in such matters, the union did not give any ground for reasonable suspicion that employees who joined the union suffered any penalty or disability, or that those who joined the association enjoyed any unusual benefits or facilities . . . The association was formed after the union had begun organising the staff and clearly in opposition to the union's activities, but its activities appeared to the Court to have been the result of a genuine, though obviously amateurish, effort to establish a representative organisation of their own by members of the staff which did not wish to be represented by the union.'

The Labour Court recommended that Hospitals Trust should recognise and negotiate with the WUI 'on condition that the union shows that a substantial proportion of the staff desire to be represented by it and not by the Association'. The Sweeps management simply ignored the recommendation, which was not binding. While the WUI failed to gain recognition by the management, it claimed credit for a 1951 pay rise and for securing the reinstatement of two women who had been sacked for going to a wedding when they were supposed to be at home in their sick beds. The pair were caught out when they were involved in a motor accident which was reported in the newspapers.

Employees allied to the union and the association would set aside their differences each September when some 750 of them would take a special train to Knock for the annual staff pilgrimage to the County Mayo shrine. Away from the soothing aura of the Blessed Virgin, however, relations between the union and the association would never be serene.

Chapter 22

THEY THOUGHT I WAS
KIND OF GOOFY

After the running of the Aintree Grand National in the spring of 1947, *Time* magazine celebrated 'the indiscriminate rain' of 'happy dollars' once again falling on Americans in the form of Irish Sweeps winnings. It told of a young Long Island bachelor named Kermit Rorkmill who was showered with $100,000 'and immediately fifteen girls called him up, including a few who had passed up his engagement ring'. Another $100,000 fell on 'two plump divorcees' labouring in a Manhattan laundromat, who quit their dead-end jobs and went shopping for fur coats. A fast-food waiter in New Jersey who won $20,000 remarked: 'I refuse to get excited, but if a guy asks for a cheeseburger and I feel like giving him a hamburger, he gets hamburger.' The report concluded: 'After a famine of six years, the Irish Sweepstakes were back.'

Within a couple of years of the end of World War II, tickets were once again being smuggled into North America on a massive scale. In July 1948 the US liner *America* docked in New York where a search turned up over a million tickets valued at $4,050,000 concealed in food cartons. Two hundred stewards and crew members were detained for questioning. One week later another liner, the *Ernie Pyle*, was ransacked from top to bottom for a secret cache of Irish Sweeps tickets, but this time the customs officers came up empty handed.

The establishment of the state-owned merchant fleet Irish Shipping Limited in 1941 opened up a new means of smuggling tickets in bulk to North America once the transatlantic sea lanes were reopened. The best-selling Irish-American author of *Angela's Ashes*, Frank McCourt, wrote of how he sailed to America on the *Irish Oak* in 1949 at the age of 19. He related how he and a priest went ashore with two Irish Shipping officers for a drink at Poughkeepsie on the Hudson River while the ship anchored overnight. Many years later the *Irish Oak*'s radio officer, Bill Jones, revealed that he had been one of the two naval men who had gone ashore, and that McCourt and the priest had been used as unwitting cover by the seamen who were making a drop of 15 cartons of illicit tickets. Jones said that his cut of the payment for smuggling the hot bundle was $100, which was as much as he earned in a month as an employee of Irish Shipping. He and his colleague loaded the tickets on to a waiting station wagon, which drove off to meet a motorboat dispatched from New York to whisk the contraband back to the Big Apple.

Five years later, in 1953, the captain of the Irish Shipping vessel, *Irish Hazel*, faced questioning on his return to Dublin after police in Wilmington, North Carolina, discovered cases of Irish Sweeps tickets deposited in a hut at the port. The value of the tickets was put at around $2 million. A car driver, a waitress and a labourer were arrested on charges of conspiracy. The captain insisted that the first he had heard of the story was when he had arrived back in Ireland, and he was sure it was completely untrue. He added that on his previous voyage the *Irish Hazel* had docked at the port of Baltimore, and that if he had heard that cases had been unloaded there he would have believed it, since almost all the crew had friends there. A spokesman for Irish Shipping denied that the United States authorities had raised the matter with the state-owned company.

When the *Irish Hazel* returned to Baltimore a couple of months later, the US authorities were lying in wait, having filed a writ to seize the Irish State's vessel. Irish Shipping was fined $10,000. It was widely believed that Hospitals Trust Limited paid the fine. A Trust spokesman was blasé about the matter, jovially telling reporters that while anyone could drop into the Sweeps office in Dublin and pick up a dozen or more books of tickets, they couldn't walk in and receive 700,000 tickets without paying for them. He added that the directors of Hospitals Trust were not bothered if tickets were smuggled into another country.

In the summer of 1948 United States customs officers sweeping the coast with their spotlight at Newport, Virginia, were confronted with the sight of four sailors on the *Irish Elm* lowering a cargo net loaded with Sweep tickets on to a smaller vessel. The US Customs made another substantial seizure the following year, this time intercepting a secret air mail delivery. A flight from London landing at Philadelphia was discovered to have tickets worth an estimated $100,000 stashed in the containers which should have held de-icer. Human lives, it seemed, had been used as chips in another Sweeps gamble.

The ugly side of the Sweeps smuggling racket was experienced at first hand by a seaman on the transatlantic route who learned that one of his colleagues was transporting tickets. After landing one consignment on American soil, the smuggler handed the seaman a $20 bill to buy his silence. The sailor unwisely informed his colleague that he wanted more than $20 to keep schtum. When the recipient of the $20 next went for a drink on dry land he was abducted by two strangers and held for several hours. When he was finally released, he told of having a pistol rammed down his throat and of being told never to breathe a word of what he knew about the smuggling operation, on pain of death.

Meanwhile, in Canada, the war on the Irish Sweeps was being intensified by the Morality Squads attached to each of the provincial police forces. In 1950 undercover Morality Squad agents managed to entrap a Calgary man into selling them some tickets. He was arrested and when the squad searched his home they found a large hoard of tickets and receipts hidden behind a false wall in his basement.

Some years later Canada's Morality Squads staged a joint operation which they insisted had 'smashed' the main distribution network for Irish Sweeps tickets across the country. The authorities claimed they had confiscated a haul of five million tickets worth over $17 million. One police chief sent out a warning to every small-time ticket tout in Canada that the authorities now had a long list of agents, so that hundreds of people could expect a knock on the door any time soon. His advice to anyone in possession of tickets for sale was to 'get rid of them before getting caught red-handed, especially now they know we have their distribution lists'.

One officer was realistic enough to admit that a battle had been won against the Irish Sweeps, but the war was far from over. He remarked: 'It would be indiscreet for us to say we've cleaned up the Irish Sweepstakes, but we've put quite a dent in it.'

Also hoping to put a dent in the sales of Irish Sweeps tickets in North America was a Mexican consortium, through the offices of a shady body called the International Sweepstakes of Mexico. At the point of start-up the Mexicans had engaged Hospitals Trust in a consultancy role. In 1948 a delegation from Dublin arrived in Mexico with a set of fresh ideas and a new design for a Mexican ticket modelled on the Irish version. The US State Department fumed to the Irish government that Hospitals Trust was plotting 'to enter into an arrangement with a Mexican lottery to exploit' the United States market by breaching the US's southern border. The Irish government hurriedly replied that it had given the matter top priority and contact between Hospitals Trust and the Mexicans had been 'terminated'.

Arthur Webb, in his authorised telling of the Irish Sweeps tale, puts a different spin on the story which may have been an attempt to rewrite history and cast Hospitals Trust in a more favourable light with the US and Irish governments. He suggests that Hospitals Trust never had any intention of helping establish the would-be rival, and that the plan from the outset was to sabotage the Mexicans with some Trojan Horse trickery. Without explaining how precisely this was executed, Webb says it worked a dream, with some monies destined for Mexico actually making their way to Ireland.

Whatever the embroidery surrounding Webb's story, a new Mexican sweepstake did begin advertising in the early part of 1948. The first draw was to be on the Handicap De Las Americas in May of that year. The prize fund was guaranteed at one million pesos. Shortly after the tickets went on sale, the sweepstake was hit by the seizure of 64,254 books of tickets valued at $1,200,000 when US Customs stopped a delivery truck near the Texas town of Laredo.

By the beginning of 1949 the International Sweepstakes of Mexico had disintegrated into a shambles, prompting headlines such as 'Operators Hunted in Mexico Sweeps' and 'Winners Unpaid in December Running—One Holding Top Tab for $100,000'. The unlucky punter left holding the worthless winner's ticket was Sid Kopytowski from the Bronx in New York. Police noted that New York had become a major, if not the main, point of distribution for Mexican sweep tickets, which Hospitals Trust would have considered an incursion on to its home turf.

Grasping at straws, Kopytowski announced through his lawyer that he would be trying to have the Mexican government make good on the promised $100,000 first prize. The Mexican ambassador in Washington quickly shut that door, stressing that his government neither backed nor authorised the sweepstake in question. There was more bad news for Kopytowski in a letter he received from the International Bank of Mexico, which said that International Sweepstakes of Mexico had vamoosed. Joe McGrath—when questioned by an American reporter on a transatlantic phone line—simply shouted down the crackly wire that the Mexicans got what they paid for, and abruptly ended the conversation.

Precisely one hundred miles west of the string of Mexican fishing villages which were to become the tourist metropolis of Cancun, lay the easternmost tip of the mobsters' paradise called Cuba. In 1955 the island was an offshore banking, partying and especially a gambling hotspot for the Mafia, who enjoyed excellent relations with President Fulgencio Batista. In 1940 Batista had become the democratically elected President of Cuba. Annoyingly for Batista, the ungrateful populace had failed to return him at subsequent elections. He stood again for the presidency in 1952, only to find himself lagging a distant third of three in the polls. Concluding that democracy doesn't work, he staged a coup and abolished it.

At the close of 1955 the following report appeared in the American press. 'Havana is now making a bid for the title of Las Vegas of the tropics. This is now a "wide open" island. The American visitor can indulge in almost any form of gambling—roulette, *chemin de fer*, dice, slot machines, horse racing, lotteries, numbers, terminals, jai alai, dog races and cockfights. A good-sized percentage of the take is collected by the government. The major portion of this goes to the charitable work being carried out by Senora Martha de Batista, wife of the President.

'The Oriental Park Oval, once one of the outstanding horse racing tracks of the Americas, had been purchased by a group of Americans and Cubans. This new company has announced a Cuban Sweepstakes to be run next April 30. The winning purse will be $50,000. According to officials, this event will be organized along the lines of the Irish Sweepstakes.'

The United States Legation in Dublin consistently lobbied both the Irish government and Hospitals Trust to bring about an end to the flagrant violations of the US postal code by the Irish Sweeps. As the drain of dollars continued apace, calls for the establishment of legalised US lotteries and sweepstakes grew louder. At the close of the 1950s, with these calls for legalisation ringing in his ears, Governor Edmund Brown of California devised a scheme to calculate roughly how much cash was leaving his state in the form of Irish Sweeps subscriptions.

The first step of Brown's attorney-general was to gather information from police, customs and revenue departments at state and federal level. They quickly established that between them, they hadn't a clue as to the true extent of the Sweeps' activities. In the grand style of FBI agent Eliot Ness tracking down gangster Al Capone, Brown's attorney-general put together a team and started from scratch with the banks. The AG's office gathered information on all bank drafts sent from California to Ireland. A clear pattern quickly emerged. The number of bank drafts destined for Ireland skyrocketed in the run-up to each of the year's three Sweepstakes, and tapered off as soon as the closing date for the draw passed.

The next phase of the investigation was to scrutinise the transactions of one sample bank in the run-up to a Sweep. They chose the Bank of America where they examined the bank drafts bound for Ireland in September 1959, ahead of that year's final Sweeps draw. It was common practice for Irish-Americans to send presents of money back to relatives in the old country, but this would normally be in regular US denominations such as $10, $20, $50 or $100. However, in the bank drafts checked for September 1959 the odd denomination of $2.85 kept recurring. Of drafts totalling more than $115,000, almost half were in multiples of $2.85. It was no coincidence that the price of a Sweep ticket was $2.85. A book cost $28.50 and ten books $285.

The AG's department traced a sample number of drafts back to the US citizens who had sent them, and each one owned up that the money was bound for Hospitals Trust. There were many other ways of transmitting money from California to Dublin which the AG's team had not examined, so the attorney-general reported back to Governor Brown that the investigation had merely scratched the top of a vast iceberg.

The final report of the investigators provides a commendably clear-cut picture of how the Irish Sweeps had become tightly integrated into the American way of life in the 1950s and 60s. It is worth revisiting it at some length. The investigators wrote: 'Californians almost invariably purchase their tickets from neighbours or fellow workers. The price varies between $2.85 and $3.00. The ticket has a number, which corresponds with a number on a stub kept by the seller. Some three to five weeks after the purchase, if all goes well, the seller again contacts the purchaser and gives him a receipt which indicates that his stub has been entered in the lottery. Tickets contain on their face a closing date.

'We spoke with a random number of these sellers and found that they were engaged in socially accepted occupations, with this as their only illegal activity. They rarely solicited purchasers of these tickets, but instead sold to their friends. These people would gradually gain the reputation of being sweepstake salesmen so that eventually they were solicited almost as much as they did the soliciting. The largest dealer with whom we spoke sold about thirty books per race, or ninety per year. This man claimed to have sold only four or five books himself, and to have given the rest to co-workers who sold them. He denied having received a commission from the sale of the other books, but admitted having posted the money and the stubs.

'Every book contains twelve tickets, each ticket selling for £1 sterling. The rough equivalent of one pound is $2.85, and the instructions are to remit this sum (or sterling) with the ticket. The seller remits money for only ten tickets. The other two tickets he may sell or keep for himself. This, plus the fact that he is entitled to a prize if he sells a winning ticket, constitutes his remuneration for his efforts.

'A few of the sellers with whom we spoke had at one time lived in Ireland, or had relatives there now. These sellers simply continued a practice begun over there, or were sent their tickets by the relative. More frequently, however, the sellers were people who had originally been purchasers of tickets and then, either dissatisfied with the slowness of getting their receipt back, or wanting the prestige which they felt could be obtained from being the person to see for a sweepstake ticket, had decided to sell tickets themselves.

'This they accomplished by talking to the person who sold them a ticket and finding an address in Ireland to which to write. Once they became established as ticket salesmen they would generally be forwarded the same number of books for each subsequent race without having to ask for them again. We encountered no instance of a seller who was originally solicited to sell tickets by an agent or an employee of the promoters. In each case the seller initiated the activity himself.

'The stubs of the tickets—called counterfoils—and the money are enclosed in an opaque envelope (a current custom is to insert the money and stubs in the fold of a greeting card) and mailed to Ireland.

They are invariably addressed to a private citizen in Ireland, usually in Dublin, and never to the Hospitals Trust (1940) Limited. There is a great variety of names to which these tickets are forwarded. We have not ascertained whether these names are those of real people, or whether they are simply mail-drops for the Hospitals Trust. Undoubtedly the purpose of using private names is to thwart the United States Post Office. If the Post Office recognizes an address as a drop for lottery mail it will stamp the mail "fraudulent" and return it to the sender, or hold it and have the sender open the mail in its presence. Since these letters are addressed to such a diversity of private names in Ireland it is difficult for the Post Office to detect which mail is sweepstake mail.

'About three months before the running of a race the tickets are received by the seller in this country. They are mailed in unmarked envelopes. Interestingly enough these envelopes are postmarked in the United States. They never come from Ireland. The most frequent postmarks we encountered were those of New York and New Jersey. However, a considerable amount is mailed here in California. All of the sellers with whom we talked denied having any knowledge of the person who mailed tickets to them, although they admitted that their tickets always came from within the United States and that they never received any directly from Ireland.

'In addition to the book of tickets, there is a piece of paper containing the address of one of these private citizens in Ireland, with the indication that remittance is to be made directly to that person. Three to five weeks after he mails his money and stubs, the seller receives in the mail, this time directly from Ireland, his receipts. This envelope generally bears no return address. The seller then distributes receipts to the people to whom he sold the tickets.

'If a person holds a winning ticket he receives notice a week or so after the race directly from the Hospitals Trust. He is sent a number of forms to fill out, which he returns together with his receipt to the Hospitals Trust. This is the first direct communication between either the purchaser or the seller of the ticket and the Hospitals Trust Limited.

'Some four to six weeks later he is sent, in a plain white envelope, a cheque in his favour, payable upon a Dublin bank, together with a slip of paper which says: "Your claim has been honoured."'

But while the AG's investigative team had little difficulty mapping the Irish Sweeps jigsaw around the well-trimmed lawns and sidewalks of suburban California, when it came to tracking through the lawless jungle of mobsters, fraudsters and smugglers, the trail went cold.

Governor Brown was informed: 'We do not get beyond the retail level. Since the sweepstake tickets are invariably posted from points in the United States it is apparent that someone originally brings the tickets into this country, and some individuals in the United States must maintain lists of the retailers in order to send tickets to the retailers through the US Mails. Since there would be no other way for them to be compensated, we must conclude that those two categories—those who bring the tickets into the country and the persons who maintain the list of retailers—are on the payroll of the Irish promoters. It is reasonable to assume, in addition, that in view of the size of this operation the promoters have administrative personnel in this country.'

While the legislators of California and other states wrestled with their consciences over the wisdom or otherwise of bringing in a legal alternative to the Irish Sweeps, the popular press was simply happy to keep publishing human interest stories concerning big winners and losers.

The *New Yorker* invited readers to write in giving their moral views on a 55-year-old dishwasher who won the handsome sum of $30,000 on the Irish Sweeps. He quit his job and embarked on living the millionaire lifestyle, trawling the best clubs, dropping hundred dollar bills as tips, and chartering a private flight to Florida. He learned from the experience that $30,000 buys you just six months of the millionaire lifestyle. After his spectacular spending spree he was back washing dishes for a living with, as the magazine put it, 'nothing to show for his fling but an ailing liver'. Instead of bewailing the fact that he had blown the windfall of a lifetime, the dishwasher insisted that he would continue to buy Irish Sweep tickets in the hope he would get the chance to do it all again. Judgmental readers were encouraged to condemn or condone the man's actions.

If the 55-year-old dishwasher felt that time was not on his side in an era when lifespans were shorter, then 78-year-old William Tyler might have been forgiven for spending his Sweeps winnings like there was no tomorrow. Tyler's story made the news from coast to coast. *Time* magazine's coverage was more lyrical than most, although it failed to mention that one of Tyler's first acts after banking his windfall was to plant his feet firmly on the ground by hiring a business manager.

'As the Lackawanna Railroad's crack [passenger train] Phoebe Snow pulled out of Hoboken and roared west last week, a private Pullman car was attached to the rear, with a party of eight elderly Negroes aboard. The leader and bill payer of the group was a tall, spare man, duded up in a blinding sports shirt and necktie, a sharp-lapelled suit, jaunty Ivy League cap and high-button shoes. He was no potentate from Africa, but William Tyler, 78, a retired Pullman porter, and he was relishing the fulfilment of a lifetime dream.

'Last spring Tyler, living quietly in a Los Angeles rooming house, hit the Irish Sweepstakes for $68,000 after taxes. Grandly, he invited his wife, his landlady and five old friends to join him on a romantic cross-country journey. Most of his companions had never been out of California and Tyler wanted them to see the rest of the country, as he had in his pillow-plumping days. "When I called the Southern Pacific to hire a car," he recalled, "I guess they thought I was kind of goofy. When the man told me it would cost around $7,500, I told him: Fine. I'll send you a check for $8,500 in case it's any more."

'From Los Angeles the private Pullman rolled to El Paso, New Orleans, Cincinnati, Niagara Falls, New York and Chicago, with leisurely, de luxe stopovers in each city. This week Tyler and friends headed for San Francisco and home. The whole excursion will cost the old porter about $15,000. Said Tyler: "I've got enough money left over to last me the rest of my life. But if I hit the Sweepstakes again in October, I'll hire another car and come back."'

While stories of eccentric Sweeps winners were always worth a few column inches, they weren't half as newsworthy as big winners whose good fortune had turned sour. Rowan Bromford of New York reached his 70th year in 1960 having led an undistinguished life. Apart from one prosperous patch when he had owned his own bar, he had made ends meet working a series of menial jobs including bellboy, janitor, doorman and cook. By his old age, however, he was broke and he had to borrow the cash to buy a third share of a Sweeps ticket, with his wife and daughter each taking another third. In October 1961 the family's boat finally came in when their ticket won $98,000. Inebriated with the sheer improbability of it all, Rowan Bromford bought a bottle of Irish whiskey and posed for a newspaper photographer. The photo made him a target.

Two years after his big win, Bromford was back in the news, but the mood of giddy celebration had long evaporated leaving a bitter aftertaste. He groused: 'From that day on it's been a constant annoyance and fight to keep the money. Panhandlers to tycoons, clubs and charities that wouldn't touch me before now hound my wife and me. People selling things from floor polishers to pool tables have been here.' But he revealed that the panhandlers and charities were the least of the worries that haunted him every day. Shortly after his big win he returned to his apartment to be confronted by a brace of 'burly men'. One produced a switchblade and said: 'Hold it, rich man.' The second thug beat him savagely and stole his wallet. Bromford spent 22 days in hospital with a fractured hand and eight stitches in his head. Just over a year later he was mugged again.

A middle-aged woman from Chicago who won the top prize of $140,000 in 1950 was overrun by so many fairweather friends, chancers and hard luck cases that, before long, she changed her name and fled her home. The corridor outside her apartment door was choked with the needy and the greedy. Shortly after her win, the long-lost brother she hadn't seen for eight years turned up asking her to co-sign a $6,000 loan for an 'operation'.

The sackfuls of letters which arrived included several from bogus charities seeking donations. One of the more intriguing came from a man offering his services as a gigilo. The missive opened: 'I have been the companion of well known actresses and I am thoroughly familiar with the elegant manners and places of life.' It closed: 'Oh, your life will be different. Warmly, Warren.' The following day a dapper fortysomething presented himself at her door, introducing himself: 'I'm Warren.'

It was all too much. The woman changed her name to Lillian and moved to the sun, sea and anonymity of Miami, Florida. By 1964 she had frittered away her large Sweeps fortune and moved back home to Chicago where she told a reporter she was considering part-time work.

The press had a field day with the horror story of 92-year-old Mary Boyle who bought a ticket on the 1963 Irish Derby in the name of her pet dog Met Jing. Before the draw took place, however, the dog died and Boyle gave the ticket to her butler. The ticket was plucked from the drum as winner of one of the $140,000 top prizes. Mary Boyle did not need the money. The socialite moved in the tight circle of billionaire

Wall Street financer and White House adviser Bernard Baruch. The many footnotes of history left by Baruch include the fact that he counselled President Woodrow Wilson at the Versailles Peace Conference in 1919, and that Winston Churchill was knocked down by a taxi on his way to meet the tycoon in 1931.

Mary Boyle didn't need the Sweeps money, but she was determined to have it. She insisted that she had simply given the ticket to the butler for safe keeping. The manservant was adamant that, following the death of her beloved pooch, the pet's upset owner had given it away for keeps. The fact that the ticket was in the name of a deceased animal didn't help the case of either party.

It ended in a manner which did nothing to heal the class divide. Late one night the grand old dame found herself out on Manhattan's swanky East 64th Street in her négligé, deposited there by her butler who had locked the front door. By the time Boyle got back with a posse of New York police the butler had packed his bags and was making his way haughtily to the door. He announced that, by way of handing in his notice, he had flushed the $140,000 ticket down the toilet.

Perhaps the most recycled hard luck Sweeps story in the American press concerned the biggest winner of them all, Emilio Scala. One typical report declared: 'He was badly stung, buying the wrong mansion in the wrong neighbourhood.' Another announced: 'He ended up selling fruit in the street.' In fact, the ice-cream man kept his fortune intact to his dying day and continued to keep open house for his family and friends in his plush mansion overlooking London. That dying day came in June 1959 and his passing was reported across the North American media, which correctly detailed that he had expired at the age of 73 from a heart attack while on holiday in his native Italy. He left £105,620 in his will.

As the post-war years elapsed, the lobby to rid the United States of the Irish Sweeps by legalising gambling found a louder voice. In the presidential election year of 1948 a group within the Democratic Party pressed for the inclusion of plans for an American National Sweep in the programme for government. It was rejected. As the election of 1956 loomed, New York Congressman Paul Fino urged the Republican Party to incorporate lottery plans in their campaign. He was rebuffed.

In 1959 Alaska joined the Union as the 49th State and quickly passed leglislation to permit a state lottery (which it never established). Fino welcomed the move in an address to the House of Representatives, saying: 'My hat's off to the State of Alaska.' The time had come, he declared, to jettison generations of hypocrisy and whisk the ground from under the racketeers. The majority in the House preferred to keep their hats firmly on, and Fino was once again sidelined.

The crusading Fino was back before the House in July 1964 armed with a bundle of statistics gathered from 81 countries around the globe, and showing how state lotteries had contributed to 'hospitals, schools, housing, welfare, charity, science, medicare, public developments and other worthwhile projects'. Once again his pleas fell on deaf ears, but by now events were beginning to overtake both Fino and his opponents.

In 1963 the legislators of New Hampshire ushered in the beginning of the end for the Irish Sweeps in the United States when they approved a state-sponsored sweepstake to start up in 1964.

The gloriously titled *Sumter Daily Item* newspaper welcomed the initiative in an editorial of February 1964. It began: 'The Granite State soon will launch a state-managed sweepstakes program that fairly can be called "gamblers' aid to education". If it works like state officials think it will, the program will provide $4,000,000 in revenue for New Hampshire schools this year and give a healthy lift to already thriving tourist business by luring betting folk from neighbouring New England states. Legislatures in Massachusetts and Vermont, evidently fearful that New Hampshire may turn out to be a Las Vegas with trees, are said to be considering lotteries of their own to keep the betting faithful at home.'

The first New Hampshire Sweepstake draw was scheduled for the following September, on a race at the State's major racecourse, Rockingham Park. A former FBI agent, Edward Powers, was installed to ensure the sweepstake was 'racket-proof'. Tickets were price-matched against their Irish Sweeps counterparts at $3 each, and they could only be purchased from special vending machines at State liquor stores and racetracks. While the six top prizes of $100,000 each fell some distance short of the $140,000 offered by the Irish Sweeps, the odds of winning were a lot more attractive. Emulating the Irish model, the tickets were drawn from a drum by pretty young women.

Observers from ten other states, including New York and California, reported back on the smooth running of the first New Hampshire Sweepstake and the ball was rolling. A referendum in New York produced a landslide in favour of starting up a State lottery there, and in 1967 enabling legislation was passed in the Big Apple.

In that same year of 1967 a senate subcomittee heard a bizarre tale of how the Inland Revenue Service (IRS) had stumbled upon one conspiracy while attempting to build evidence of another that was completely unrelated. The IRS placed an electronic bug expecting to tape-record an expected bribe attempt, but the bug picked up the wrong conversation. But what a conversation! It was between convicted fraudster Edward Vitale and his lawyer, Municipal Judge Russell Swarthout, and the pair were discussing their plot to conceal a chunk of Vitale's Irish Sweeps winnings from Revenue.

The story had begun in October 1960. At the time Edward Vitale was serving time behind bars for making 'false, fictitious and fraudulent statements and representations to a federal officer'. Word reached him in his prison cell that he had won a top prize of $140,000 on the Irish Sweeps. Vitale owed $300,000 in back taxes, but he was determined to keep his winnings, or as much of them as possible. He channelled the money into a Detroit bank through an attorney called Hoffiz, who took a hefty $15,000 fee and handed the delicate matter over to Swarthout.

When Vitale was released on parole in 1962 he and Swarthout wasted little time in buying an eaterie called Herc's Snack Shack with $20,000 of the winnings. The documentation was arranged to disguise Vitale's ownership. Swarthout filed the fraudulent documents with the IRS, and went to jail when the scheme was rumbled by the misdirected electronic bug. While the IRS were deliriously happy with the unintended outcome, one senator complained that it showed the 'absolute uncontrollability' of electronic snooping devices.

While Edward Vitale was already a convicted criminal at the time he hit the Sweeps jackpot, Frank McNulty had the Irish Sweeps to thank for landing him behind bars. A machinist in his sixties from Oakland, California, McNulty won a big prize of $128,410 in 1973. The Internal Revenue Service were soon knocking on his door, demanding a tax payment in the region of $35,000. McNulty told them that he had transferred his winnings straight into a bank account in the Channel Islands tax haven of Jersey. He argued that since the money had never entered the United States, the IRS was entitled to nothing.

On St Patrick's Day 1975 McNulty was jailed for five years on a conviction of tax evasion. He was freed after serving three years in 1978, on the expectation that he would settle his tax bill which had now doubled with interest and penalties to $70,000. His freedom was short lived. Still refusing to pay, he was returned to jail where he remained until his release on the day before St Patrick's Day 1979. The judge said that keeping McNulty imprisoned would no longer serve justice, but he warned him that he would have no peace until he settled with the IRS. The judge added that there was little prospect of McNulty ever being able to join his money abroad, as it was unlikely the United States authorities would issue him with a passport until he had paid up his due.

A camera crew from CBS Evening News were waiting to interview the now 67-year old as he walked free almost four years to the day after his jail sentence. Insisting that he had right on his side, he announced: 'I won't let a bunch of crooks and liars take the money away.'

Two years later he was living contentedly with his wife in a mobile home in California's San Joaquin Valley. He was happy to reveal that he was siphoning money into the United States from his Jersey account, where his nest egg was earning very high interest. He remarked: 'I bring in what I want to. Absolutely. There's no law says you can't.' An IRS official admitted that they had failed to collect a single cent of a tax bill that now topped $100,000. McNulty confidently predicted that they never would, saying: 'I don't owe them one Lincoln penny.'

THE FIRST CROWD I FLEW
TO THE CAYMAN ISLANDS
WERE SWEEPS PEOPLE

If the 1930s was a decade of heady adventure for the promoters of the Irish Sweeps, the 1950s was the decade when Joe McGrath and his fellow Hospitals Trust directors embedded themselves deep in the foundations of the insulated Irish economy. Illegitimate money from North America and elsewhere was poured into a range of legitimate concerns in Ireland, including the glass, textile and bloodstock industries. The imposing Hospitals Trust headquarters in Ballsbridge was built on a scale to reflect the lofty role the Sweeps occupied in Irish life. Even the mixing of the millions of counterfoils reflected the industrial character the Sweeps had assumed. The process still went on over three days, but the costumed girls pushing miniature carriages on rail tracks had been replaced by noisy pneumatic mixing machines that swirled the tickets about in tornadoes of turbulent air.

Despite constant unwelcome pressure on the Irish government from the United States authorities to curb the activities of Hospitals Trust, and despite embarrassing episodes such as the Trust's involvement with the Mexican International Sweepstakes racket, the perceived link between the Trust and the State was so tight that it was hard to tell there wasn't an exact join.

One woman who clearly believed the Sweeps were an arm of the State was Sheila O'Shea, who wrote to Taoiseach Éamon de Valera in January 1958. From the outset the Hospitals Trust's recruitment policy had been weighted in favour of women who had participated in the struggle for Independence, either by direct action or as the supportive wife or daughter of a freedom fighter. O'Shea had been one of those women getting temporary work in the busy period before each draw.

However, by 1958 she was of retirement age. She felt she deserved a military pension in her own right, but this had been denied her. She was in receipt of an old age pension, but this had been slashed from 25 shillings a week to ten shillings because of her small income from the Sweeps for a few weeks' work three times a year. Her request put directly to the leader of the country was, would he either see that she got her full old age pension, or else would he get her a full-time job with Hospitals Trust?

As the Hospitals Trust extended its tentacles into the diverse nooks and crannies of Irish society, a few voices were raised that its core mission to fund the hospital system was becoming a fading afterthought. By 1953, despite the evident wealth of its directors and the strength of its industrial investments, the Trust's contribution to the State's hospital building programme was falling far short of target. When *The Irish Times* canvassed a range of 'prominent people' about how to tackle the problem, most declined to comment. Criticism of Hospitals Trust was not to be dished out lightly.

The Irish Medical Association (IMA) had never been friendly to Hospitals Trust. Before the advent of the Sweeps, the medical elite had run the hospitals as independent fiefdoms and generally operated as a separate sovereign entity to the State. The Sweeps cash had brought state interference, with the government acting as the paymaster of the new funding stream. So it was in the interests of the IMA to point out that not only was Hospitals Trust short-changing the hospitals, but the money actually reaching the system was being unwisely spent.

A spokesman raised the fact that there were still 'appalling conditions unremedied by Sweeps funds' in the voluntary hospitals. In the view of the IMA, the ambitious hospital building programme was part of the problem, not part of the solution, because too much of the Sweeps money had gone into bricks and mortar, and not enough into hospital staff and patient beds. He charged: 'The IMA has never been consulted on the spending of the Sweeps money, but we think the problem might be solved by cutting down on contracts, by stopping the duplication of State hospitals throughout the country.'

When *The Irish Times* asked the Hospitals Trust to comment on the criticisms by the IMA, the Trust said that the person to talk to was Viscount Powerscourt, chairman of the Associated Hospitals

Committee, who would 'have an important contribution to make'. Viscount Powerscourt, however, felt he had no contribution to make. *Irish Times* readers weren't short of solutions to the hospitals crisis. One, calling himself Jackeen, suggested that the Sweeps promoters could help by creaming off less profits for themselves, and the government could abandon its practice of deducting stamp duty from the relatively small amount going to the hospitals.

Mrs Kathleen Gibbons of Enniscorthy in County Wexford suggested a three-pronged approach to raising extra funds, which could be implemented on a community level across the country. The first was: 'Organize a Silver Circle.' A silver circle was usually a series of four prize draws over four weeks, with subscribers buying four 'lines' in advance to cover the four draws. Mrs Gibbons's second strand was for communities to organise 'a whist drive with cup of tea at half-time'. The final part of her strategy was to hold 'a raffle of tickets for latest model motor car'. She omitted to mention where the motor car might be sourced from.

In 1956 Hospitals Trust published a self-serving book entitled *Ireland's Hospitals 1930–1955* with a foreword by Joe McGrath. He wrote: 'The Sweepstakes are still very necessary. Great though the figures [raised] be, the humanitarian purpose that inspired this venture must never be overlooked—the purpose of helping the sick poor.' But it was increasingly plain to see that Hospitals Trust was falling short of meeting that prime directive, with the result that the capital's voluntary hospitals were failing to provide an adequate patient service. In 1959 an *Irish Times* editorial jabbed a finger of blame at the way in which the Sweeps funding had been mismanaged.

The paper called for the merging of several Dublin voluntary hospitals to end some of the duplication pointed out by the Irish Medical Association in 1953. The editorial said there was a growing momentum towards integration in the late 1920s and early 1930s, but that reform was 'postponed when the success of the Sweepstakes seemed to promise a Golden Age'.

With the hospitals' share of the pot shrinking in real terms since the early years of the Sweeps, the promised golden age had never fully come to pass. The leader writer wrote: 'Valuable, however, as the contribution of the Sweepstakes has been, it has not been sufficient to put and keep the hospitals in the black. Doubtless, if all the money had gone to the maintenance and improvement of the voluntary hospitals—as was the original intention—they would be thriving; but much of it went towards the foundation of new hospitals in the city and throughout the country. The Government took a substantial levy in the form of stamp duty and, in the nature of things, a good part of the share allotted to the voluntary hospitals in Dublin was, in a sense, wasted on the purchase of equipment by each individual hospital which would have been redundant if they had been gathered into a single big unit.'

In asserting that the Sweeps money had been mismanaged, *The Irish Times* editorial echoed the sentiments of Professor V. M. Synge three years earlier. Synge blended his criticisms subtly into a speech broadly praising the way the Sweeps money had built 'beautiful hospitals and sanitoria', and continued to do 'good work'. In regretful tones he then delivered the sting in the tail. 'If they had been built with a little less luxurious architecture, more money might have been available to keep the Dublin hospitals up to date.'

As the 1950s progressed the chief concern of the directors of Hospitals Trust was to keep the profile of the Irish Sweeps up to date, as the gaming marketplace became ever more crowded. While the pro-gambling lobby in the United States built up a steady head of steam, the competition in Britain grew. In existence since the 1920s, the English football pools flourished in the post-war years, their visibility boosted by the fact that they were a regular weekly fixture. In 1956 the Macmillan government introduced Premium Bonds, offering patriotic Britons repeated entries in a big prize draw while at the same time putting away savings and fighting the scourge of inflation.

The Irish government was quick to pick up on the idea and the first Irish Prize Bonds draw, for top prizes of £5,000, took place in September 1957 attended by 'Ministers of State, ex-Ministers, a scattering of High-Ups in the banking world and all sorts of rich looking men'. The two rich-looking men mentioned before all the others in that newspaper report were Joe McGrath and Spencer Freeman 'whose silvered locks any woman might envy'. The draw, by pretty young women from six drums, was clearly modelled on that of the Irish Sweeps.

The Irish prize bonds were too puny to be of any consequence to McGrath and Freeman, but they decided a new publicity campaign was needed to maintain visibility abroad. That new campaign rested on sports sponsorship. In 1958 Hospitals Trust began sponsorship of the Irish Hospitals £5,000 golf championship at Dublin's Woodbrook course. The Hospitals tournament, held the week after the British Open, acted as a replacement for the Irish Open which had been suspended indefinitely in 1953 due to a lack of funding.

In January 1959 when Ireland's Canada Cup winning team of Christy O'Connor and Harry Bradshaw flew to New York for a celebratory banquet in their honour, their return flights were provided by Hospitals Trust. In return, the pair were asked to persuade some leading American golfers to compete in that year's Woodbrook tournament. Some of the world's top golfers did participate in the event, which ran for five years up to 1962.

After the 1962 Woodbrook event, Hospitals Trust withdrew from golf sponsorship in order to focus its profile-building on the world of horse racing. The plan to switch the 1962 summer Sweep from the Epsom Derby to the Irish Derby was announced in May 1960, when the Trust said it would add £30,000 to the prize fund, making the Curragh race 'the most valuable horse race in Europe, if not the world'. The race would be renamed the Irish Sweeps Derby. The Trust pointed out that since the Irish Derby took place later than the Epsom race, the extra three weeks would ease the workload on its employees. A spokesman for Bord Fáilte, which had suggested the move to the Trust, welcomed the initiative as 'of considerable benefit to our tourist promotional work abroad'.

The Curragh racecourse was given a complete facelift to make it a fit setting for Europe's richest race and the record crowd it was expected to draw. To accommodate the multitudes descending on the course, a new platform was constructed on the main Cork railway line and a special pathway cut out for those alighting there to make their way to the stands. A CIÉ special train carrying VIPs from Dublin to the Curragh broke down after travelling barely a mile, and a replacement diesel engine was sent to rescue the dignitaries.

An impressive new stand was erected to afford punters a clear view of the final furlong. The capacity of the reserved enclosure and the grand stand enclosure was expanded by a factor of four to eight. The catering facilities were the best ever assembled at an Irish racecourse, with self-service for those with an eye on their budgets, and waitresses serving a four-course luncheon from 11 am to 3 pm. One of the bars featured a counter 300 feet long, which was described as 'easily the longest in Ireland'.

Many years later Sydney Robbins, the first secretary of the newly formed Irish Racing Writers' Association, recalled how Spencer Freeman had considered taking radical measures to ensure the army of visiting journalists would dispatch their reports across the globe with something like military precision. Robbins wrote: 'One of the things that bothered Captain Freeman and Joe McGrath was "drink". The Sweeps organization had some considerable experience of Ireland's favourite pastime—I don't mean in a personal capacity of course, but had been reluctant spectators to some remarkable feats in this regard by pressmen and numerous enthusiastic helpers in the early ballyhoo days of the Irish Sweeps promotions. Not surprisingly, therefore, the Hospitals Trust and Mr McGrath, I believe, in particular, were inclined to be very cautious in this matter, thoughts of an open-air Bacchanalian orgy on the Curragh plain no doubt not being far from their minds.'

Although 'it took some persuasion', Robbins eventually managed to convince Freeman that 'the 1960s brand of journalist bore no relation to their less sophisticated predecessors'. He continued: 'Anyway, as I pointed out, it would look bad if people like Peter O'Sullevan and John Lawrence were to be handed vouchers in case they wanted to slake their thirst. Somewhat reluctantly, it was agreed that a free bar would be available for those who had the necessary credentials for entry to the marquee across the road at the back of the grandstand.'

As it turned out, the necessary credentials were in abundant supply. Robbins recalled: 'Correspondents with Dublin accents appeared claiming to represent the *Bombay Express* or *Pravda*. Where they got their badges has always remained a mystery. One of the tricks was to have your fill of food and drink and then pass the badge on to your friend, who in turn would do the same. In any event, the Sweeps kitchen staff were called on to serve almost twice the anticipated number of meals.'

Robbins, who as secretary of the Racing Writers' Association nominally had some influence over the freeloading Irish journalists, concluded his account: 'The only thing I can never understand is why Captain Spencer Freeman never asked for my co-operation in any further ventures.'

Whatever his reservations about the behaviour of the Irish journalists, Spencer Freeman was delighted with the outcome of the first Irish Sweeps Derby. The total prize money for the previous Irish Derby had been £7,000. The first sponsored by Hospitals Trust was worth £60,000, far outstripping the £33,000 pot for that year's Epsom counterpart. The race received worldwide press coverage and interest from TV stations. The ABC network in the United States negotiated the rights to broadcast future Irish Sweeps Derbies. The big race subsequently went out live at breakfast time on America's eastern seaboard in an era when live transatlantic broadcasts were a big deal.

By 1962 a growing proportion of the publicity generated for the Irish Sweeps from the hospital sector was of the negative variety, so when a good news story came around that year, the Hospitals Trust was quick to take credit, no matter how tenuous its claim might be. After spending six years in Dublin's Mater Hospital, 17-year-old Tony O'Rourke of Castletown-Kirkpatrick in County Meath returned home after surviving 'the most intricate heart operation' ever carried out at the hospital.

Hospitals Trust fired out a telegram to the newspapers asking them to publish the Trust's 'warm congratulations' to the 14 strong medical team who had performed the operation. The telegram said: 'This makes worthwhile everything the Sweepstakes organization has contributed to healing the sick and marks a benefit to all mankind.'

This piece of self-congratulation cut no ice with J. J. Hillary of Dublin who crunched the latest numbers published by Hospitals Trust and took his results to the press. He noted that out of a total take of £6,011,708 on the previous Sweep, only £3,251,500 had gone into the prize fund. The hospitals' cut was £1,098,339 before the government took its chunk of stamp duty. This left the considerably larger figure of £1,325,756 going into the coffers of Hospitals Trust as 'expenses'. Hillary asked: 'Are not the "expenses" rather excessive?'

In support of his point, he showed that the average amount going into the prize fund over the previous 104 sweeps since the very first, was 14 shillings out of each 20 (20 shillings making up one pound). For the first sweep of 1962 the sum going into the pot was just 11 shillings. He concluded: 'The expenses seem to be increasing. Could not these be cut down to allow more to be returned to the investor and increased sums allowed to the hospitals fund? Four millions seems a large sum to be used annually for the running of three sweeps.'

The Hospitals Trust's takeover of the Irish Derby only served to bolster Joe McGrath's position as 'the Napoleon of Irish racing', as he was described by one commentator. In addition to being the country's top breeder, he was the top owner in seven of the 19 seasons from 1947 to 1965. He served as chairman of the Racing Board and president of the Bloodstock Breeders' Association. His sons Joseph, Seamus and Paddy followed him into the bloodstock game, with owner Patrick and trainer Seamus winning the 1973 Irish Sweeps Derby with Weaver's Hill.

In 1950 Joe McGrath sold his stallion Nasrullah to a breeder in Kentucky where the horse supercharged the US breeding industry. As his son Paddy later explained: 'At that stage American breeding had reached the stage where the local stock was producing either a brilliant horse, a useless one or a nut. The Nasrullah line linked with the American bloodstock lines and gave a whole new impetus to the United States industry.' In the nine years before his death in 1959, Nasrullah topped the sire list five times, giving rise to a line that included the thoroughbred champions Bald Eagle, Jaipur, Red God, Bold Ruler, Noor, Mill Reef, Secretariat and Invasor.

Captain Spencer Freeman had also immersed himself in the world of bloodstock, living the life of a country squire on his sprawling stud farm at Ardenode, Co. Kildare. He hunted with the Kildare Hounds and captained his polo team in jousts in the Phoenix Park. The Freemans advertised occasionally for staff ranging from stable lads to cooks to parlour maids. One for the latter, from 1953, read: 'Two in family. Comfortable, warm home. Good food. Liberal outings. Transport to Mass. Wages (commensurate with ability) with bonus. Use of bicycle. Applicant must be thoroughly experienced and furnish personal references. Aged between 25 and 40.'

Two decades later, in 1971, live-in housemaids had become virtually a thing of the past in a modernising Ireland, but not in the cosseted world of the Freemans, who by now had swapped their stud farm in Kildare for stately Knocklion House in south Dublin. A classified ad of that year invited applications for: 'One of the Most Desirable and Best Paid Jobs in Dublin.' Mrs Freeman advertised: 'Light housework. Three other domestic staff. Sitting room. TV. Radio. Transport to Mass etc. Alternative weekends also weekly half-days off. Only two in family. Comfortable and warm house. For this very "cushy" job only experienced maids over 30 years old should apply.'

Big Joe McGrath was not around to meet the Spencers' new housemaid or see his sons Patrick and Seamus sweep to victory in the 1973 Irish Sweeps Derby with Weaver's Hill. On a spring day in 1966 at the age of 80, he drew the final breath of a long, extraordinary life. Still turning up for work each morning at his Ballsbridge headquarters, he was taken ill at the desk from where he had masterminded his fantastic global scam in the post-war years.

Government ministers, leading churchmen and captains of industry led the clamour to pay tribute. The President of Ireland, Éamon de Valera, saluted Big Joe's heroic deeds, his noble spirit and his good works. De Valera said: 'I am very sorry to hear of Joe McGrath's death. He has been one of the big men of our time, in the foremost ranks, first in the political and then in the industrial and social fields.' McGrath's old cabinet colleague Ernest Blythe said: 'As he acquired wealth, his generosity increased.' Spencer Freeman, the last of the Sweep's founding fathers, said in admiration: 'He was a glutton for work.'

McGrath was barely cold in the grave when an article in the influential US business magazine, *Fortune*, accused him and his organisation of a different type of gluttony. In late 1966 the Irish-born journalist Thomas O'Hanlon wrote an exposé for the publication attacking the smuggling activities of the Hospitals Trust and the excessive profits extracted by its directors. Swatting away the charitable façade, *Fortune* baldly characterised Hospitals Trust as 'a private company run for profit'. The Irish newspapers were defensive of Hospitals Trust, which was a heavy advertiser. A typical rebuff from the Irish media was that the accounts supplied by Hospitals Trust 'do not lend facts to support the *Fortune* criticisms'.

There were criticisms from closer to home the following year, 1967, when the Workers' Union of Ireland resurrected its long-running dispute with Hospitals Trust over union recognition. The WUI returned to the Labour Court claiming that it was being denied the right to negotiate conditions on behalf of seven night cleaners. The other 52 night cleaners employed by Hospitals Trust were represented by the House Association.

As part of the union's submission to the Labour Court, branch secretary Michael Cassidy said that the entire Hospitals Trust workforce was cowed by a work environment of 'favouritism, servility, ingratiation, paternalism and nepotism'. Whatever the truth or otherwise of this claim, the unhappy reality for the WUI was that it did not have the support of the majority of Hospitals Trust workers. There was a widespread view in the lion's share of the workforce represented by the House Association that the union agitators were in danger of jeopardising jobs at a time when ticket sales were in sharp decline in North America, Britain and elsewhere.

The new boss of the Hospitals Trust, Paddy McGrath, was as dismissive of the union as his late father Joe had been. He sent a letter to be read out at the Labour Court. It stated flatly: 'We have negotiated with the House Association on the matters alleged to be in dispute and on several other matters. If we are obliged also to negotiate with the WUI we would be negotiating twice on similar matters with two bodies for the same employees.'

As it had in 1950, the Labour Court recommended that Hospitals Trust talk to WUI representatives. As they had in 1950, and ever since, the directors of Hospitals Trust simply ignored the recommendation. The Fianna Fáil Minister for Labour Paddy Hillery said he approved of the Labour Court recommendation, but ruled out putting any pressure on Hospitals Trust to comply. The Fine Gael leader Liam Cosgrave came out firmly on the side of Hospitals Trust and against unpatriotic lefties, saying: 'There is nothing anti-trade union in this. It is an Irish industry established by Irishmen and should not be sabotaged.' He reiterated: 'I do not want to see it sabotaged for theoretical reasons.' Labour TD James Tully offered his definition of the term 'house association' as 'a bosses' union' while his party leader Brendan Corish told the Dáil: 'It is a phoney association. It is not a union.'

The WUI threatened strike action in advance of the end-of-year Cambridgeshire draw unless Hospitals Trust complied. The Sweeps promoters refused to budge and the WUI backed down. Paddy McGrath's hard-bitten image with Ireland's trades unionists was not improved by his public jokes about his role as the big boss of 'the McGrathfia' and the fact that his close friends referred to him as the 'Godfather'.

The animosity towards the union from many in the House Association was showcased on the letters pages of the newspapers when the WUI went back to the Labour Court in 1969 alleging that certain favoured employees of the Hospitals Trust secretly enjoyed better wages and pension provisions than their colleagues, thanks to under-the-counter 'grace and favour' payments from management.

Betty Ray, on behalf of the House Association, attacked the union for stirring things. She wrote: 'Hospitals Trust have been very good employers as far as my age group and others are concerned. If I left tomorrow or Hospitals Trust folded up (God forbid) both I and a good 50% of the staff (old and young) would find it impossible to obtain employment with so many facilities and good wages. My suggestion to Mr Cassidy is to instruct his minority members of Hospitals Trust to get on with it and refrain from trying to cause dissension amongst the staff. I think there is enough dissension in the world today without the "fly in the ointment" working overtime. I, for one, do not feel like signing on, all because of a few philistines.'

Betty Ray's fears about signing on the dole were not groundless. Ticket sales for the previous Lincoln Sweepstake were down by the very significant sum of almost half a million pounds. This did not prevent Michael Cassidy of the WUI from returning fire, again via the letters pages of the national newspapers. He said that previous good work by the union had helped to relieve a regime of 'tyranny' for the Ballsbridge workers. He accused management of manipulating the House Association, and he pointed out that even philistines are entitled to the basic constitutional right of representation.

While Hospitals Trust shrugged off the ruling of one court in 1967, it was more than happy to accept the final verdict of another. A New Yorker by the name of Isaac Wunder appeared in Dublin's High Court claiming he was the holder of a ticket which drew Kelling, the winner of the 1950 English Cambridgeshire. Wunder's grievance was that Hospitals Trust had refused to pay out on his big win for fully 17 years. His case was somewhat undermined by the fact that over the course of those years the High Court and Supreme Court had thrown out his claims to hold 19 other winning Sweeps tickets.

The Hospitals Trust's lawyer, Declan Costello, produced the winning counterfoil for the 1950 race, which had been held by a subscriber in Canada. He also produced a receipt from the winner acknowledging payment to him of £25,000. Presiding Justice Murnaghan told Wunder: 'You are more to be pitied than anything else. You have spent a lot of money pursuing actions which are in your own mind and nowhere else. I am very sorry for you but I have come to the conclusion that you are suffering from a delusion. I believe that you believe everything you say is true. The trouble is that I do not believe it is true. I think you are making a mistake, an unfortunate mistake which has cost you a great deal of money.'

Wunder told the judge that the ticket at issue, the twentieth he had taken to court, was the very last one on which he was making a claim. Justice Murnaghan said he was awarding costs to Hospitals Trust, and Wunder responded that he would be lodging an appeal against that decision with the Supreme Court, which had dismissed all his previous claims.

His Supreme Court appeal was heard in January 1968 and fared no better than his previous ones. Upholding the High Court decision, Chief Justice Cearbhall Ó Dálaigh confirmed to Wunder that he was indeed delusional and urged him 'to place his affairs in the hands of some friend or relative before he renders himself penniless by his pointless action'.

With the advent of legalised gambling in the United States, and the growing popularity of the football pools in Britain, subscriptions to the Irish Sweeps began to slump by the mid-1960s. In an attempt to plug the shortfall, in February 1966 Paddy McGrath presented a plan to Health Minister Donogh O'Malley which involved doubling the number of annual Sweeps races from three to six. In addition, McGrath proposed to spread out the drawing of the tickets for each race over a number of weekends. This weekly sequence would put the Irish Sweeps on the same regular footing as the English football pools and some of the new United States lotteries, giving the Sweeps a continuity more suited to a world that had moved on since the 1930s. McGrath won O'Malley's support for the scheme by telling the health minister that the expanded format would raise an extra £2 million a year for the country's underfunded hospital-building scheme.

The Department of Justice, under Minister Brian Lenihan, was hostile to McGrath's plan. In a memorandum to government in November 1966 department officials suggested that the real intended beneficiaries of the expanded Sweeps would be the McGraths and their partners at Hospitals Trust. The memo argued that the legality of the proposed new prize plan was 'open to question' and that the new arrangement mooted by Paddy McGrath, 'like the scheme for the ordinary Sweepstakes, is such that a substantial profit for the promoters can be wholly concealed'. The department calculated that the true amount of this concealed profit would be in the region of £900,000 annually, quite apart from the large sums claimed for a variety of expenses and directors' salaries.

The Department of Justice informed the government that it simply did not believe Hospitals Trust could be trusted to supply honest figures. It said: 'Consideration of the promoters' profits is made more complicated by the fact that the estimated ascertainable profit . . . from the new scheme is based on the promoters' own statements and estimates of income. Here, the Minister thinks it necessary to repeat the view that these statements and estimates seem exceptionally difficult to accept.'

The department finished its attempted demolition job on McGrath's scheme by pointing out that if it was approved, the Irish government would be giving Hospitals Trust the go-ahead to further damage Ireland's reputation abroad. It made clear that if the scheme was purely targeted at Irish sales, every household in the country would have to buy two tickets a week in order to raise the funds puffed-up by Paddy McGrath. The memo continued: 'And if the answer is that the promoters' real intention is to go outside the State for a substantial part of the income, the Minister is of the opinion that the Government would wish to consider the implications of that.'

Jack Lynch replaced Seán Lemass as the leader of Fianna Fáil and Taoiseach in November 1966. In December Lynch's new cabinet overruled the advice of the Justice Department and approved Paddy McGrath's plan to double the number of Sweeps. The government's sanction of the new Sweeps scheme drew an angry response from an alliance of charities and associations which had been holding modest fundraising lotteries since the restraints on small-time gaming had been loosened a decade earlier. The Federation of Voluntary Charitable Organisations was founded to represent the interests of a range of agencies stretching from cultural bodies like Gael Linn and the GAA to medical concerns such as the Central Remedial Clinic and the Irish Wheelchair Association. The government bowed to the rainbow lobby and put Paddy McGrath's expansion plan on the back burner.

As a sop to McGrath, Hospitals Trust was given permission to add a fourth Sweeps race to the annual schedule, with the first taking place at Leopardstown racecourse during Christmas week 1969. With a prize fund for the runners of £10,000, the promoters claimed that the new Sweeps Hurdle would be 'the most valuable hurdle race in England or Ireland'.

A winner of a £50,000 first prize on the third of the new Sweeps hurdle races was a porter at a Detroit car dealers. James Stultz received news of his good fortune three weeks after he and his wife Cora went through divorce proceedings. Cora immediately started court proceedings claiming that her ex-husband should have listed his Irish Sweeps ticket among his assets before their property was divided some weeks before the race was run.

The judge told the former Mrs Stultz that she should have sought the inclusion of her husband's ticket among the couple's joint property. She must have known he had it since he had entered every draw for the past 14 years. The judge admonished the ex-wife, ruling: 'She's not entitled to one penny more than she's already received. He had no knowledge the ticket would be a winner. I wonder if she would have been willing to take the ticket instead of getting their house in the settlement before it became a winning ticket.' In conclusion, the judge waxed scriptural, saying: 'What God giveth, man taketh not away.' A relieved James Stultz announced that he would be taking 'a long vacation' with his newly secured wealth.

The new end-of-year Sweeps Hurdle was an attractive fixture for a four-man syndicate that formed in the mid-1960s to take on Hospitals Trust's chicken pluckers at their own game. In an interview for this book, the late Jim Aiken explained how he had joined forces with three other entrepreneurs to track down the holders of hot tickets. A physics teacher with an exceptional head for figures, Aiken quit his teaching job in 1965 to become a concert promoter. By the 1980s he would be the biggest in Ireland, staging huge outdoor concerts by such acts as U2, Bruce Springsteen and Queen.

As he was finding his feet in showbiz, he became friendly with Tom McCluskey who ran the Beechmont Ballroom in Navan. McCluskey felt there was money to be made by buying a half-share in tickets bearing the names of favourite runners. He asked Aiken and another small-time promoter if they had the money to help make up a pool of £40,000 to spend on tickets. Aiken and the other promoter managed to scrape together the guts of £10,000 between them. The fourth member of the syndicate was a bookmaker. Aiken said: 'The theory was to buy a share in tickets on all the fancied horses for under £42,000. The idea was that if you bought a half-share of every ticket there was, you had a return of £42,000. So if you could buy those for £30,000 you were an absolute cert to make £12,000. It was irresistible. If you could buy them for less than £42,000 it was an absolute cert you were going to win.'

The Irish Sweep had a special allure for the four venture capitalists. Aiken explained: 'It generated excitement. You heard that someone had won the Sweep. That's why they had a farm, or a better shop, or why their children went to school. The Sweep offered a way of emerging from the poverty around.'

Tom McCluskey had done his homework. He was aware that when the 100/1 rank outsider Caughoo won the 1947 Aintree Grand National, the chicken pluckers who had bought shares in tickets on all the fancied horses had lost a fortune because they hadn't bothered to cover the long-shots.

According to Jim Aiken: 'Tom McCluskey said that the only Sweeps worth going on were the quality ones, so we went on the Derby and the Sweeps Hurdle because you could follow definite form lines. We left out lotteries like the Grand National. In the case of the Sweeps Hurdle, we knew that Persian War would probably win it [in 1970] and it did. We might take a flyer on the Grand National if we saw a likely horse, but there was no way you could balance your books on the National.'

Aiken enjoyed the cat-and-mouse game his syndicate played with Hospitals Trust. He recalled: 'We'd go to the Sweep, listen for the draw, get the details and scribble them down. Then I'd go to Canada. Or someone would go to Canada, the US, England, Scotland. You'd hear such a person lives at such an address. Horse is Sindar in the Derby. You immediately knew Sindar was 7/1 so we'd pay about £4,000 for half a 7/1 shot. It was a mathematical thing, but in my case it was something to do that was different.

'One time I was asked to leave the Sweeps headquarters in Ballsbridge. I was taking notes and this fellah comes over. I said I'm only taking notes for the Northern papers. He says: "You're Not!"

'As the horses came out I'd write them down. I'd ring whoever and say "Make a move, one has been drawn outside Toronto." If you didn't get the favourite you could call the whole thing off, but if you got the favourite you could attempt to balance it. It was more exciting than wise. One Christmas Eve in Bristol chasing a ticket-holder, I couldn't get home to Belfast so I got to Cork. I hired a self-drive car and drove the length of the country from Cork to Belfast. I got home and the wife just said: "I thought you weren't coming home for Christmas." She was very tolerant!'

There were many frantic trips to the United States and Canada as Aiken attempted to doorstep ticket-holders in the short window between the drawing of the tickets on a Tuesday and the running of the race the following Saturday. He explained: 'Between the draw and the race it was unbelievable the things we did to get to the holders. It wasn't as easy to get to Toronto back then as it is today. We had an opening question for every ticket-holder. It was: "Would you bet £10,000 on a horse?" The £10,000 was the sum we were offering them for a half-share of their ticket, or two grand or four grand depending on the horse. If the horse didn't place, all they'd get would be £400 for drawing a runner in the race. Everyone looked at you at the start and said no way am I going to sell. Good luck! But invariably they took the sensible view and sold. You'd search for ones that potentially would win and then you might take out insurance on outsiders. For example, rather than buying half a ticket on an outsider you might back it at 100/1.'

He continued: 'People with tickets were glad to have us call offering insurance. You brought them to a bank. You'd have arranged the transaction in advance with a local bank. You brought them to the local bank and showed them the cheque. The bank confirmed that the cheque was valid and you'd tell them that the moment they signed over half of the ticket, the money would immediately be made available into their account. They'd sign and you'd give them their letters of credit. People were delighted. Tom McCluskey was the manager of the consortium and he'd hold the legal documents. He supplied us with the documents. You'd sign a contract saying: "I, Damian Corless, have drawn such a ticket and I am now prepared to sell 50% of it and I instruct the Irish Hospital Sweeps to send 50% of proceeds that occur from this ticket to such an account at Bank of Ireland and so on."'

After several years of criss-crossing the Atlantic to pluck the chickens, Jim Aiken decided there had to be an easier way to make a living. He recalled: 'It was a lot of work for the return. I remember after one Sweep the four of us shared £6,000 and after another we had only £4,000 to split between us. It was a lot of work but it was part of being smart. We had discovered that if you carried it through to the end then you had this thing that all gamblers want—an infallible system.'

However, as he reflected ruefully, the system was only infallible if you carried it right through to the end, which meant taking out adequate insurance against the most freakish results. He recollected: 'One of the McGrath-owned horses won a Sweeps race at odds of 33/1 and we had no ticket on the winner. I had a little insurance on it but the whole Sweep was a huge loss because we had neither bought part of a ticket nor insured against it (by placing a bet with a bookmaker). At the start of the race the favourite's tail caught in the gate and his race was over. That dampened our ardour because we ended up giving back most of what we'd made over the previous number of years.'

There were other reasons Jim Aiken decided to call it a day in the Sweeps game. He revealed: 'We were trampling on other people's toes, and they didn't like this. We were coming in to American and Canadian cities and instead of one person buying and selling tickets you now had two, creating a bit of a market. In Chicago, for instance, the whole sale of tickets was controlled by the Chicago Transit Authority. Somebody in there had the sales rights and they jealously guarded that. They wanted nobody stepping in. I remember one time I found a winner in Chicago. Eventually I got a call to my hotel room. The caller wanted to know what I thought I was doing.'

In the 1990s it emerged that a so-called golden circle of Irish businessmen had evaded their Irish tax liabilities by concealing large sums of money in offshore Ansbacher accounts based in the Cayman Islands in the Caribbean Sea. The man who hatched the plot in cahoots with Taoiseach Charles Haughey's bagman Des Traynor, was Cayman banker John Furze. Jim Aiken recalled that many years after his Sweeps syndicate disbanded, he was flying above the Caribbean with a veteran pilot. The concert promoter recollected: 'The pilot said I see you're having problems in Ireland with the Cayman Islands. I used to fly John Furze to the Caymans.' The pilot then added: 'The first crowd I flew to the Cayman Islands were Sweeps people.'

In 1970, with great fanfare, Hospitals Trust introduced a new super-prize with the express purpose of winning back market share on the eastern seaboard of the United States where the New York lottery with its $1 million prize fund had put a severe dent in Irish Sweeps ticket sales. The super-prize of £200,000 was on top of multiple first placed horse prizes of £50,000. While the super-prize gimmick gave a temporary boost to ticket sales internationally, the United States market would never recover. The first winner of the super-prize was a woman from Canada, as were ten of the first 16 super-prize winners, with only three coming from the United States and two from Britain.

For Hospitals Trust Limited the climate was about to get even harsher in the 1970s, as black storm-clouds gathering over Canada began to roll eastwards across the Atlantic.

Chapter 24

I HAVE BEEN INTIMIDATED IN REGARD TO THE HOSPITALS SWEEPSTAKES

Late in 1972 the *Sunday Independent*'s top sleuth Joe MacAnthony began to dig into the affairs of Hospitals Trust at the suggestion of his editor, Conor O'Brien. Many years later, in an interview with the film-maker Bob Quinn, MacAnthony revealed that initially he had little enthusiasm for the assignment.

He told Quinn: 'I didn't want to do the Sweepstakes story. Conor O'Brien came to me and said why don't you do a story on the Sweepstakes and I thought okay I'll have a look. And I had a look and I couldn't find anything. But there was one aspect of it that touched me. Mary Maher who was a journalist at *The Irish Times* spoke to me about the condition of the women in the Sweepstakes and how badly off they were, and miserable pensions and stuff like that, and that started me into it and it also provided me with a primary source. And when I started from the primary source I started to gather stuff, and I got a TD to bring documents out of the Dáil library, to smuggle out the reports they gave to TDs but kept from the public.'

As he dug back in time to the pre-Sweeps lotteries held by Richard Duggan in the 1920s, he was struck by some of the examples of sharp practice he came across. He said: 'Duggan would hold a lottery for a hospital in Dublin. The draw would take place in Switzerland and someone with a PO box number in Egypt would win.' He added that in another instance: 'The Superintendent who was supervising the draw by some strange quirk held up a ticket which happened to be his own son's, and he won a large prize. The more you looked at it the more you saw what was crooked about it.

'So I went first of all to Canada because by that time Canada was the main centre for the Sweepstakes. I investigated it there, where I learned how the operation worked. Then I went to the United States and I went to the newspaper libraries in New York. And then I read all the Dáil debates from 1922 onwards. And I got sources who could tell me what went on within the Sweeps. So I was fairly confident that I had the goods. But they were worried in the *Independent* for two reasons. One, the McGraths who ran the Sweepstakes were close friends with the Murphys who owned the *Independent*, so the possibility existed that the story would never get into the paper. The other one was the legal aspect. [The lawyer] said he wanted proof and I brought in a suitcase full of documents, and he went through it. . . . And he said it's all right, run it. But we couldn't run it and tell the Murphys who owned the *Independent*. So we decided to run it without telling them. Conor O'Brien was the man who made this enormous, risky choice. He rang my wife Barbara while I was away and said it was the most extraordinary story he'd ever read. So he ran it entire because if he'd cut it in half they'd never have let the second half get out.'

Conor O'Brien's instincts were proven spot on. In MacAnthony's own words 'all hell broke loose' when the 7,000 word exposé appeared on Sunday 21 January 1973. His devastating report began: 'Following months of investigation into the Irish Sweepstakes, it can now be established that Irish hospitals are receiving less than 10% of the value of tickets marketed in their name throughout the world by Hospitals Trust (1940) Limited. From interviews with the US Postal Department and with police across Canada—where most of the tickets are sold—it seems clear that more than 90% of the value of tickets entered in each draw is being written off, mainly to expenses, at a rate of more than £150,000 a week. Our investigations show also that the persons legally responsible for managing and controlling the Sweepstakes—the Associated Hospitals Committee—are not fully aware of the true figures involved in the operation of the Sweep. Nor are Dáil deputies—even though it is Dáil Éireann which provides the authority by which the Sweepstakes are run. These disclosures are only part of what must be one of the most extraordinary, yet least publicised, stories in modern Irish history. For the facts show:

• That the Act which licenses the Sweep was so framed as to prevent the Irish public knowing the real amount of money spent in running the scheme.

• That the figures published by Hospitals Trust (1940) Ltd after each Sweepstake are considerably less than the true amount involved.
• That the hospitals receive only 75% of the sum described as the Hospital Fund—because the only tax on the Sweep is taken from the hospitals, not the organisers.
• That agents of Hospitals Trust Ltd are engaged in selling tickets abroad at prices far above those sanctioned by the Minister for Justice.
• That leading shareholders in Hospitals Trust Ltd have also been involved with a bookmaking group in buying up ticket shares which allows them to win their own prizes.'

MacAnthony went on to calculate that the McGrath family alone were increasing their wealth at the rate of £8,000 with each passing day while most retired Hospitals Trust employees with over 25 years of service were struggling to get by on a pension of £4 per week. He quoted an investigative piece, which appeared in an American edition of *Readers Digest* but which was never circulated in Ireland, as describing the Irish Sweeps as 'the greatest bleeding hearts racket in the world'.

He continued: 'The owners of the Hospitals Trust (1940) have amassed wealth close to one hundred million pounds which makes them not only the richest people in Ireland by far, but also places them in a bracket with the wealthiest in Europe. The leading shareholders in the group—the McGraths—have seen assets and earnings increase at a rate of more than three million pounds per year, which is the same as what the Irish hospitals received from the Sweeps in 1971. Similarly, the next biggest shareholders—the Duggans and the Freemans—have increased their combined wealth by almost the same amount.'

MacAnthony pointed out that the *Readers Digest* had estimated the late Joe McGrath's salary from Hospitals Trust at the astronomical sum of £100,000 a year, plus unknown expenses. He quoted Section 2 of the Public Hospitals Act 1933 which governed the running of the Sweeps. It said: 'When calculating for the purposes of this Act the amount of the money received from the sales of tickets in a sweepstakes, the value of the tickets issued free of charge by way of a reward to a seller of tickets shall be excluded from the calculation, and there shall be deducted from the nominal selling price of all other tickets all commissions, prizes and other remuneration given in relation to the selling of such tickets.'

He continued: 'Because of this, the Sweeps promoters operate two sets of expenses, only one of which ever appears in the published balance sheets. And even the published accounts are restricted to Dáil deputies and those directly connected with the Sweep. There are strong indications that the hidden expenses take a hefty slice of the Sweeps revenue.'

MacAnthony revealed that the Canadian police told him they believed that more than a third of the Irish Sweep tickets purchased by Canadians never made it into the draws held at Ballsbridge. He stated that the Irish Sweep operated 'the largest smuggling ring outside the Mafia', paying bribes to seamen, longshoremen, railway workers, postal staff and customs officials.

The journalist explained that those who controlled the distribution of Irish Sweep tickets in Canada could accumulate fortunes. One police officer related to him how he had raided the home of a major distributor in Quebec. During the raid the officer noticed that the householder's pet dog had soiled an expensive oriental rug on the floor. When the policeman pointed this out to the distributor, the man laughed and said that whenever that happened he simply rolled up the rug, threw it out and bought a replacement. The Canadian police provided many more stories of wealthy distributors, leading them to conclude that many of the ticket sellers kept their hands on the money they were entrusted to send to Ireland.

A former chief of Montreal's Morality Squad told MacAnthony that he had seized so many tickets for one draw in 1966, that the confiscated tickets had a combined value higher than the entire proceeds listed by Hospitals Trust for the draw. In a separate raid he uncovered receipts supposedly issued from Hospitals Trust in Dublin for tickets which had been sold just four days previously. It was not possible that the counterfoils could have made the round trip to Ireland and back in only four days, so the receipts were clearly bogus and the money had been pocketed. The former policeman told of an incident where he had seized thousands of ticket stubs with a face value of over $10,000 following a tip-off which he believed had come from the agent in possession of the stubs. With the stubs confiscated, the agent wouldn't be able to send them to Dublin, but he would be able to keep the money he had collected if he claimed that it too had been seized by the police.

A senior officer in Montreal said: 'You can't control an operation like what the Irish Sweep are doing here without a lot of money sticking to people's fingers. It's a lot of tripe to say it's on the up and up. From what I've seen, I'd put the money going back to Ireland at around 90 cents out of every three dollars spent on tickets.'

MacAnthony went on to reveal that businesses and individuals providing 'convenience addresses' for tickets arriving from abroad were receiving 15 new pence commission for each book passed on to Hospitals Trust. He claimed that the owner of one sports shop on Dublin's Capel Street was earning the hefty sum of £15,000 per year by processing Sweeps mail. He revealed that the fabricated Mr Moran of Merrion Road in Dublin was, in fact, Hospitals Trust boss Patrick McGrath who was receiving secret commissions. He pointed out that the bribes and commissions excluded from the accounts published by Hospitals Trust were a major drain on the money which was supposed to go to the hospitals and into the prize fund.

The *Sunday Independent* journalist then accused the Hospitals Trust of breaching the provisions of the 1956 Gaming and Lotteries Act which stated that not more than 40 per cent of any lottery proceeds could be deducted as expenses. He estimated that 40 per cent of the proceeds went missing in the form of pay-offs before the promoters creamed off their published expenses.

MacAnthony discovered that Hospitals Trust had evolved a sophisticated banking system to make it virtually impossible to follow the money trail. He wrote: 'The companies which receive Sweep lodgements are not even of the same nationality. The complicated procedure is as follows. On one day the cash received from abroad goes to the Bank of Ireland. On the following day the cash received is lodged with an American company. The day after that, the money goes to a British company. This system of alternating lodgements with companies of different nationalities is followed all year round.'

MacAnthony demonstrated how the Department of Posts & Telegraphs worked in league with Hospitals Trust to flout international postal law. Some years earlier a bundle of Sweeps mail addressed to a non-existent address had found its way to the offices of the *Irish Press* newspaper group. According to international law, this mail should have been returned to sender. Instead, the department dispatched a postal official to collect the consignment and drop it at the headquarters of Hospitals Trust. He pointed out that a Post Office van called at a number of Dublin hotels on a regular basis to pick up mail intended for Hospitals Trust.

The journalist identified a number of American states as non-hostile to the Sweeps, including Arkansas, New Mexico, Michigan and Wyoming. Sweeps tickets could be posted to these states without much fear that the mail would be intercepted. Other states, including New York, California and Texas, were classified by Hospitals Trust as hostile, and mail had to be first smuggled into these locations before being put in the local post.

MacAnthony said that after the United States and Canadian authorities had identified the state-owned Irish Shipping vessels as a major smuggling conduit, Hospitals Trust had switched to using foreign freighters. He cited the last ship to be accused of transporting Sweeps tickets into the US as an Icelandic vessel. The last big seizure of tickets in Canada had been shipped from Britain labelled as 'jellies'.

The journalist then took a swipe at the members of the Associated Hospitals Committee, a body he described as 'little more than a rubber stamp' for the underhand activities of the Sweeps promoters. He said that the committee members were entitled to demand a complete set of accounts for every draw, but had never done so as far as the records showed.

The *Sunday Independent* backed up MacAnthony's exposé with an editorial by Conor O'Brien calling for 'an end to begging'. It posed three questions. 'The first question is: does the revenue brought in by illegal Sweep activities abroad still justify a Government involvement which clearly brings its own name into disrepute? Given mounting criticism in Canada and the view of a Department of Health spokesman that the Sweep's contribution to Irish hospitals' expenses are now "insignificant" the answer must be no.'

The second question set by O'Brien was could an alternative fundraising mechanism to the Irish Sweeps be put in place? The answer given by the *Sunday Independent* was that yes, a national lottery should be established.

The third question posed by the newspaper concerned the issue which Hospitals Trust had used to blackmail successive Irish governments over the course of more than four decades. 'If the Sweep's activities abroad were to cease, could alternative employment be found for the 1,000 people currently employed in its operations? The answer to this question, as with the previous one, lies in the creation of the National Lottery. Most of the Sweep workers could be re-employed in such an undertaking with the added benefit of belonging to the civil service to give them security on retirement, which is not the case in their present situation.

'In addition to these considerations, the Government must also have regard to its own pride and image abroad. We are rapidly developing into a modern industrial nation with all the prestige that such a position endows on a people in the world today. Yet, along with the Mafia and a tiny few Caribbean islands, we still persist in seeking the world's charity to maintain our health services. And we are prepared to countenance illegalities in order to do so.

'This simply will not do. It is about time that our representatives in Government decided that we are an independent nation, depending on ourselves for sustenance and not on other people's sympathy. The poor mouth is no longer representative of the New Ireland. Those charged with ordering our affairs should realise so and act accordingly.'

The *Sunday Independent*'s editor, Conor O'Brien, had taken the courageous decision not to give advance notice to the newspaper's owners, the Murphy family, who were close friends of the McGraths.

According to Joe MacAnthony: 'The story was told to me that Mrs McGrath and Mrs Murphy used to go to mass in Foxrock and they would go up and get Holy Communion. Apparently Mrs Murphy was there completely unaware of this story and she took Holy Communion, and Mrs McGrath was beside her and she took Holy Communion, and she nodded at Mrs McGrath and Mrs McGrath looked at her and stomped off. All hell broke loose. Major Murphy, who was the major shareholder, came in to Conor with a statement saying "Major Murphy had no knowledge of this story being published in the *Sunday Independent*." He was trying not to lose his friendship.'

Whether the Murphy family lost for ever the friendship of the powerful McGraths, their newspapers lost the advertising revenue from the McGraths' string of businesses which was withdrawn following publication of the story. Soon after, the Murphys sold their holding in the Independent Group to businessman Tony O'Reilly. The sensational revelations about the activities of Hospitals Trust were not picked up by the self-proclaimed newspaper of record, *The Irish Times*, and received either muted or no coverage in other media outlets.

Some months after MacAnthony's Sweeps exposé, the editor of *Profile* magazine commissioned Thomas O'Hanlon, who had earlier penned a hostile feature on Hospitals Trust for *Fortune* magazine in the United States, to review a biography of Drew Pearson which named the influential columnist as a major player in the Sweeps racket. The cover featured an image of the late Joe McGrath, who was labelled 'Mister Sweep'. When the magazine's publisher, Hugh McLoughlin, found out about his editor's plans, he pulled the edition from the shelves, remarking: 'It's a second-hand story. There's nothing illegal about the Sweeps in this country. It may be illegal abroad.' The July 1973 issue of *Profile* reappeared minus the Drew Pearson article and with a new cover. MacAnthony's exposé was picked up across the Atlantic by *Newsweek* magazine, which stated that his story left the Irish Sweeps with a 'badly tarnished' image.

Joe MacAnthony took six months off to write a book exposing the inner workings of Hospitals Trust, but failed to find a publisher. After he returned to the *Sunday Independent*, he turned his inquisitive instincts to probing the financial dealings of the Fianna Fáil politician Ray Burke. Burke was elected to the Dáil in the general election of 1973, taking the seat held by his father P. J. Burke. MacAnthony wrote a front page exposé headlined 'Conflict of Interest', followed by a second piece which attempted to link planning corruption and politics in County Dublin.

McAnthony produced an extract from the accounts of the construction company owned by Mayo builders Tom Brennan and Joe McGowan who had been friendly with Burke's father P. J., who was also from Mayo. The extract showed that the strapping sum of £15,000 had been paid to Burke under the vague heading of 'planning'. The recently established Garda Fraud Squad launched an investigation lasting several months. The focus of the probe was the close relationship between Burke and the two developers and whether they had bribed the politician. Burke had been using his position as a member of Dublin County Council to secure the rezoning of lands owned by Brennan and McGowan for residential development in the north Dublin district of Swords. At the same time Burke was double-jobbing as an estate agent for the pair, selling the houses they built on the same lands and across the greater Dublin area. Brennan and McGowan had secured options on agricultural land in north Dublin that was never intended for housing development. The two builders then moved to have it rezoned with the backing of county councillors, often against the advice of the council's own planners. McAnthony revealed that around the time of the £15,000 payment Burke had seconded a motion to rezone Brennan and McGowan land at Mountgorry, east of Swords.

Another branch of the Garda investigation aimed to find out how Burke had come by his grand new home, Briargate, in Swords. The house, on an acre of rolling grounds, was designed and built for Burke by a Brennan and McGowan company, Oak Park Developments, in 1973, the year he entered the Dáil. Detectives interviewed Brennan, McGowan and Burke, questioning the TD several times. It would emerge many years later that Burke and the builders had lied to the police and supplied bogus bank documents. Decades later the Flood Tribunal found that the transfer of Briargate to Burke amounted to a corrupt payment. The tribunal also ruled that Burke received more than £160,000 in corrupt payments from Brennan and associates through a series of offshore accounts. The tribunal said it was satisfied the payments were for political favours.

MacAnthony later remarked of his Burke story: 'I thought, we have him. There is no question that we have him dead to rights.' However, a policeman close to the investigation informed him bluntly: 'Forget it. No, he'll never go to jail. Nothing's going to come out of it.' In a separate interview the journalist added: 'What puzzled me about the Burke case was that I had found the document in the Companies Office that damned him. And still nothing was done. Just as the [Garda] predicted. Certainly, if I had stayed with the *Sunday Independent*, I would have stayed on his tail, and on those who made contributions to his phantom political fund. I put down the welter of corruption in Irish politics to Burke's escape from retribution after that exposure in 1974. It gave everybody in the game a licence to steal.'

MacAnthony reflected: 'My life was pretty much over as a journalist in doing the Ray Burke story.' His working relationship with the *Sunday Independent* deteriorated, a position with RTÉ television fell through, and the writer went into what he described as 'professional exile' in Canada.

Six weeks after the *Sunday Independent* attacked the grandees of the Associated Hospitals Sweepstake Committee for failing to regulate the activities of Hospitals Trust, the committee set up an investigative subcommittee. In June 1973, six months after MacAnthony's report, the committee responded to his criticisms with the publication of a document entitled 'Irish Hospitals Sweepstakes: The Facts'. The Hospitals Committee's banal response was little more than a synopsis of the law governing the Irish Sweeps, laying stress on the role of the auditors to keep the promoters honest and above board.

The publication of the *Sunday Independent* report did, however, turn the Hospitals Trust into a legitimate target for others who had previously kept their reservations to themselves for fear they would be accused of sabotaging the national interest. In March 1973 the Labour deputy Dr John O'Connell announced that he would be submitting a private member's bill to the Dáil proposing that the Sweep should be nationalised. Six months later an editorial in the *Journal of the Irish Medical Association* declared that the funds raised by the Irish Sweeps were now 'peripheral' to the financing of Ireland's hospitals, and that the little money raised by the Sweeps should be used to fund academic medical research. The editorial concluded: 'The reasons for the existence of the Sweepstakes needs to be redefined if we are to maintain the faith of the subscribers. It is necessary to show that the funds are collected for some worthy cause.'

In 1973 a Fine Gael/Labour coalition government led by Liam Cosgrave ousted a Fianna Fáil government which had been in power for 16 years. With Joe MacAnthony's charges against the Sweeps now in the public domain, members of the Fianna Fáil Party now in opposition felt free to add to the verbal attacks being made by Hospitals Trust's traditional enemies in the Labour Party. The former Fianna Fáil justice minister Des O'Malley now voiced criticisms in public that he had previously made only in private to his cabinet colleagues.

Years later O'Malley revealed details of his difficult dealings with Hospitals Trust and his own civil servants while Minister for Justice. He said: 'I had to read the deed [for the Sweeps] around four times a year. And I began to read the deed, which perhaps my predecessors hadn't done. And I began to ask questions about it and I discovered the hospitals were receiving very little money but an awful lot of money seemed to be flowing around. I queried it first in the Department of Justice and the answer was that the deed is the same as it was for the past thirty years—just sign it and be done with it. I found that the only real sanction I had, if you were making inquiries into the Sweeps, was to refuse to sign the deed.

'So I hinted in that direction on one occasion and Paddy McGrath came rushing in to me in the Department saying this was terrible . . . and that it would lead to the immediate unemployment or disemployment of 800 or 900 women working in the Sweeps office in Ballsbridge, and that I couldn't contemplate that. And that even if I could, other members of the Government wouldn't. And therefore I couldn't do it, I was told.' Remarking that the Sweeps promoters had their 'tentacles' in every corner of Irish industry, O'Malley observed: 'They weren't shy about exercising the economic and social power that their position gave them.'

In a 1973 Dáil debate, O'Malley put pressure on his Fine Gael successor at Justice, Paddy Cooney, to furnish details of the management fees paid to the promoters of the Irish Sweeps. Cooney told O'Malley that the accounts supplied by Hospitals Trust were available for inspection in the Dáil library. O'Malley's party colleague Dr Bill Loughnane declared 'there is something phoney' about the finances of the Hospitals Trust, pressing the minister: 'Is it not worthy of investigation?' Meanwhile, the surprise appointment of Paddy McGrath to a seat in the Senate by Taoiseach Liam Cosgrave was taken as a vote of confidence in the Sweeps promoters. According to the *Irish Independent*: 'This, according to some opposition critics, has given the matter of the Sweepstakes a whole new dimension and could well inhibit a full review of the operation of the Sweeps.'

At the beginning of 1976 the Federation of Voluntary Charitable Organisations objected to the revelation that Hospitals Trust had sought permission from the Fine Gael/Labour government to operate a weekly national lottery based on greyhound racing. Some years earlier the federation had successfully blocked Paddy McGrath's plans to double the annual number of sweeps from three to six. The federation issued a statement saying it had made 'strong representations' to the Taoiseach and the Minister for Justice that Hospitals Trust's plan 'would have a disastrous effect on the many charities who depend in varying degrees on income from lotteries'. The bodies represented by the federation were restricted by law to offering a top prize of £500. A spokesman argued: 'Who will continue to subscribe for a possible prize of £500 if someone else can offer prizes greatly in excess of that sum?'

Two days earlier Hospitals Trust had announced that the Ballsbridge operation was in danger of closing if it were not granted permission for its greyhound lottery. To back up its case, the Trust announced at the same time that it was putting its 700 staff on a two-day working week. The federation countered that a Hospitals Trust weekly lottery would 'virtually ensure' the closure of many small charities. Once again the federation succeeded in frustrating a scheme proposed by Hospitals Trust.

Later in 1976 the Fine Gael/Labour coalition did oblige the Sweeps promoters, passing a new Public Hospitals Act which allowed Hospitals Trust Limited to increase the cut they took for expenses to 40 per cent of what was left after they took their secret expenses. As the legislation was debated, Fianna Fáil again went on the attack. That party's P. J. Lawlor charged: 'We have a situation here whereby the Government and the Minister for Justice have the embarrassment of trying to explain in this House that with their concurrence a scheme has been worked out with Irish Hospitals Sweepstakes whereby the tax authorities in the US and in Canada are being fiddled. That puts it in black and white.' Des O'Malley quoted from Joe MacAnthony's *Sunday Independent* feature of three years earlier, pointing out the journalist's contention that the Sweeps promoters were understating the gross income for each sweep by one-third.

Even though the legislation was being put forward by a government that incorporated the Labour Party, deputies from that camp came out strongly against it. Labour's Dr John O'Connell got the rapt attention of every deputy in the Dáil chamber when he stated: 'I have to confess to having grave reservations about this Bill. I feel that to say otherwise would be dishonest. I am aware of the fact that we are in a dilemma because I recognise that if this is not agreed in this House we may find over 700 people unemployed. It seems to me, and I must be frank, that it is putting the revolver to my head, that unless I agree to this we will have over 700 people unemployed. Believe you me, sir, I have been intimidated by people in the last few months in regard to the Hospitals Sweepstake telling me that unless I voted for this there would be serious repercussions. I am not happy with the whole operation of the Sweepstake. There is a smell about it. It has damaged our good name abroad and I do not think . . .'

At this point O'Connell was interrupted by Justice Minister Cooney, who asked him to repeat what he had said about intimidation.

O'Connell replied: 'Yes, I have been intimidated by people—not in the House—that there would be serious repercussions if I did not vote for this Bill. I would be smeared in my constituency—this was conveyed to me just two weeks ago, last Sunday week—that I would be smeared in my constituency and everything done to get me out. As I said, I am not happy about the Hospitals Sweepstake. It has a smell about it. It has damaged our good name abroad. I do not think we can be proud of the fact that the sweepstake operates properly. I have grave reservations about the whole of the Hospitals Sweepstake. People abroad are under the impression that the Hospitals Sweeps finance our hospital services. That is the great myth.' O'Connell added that the directors of Hospitals Trust Limited should be forced to disclose all donations made to politicians.

Justice Minister Cooney responded: 'This is possibly the most serious statement I have heard in this House, and there have been many serious statements made in the course of my comparatively short time here. I think if a Member of Parliament is subjected to that pressure it is intolerable, but it is incumbent, more than incumbent, it is absolutely vital that that Member would make his complaint to the authorities of the State so that criminal proceedings could be taken against those responsible for this intimidation.'

The attacks on Hospitals Trust were taken up in the Dáil by Deputy Peter Callanan who remarked: 'If there is anything fishy about the sweepstake—which has State sponsorship behind it—certainly people are likely to talk and they are talking. I can assure the House that they are talking down the country about this, and about the amount of profit being made by directors and so on in that organisation.'

When the bill reached the Senate, John Horgan of the Labour Party announced: 'Even though the whole Sweepstake operation is one which is to a large extent abhorrent to me, I could not vote against this Bill in conscience because of the very substantial implications, particularly with regard to employment.' Senator Mary Robinson clearly had in mind Joe MacAnthony, who had been forced to move to Canada in search of work, when she stated: 'There is an underlying element of disquiet and cause for concern. We know that those journalists who have sought further information and who have investigated the operation of the Irish Hospitals Sweepstakes have not furthered their careers in doing so. Indeed, if anything, they have either changed their immediate employment or left the country entirely.'

Chapter 25 ∾

GET RID OF IT! YOU SHOULDN'T HAVE IT. DON'T USE IT!

In March 1973 the £200,000 super-prize introduced three years earlier was scooped for the first time by an Irish citizen. Described as 'a 53-year-old disabled bachelor' from the Curragh in County Kildare, Michael Conroy received a threefold bounty of good news. In addition to his £200,000 jackpot he learned that he was entitled to an additional £4,000 seller's prize for selling the ticket to himself, and on the same day he learned of his win, his solicitor informed him that he had been awarded £10,000 for injuries he had sustained in a road accident two years earlier.

Conroy told reporters when he heard of his huge windfall: 'I was knocked stupid. Imagine being told that sort of news. I just couldn't believe it.' He also revealed that one of the first people to call in offering congratulations was his next door neighbour Joe McGrath Jnr, son of Big Joe, who was the owner of Conroy's house.

In 1975, in an attempt to boost flagging interest in the Irish Sweeps in the United States and to offset the effects of doubling the price of a ticket from £1 to £2, the super-prize was nominally doubled to £400,000. However, the former justice minister Des O'Malley pointed out that the new jackpot was a dupe of smoke and mirrors trickery by Hospitals Trust. When the super-prize had been £200,000, the entire bonanza went straight to the winner in a lump sum. In stark contrast, the winner of the new £400,000 prize received only £75,000 upfront, followed by a series of smaller annual instalments for the remainder of their life.

O'Malley noted: 'From the point of view of the promoters or those providing the prize, the cost of the annuity clearly will vary enormously depending on the age of the winner of the super-prize. You can buy quite a substantial annuity for an 80-year-old man or woman comparatively cheaply ... It seems, therefore, there is a great element of luck, so far as the promoters of the Sweepstakes are concerned, in who wins. The cost of providing the annuity will vary enormously depending on the age and the health condition of whatever person is lucky enough to win. It seems to me that the original intention, and the intention which was carried out when the super-prize was £200,000, was that the prize would be paid to the person and he could do what he liked with it. If he wanted to buy an annuity himself, or to invest it, he was free to do so. I do not know why that should not now be the case, and why there is a payment of £75,000 and a life annuity is substituted for what is advertised as a prize of £400,000.'

The first winner of the deceptive £400,000 super-prize was a dentist from Florida who was visiting Dublin for a dentistry convention. He bought his £2 ticket from the head hall porter at Jury's Hotel in Ballsbridge, about a hundred metres from where it was soon after plucked from the drum at Hospitals Trust headquarters. The doubling of the ticket price and the supposed doubling of the super-prize did not halt the decline in sales. The declared proceeds on the 1975 Lincoln Sweep were down almost £600,000 on the same race the previous year.

In the run-up to the 1975 Lincoln Sweep, the 200 or so members of the Workers' Union of Ireland employed at Hospitals Trust served strike notice, prompted by grievances over pay, conditions, the short-time working week, and the Hospitals Trust's continuing refusal to recognise the union. Fearing that the strike would hit revenues from the Lincoln Sweep, management finally agreed to treat the union on an equal footing with the House Association.

The truce between management and the union was short lived and in 1977 Hospitals Trust was hit by the first strike in its long history, with WUI members picketing for the payment of wage rises due under the national pay agreements of previous years. Hospitals Trust pleaded that times were hard and it couldn't honour the wage agreements.

Four weeks into the strike, the journalist Nell McCafferty visited the striking women on the picket line outside the Ballsbridge HQ. She was told that every single woman on the line was a widow or a spinster and that they were now eating into their meagre savings to sustain their protest. One woman who had worked there for 22 years announced that she had just £1.25 left in her Post Office savings book. One widow attacked the Trust's employment policy, explaining that the widows found themselves 'fighting each other for seven weeks' work a year' and then weren't adequately paid for those few weeks.

The picketers were supplied with soup and sandwiches by ex-employees of the Trust, while construction labourers working on the building next door emptied a bucket of liquid on the head of one employee who passed the picket. 'And they told him it wasn't spring water', chuckled one of the women. A passing bus driver brought his vehicle to a halt, blocking the car of a Hospitals Trust executive while the conductor very slowly went into a shop to buy a carton of milk. On another occasion the Labour Party leader Frank Cluskey joined the picket to show his support.

The back pay issue was eventually settled and the strike lifted, but the Hospitals Trust workforce continued to dwindle, dropping to just 325 employees the following year from a total of 900 in 1975. In an attempt to raise extra income in the small Irish market, Spencer Freeman approached the Federation of Voluntary Charitable Organisations with a proposal that Hospitals Trust would take over the running of their small-time lotteries, guaranteeing each body a fixed income from weekly draws for the maximum prizes of £500 allowed by law. Hospitals Trust believed that if it could get its hands on the 84 licences held by the voluntary groups, it could hit the ambitious target of selling 500,000 tickets a week. The Trust's plans were scuppered when two of the biggest voluntary groups, the Central Remedial Clinic and the Rehabilitation Institute, announced a joint 'instant win' lottery involving sealed cards. The two bodies pointed out that the 25 to 30 per cent they would be taking in running expenses was far lower than the latest 40 per cent slice that Hospitals Trust had negotiated, and that one in seven cards would pay out some level of cash prize, which contrasted with the astronomical chances of winning on the Irish Sweep.

In 1978 Hospitals Trust attempted to revive its earlier plan to increase the number of annual Irish Sweeps draws to six. In late 1966 the incoming Fianna Fáil cabinet of new Taoiseach Jack Lynch had approved Paddy McGrath's proposal for six draws, but the government had put the scheme on the back-burner following protests from the Federation of Voluntary Charitable Organisations who insisted their small lotteries would be badly damaged. Now, in March 1978, and making no mention of negotiations with the government, the Trust announced there would be six Sweeps draws in 1979.

The promoters' plan to hold six Sweeps in 1979 lay in tatters before that year was very old when 600 Dublin postmen went on strike in January, claiming they were owed £10 each for working overtime delivering Christmas mail two weeks earlier on 23 December. One week into the strike a 30 ton mountain of undelivered mail had built up at the capital's Central Sorting Office. One Dublin employer whose business was brought to a standstill said he would personally contribute £100, if 59 other firms would do the same, to pool together the £6,000 the strikers claimed was owed to them.

His scheme attracted little support from either the striking postmen or the company bosses. Indeed, the chaos worsened when hundreds of female telephonists employed by the same Department of Posts & Telegraphs escalated the chaos with a series of lightning strikes in pursuit of equal pay with male colleagues who were earning £6 a week more for doing the same job.

As the weeks of industrial action dragged on, the original 600 striking postmen were joined by over 12,000 other Posts & Telegraphs workers, and the original demand for an extra £10 became a general claim for wage increases of up to 51 per cent. Some years later Paddy McGrath lamented: 'What really began to kill the Sweep was the prolonged postal strike of 1979. We lost 40% of our overseas business because the local post offices (in North America, Britain and elsewhere) would send the tickets back. They were not accepting anything for Ireland. We never recovered from that.'

Two of the intended six draws for 1979 had to be cancelled, at a cost to Hospitals Trust that Paddy McGrath estimated at £1,300,000. Two hundred and fifty of the remaining 300 employees were laid off for the duration.

By the end of 1979 the Sweep was up and running once again, but there were clear signs that the operation was on its last legs. Nine years after it was created to rekindle waining interest in the Irish Sweep, the super-prize was abandoned. Where once there had been 20 top prizes, each worth a fortune, now there remained just three of £100,000 each. The total prize fund for the final Sweep of 1979 was £561,800, but the amount being claimed by the promoters for administration was more than £727,000, providing more ammunition for those who said it was time to wind up the ailing enterprise. Paddy McGrath faced increasingly sceptical questioning from interviewers. He told one: 'I know I'm honest. To make sure that everyone is always honest we have an audit daily to make sure that the returns are always correct.' He claimed it was not possible for the promoters to 'skim off' cash.

Paddy McGrath may have become adept at batting away the mildly impertinent questions of tame interviewers, but when an investigative team from RTÉ 's *Politics Programme* began digging up dirt on the Irish Sweeps in 1978, the promoters showed that, when roused, they could scrap as dirty as the meanest street-fighter.

A former chairman of the RTÉ Authority kicked off the TV investigation by supplying reporters Michael Heney and Charlie Bird with a copy of a 1966 memorandum drawn up by the Department of Justice under Minister Brian Lenihan. Among other criticisms, the confidential memo to cabinet said that the acounts furnished by Hospitals Trust could not be trusted and that the illegal activities of the Sweeps' agents were tarnishing Ireland's reputation around the world. 'It was very, very revealing,' Bird later remarked.

John Horgan, a former journalist who had been elected a Labour Party TD in 1977 and who was highly critical of the Sweeps, recalled years later: 'There is documentary evidence that when this programme was mooted the Sweeps heard about it, because I presume RTÉ approached them. They made an approach to the Director General to express their concern. This concern was communicated to a meeting of the editorial committee as it was at the time. You could see danger signals flaring all over the place. Government memoranda to cabinet were as scarce as hens' teeth at the time. Most of us who worked as journalists had never seen one. The idea a media organization had one and might be thinking of using it was almost unknown.'

Charlie Bird elaborated: 'We went to the powers that be in RTÉ at the time and showed them this and they were horrified and aghast, first of all that we would have such a memorandum, and they basically told us, get rid of it! You shouldn't have it. Don't use it!'

Michael Heney recalled: 'We very quickly realized that we were into something explosive, sensational, quite extraordinary. We had the lists, we had the names, the addresses, the places. We had the events, we had the smuggling, we had the paybacks, the kickbacks, the money paid to the hauliers. We had chapter and verse.'

The reporters from the *Politics Programme* interviewed officials in Canada and the United States, filming an in-depth exposé of the Sweeps' operations. Their final port of call was Rotterdam in the Netherlands in December 1978 where they staked out a freight container holding $6 million worth of Sweep tickets which was bound for New Jersey in the United States. The contraband was concealed in a consignment of dried milk powder. The investigation which had taken five months was at an end. The only question that remained was whether the TV crew from Ireland should tip off the Dutch authorities about the scam.

Thirteen years later, Michael Heney wrote in the *Sunday Tribune*: 'Someone somewhere in RTÉ decided that it would not be "patriotic" to inform to a foreign government. So the moment passed. The Sweeps tickets reached their destination. Journalism had met the Sweep head on and the Sweep won. And in the event, it was to take thirteen years and the demise of the Sweep itself to enable the story then being researched to be told on RTÉ.'

Five months in the making at considerable cost, the forensically researched documentary was axed. Excerpts were salvaged for a *Today Tonight* special report broadcast 13 years later in 1992, long after Hospitals Trust had gone to the wall. Just as the Sweeps' promoters had punished the *Sunday Independent* in 1973 by withdrawing advertising, they had forced the national broadcaster into a craven climbdown by threatening a similar retribution. John Horgan observed: 'Big advertisers do exercise big pressure and it is part of the business of a public service organization to stand up to that.'

Michael Heney remarked regretfully: 'We should have broadcast it. We should have broadcast something close to what we presented to our management. The fact that we didn't was a failure by the State broadcaster.'

Chapter 26

FIFTY YEARS TO BUILD IT AND FIVE YEARS TO BLOW IT

Citing the hole punched in Hospitals Trust's finances by the 1979 postal strike, the company pressed the government to approve three annual Shamrock Sweeps. Official sanction was granted for the new mini-draws which featured £1 tickets and a modest top prize of £20,000. Hospitals Trust gave an undertaking that no tickets would be sold abroad. There was little pretence that the Shamrock Sweeps would raise money for Ireland's hospitals. Their purpose was to keep the severely shrunken workforce at the Trust in gainful employment.

The sticking plaster solution of the Shamrock Sweeps failed to keep the workforce intact and in September 1980 Hospitals Trust laid off 180 staff on a temporary basis. Pressed on its plans for 1981, management refused to commit to staging any sweeps in the coming year.

Labour TD John Horgan, a long-time critic, launched a blistering attack on the promoters in the wake of the latest spate of lay-offs. Demanding a 'long overdue' public inquiry into the company's activities, Horgan charged that the entire history of Hospitals Trust was 'a sorry litany of broken promises'. He continued: 'Over the years the need to safeguard employment in the Sweeps has been a gun held to the head of successive governments by the Sweeps' promoters in their plea for ever greater licence to increase the proportion of receipts which can be put towards the paying of the Sweeps' expenses. The emptiness of that bluff can now be clearly seen.' He closed by claiming: 'The attitude of the Sweeps to its employees is nothing short of disgraceful.'

A Hospitals Trust spokesman countered that the company was not surprised by Horgan's attack as he was one of a small band of public representatives whose 'antipathy' towards the company was well known. He continued: 'Mister Horgan, I presume, would suggest that he has issued his statement in the interest of the workers employed in the Sweepstakes. What he is doing, in reality, could result in a lessening of public confidence, thereby making it more difficult to preserve jobs.'

The bad news for the McGrath, Duggan and Freeman families in 1980 didn't end with the growing crisis at Hospitals Trust. For decades the three families had ploughed the wealth generated by the Sweep into a range of Irish industries through their vehicle Avenue Investments. With a workforce of over 6,000 that dwarfed the few hanging on at Hospitals Trust, Waterford Glass was perhaps the most prestigious and profitable business in the families' portfolio. However, in 1980 the crystal company's profits dipped for the first time since the 1950s. Financial commentators also began to question whether Avenue Investments was overstretched and unwisely getting into businesses where it had no track record.

As recession gripped Ireland in the early years of the 1980s the extensive domestic business empire built by the Sweeps families was dismantled, with companies and lands sold off to clear Avenue's large debts. Apart from the worsening business climate, the three founding families made it clear that there were now some 50 McGrath, Duggan and Freeman grandchildren with an expectation of an inheritance. When Waterford Crystal was put up for sale in 1984 politicians of all hues voiced their concerns for jobs in the region where unemployment already stood at 20 per cent. A Waterford Workers' Party representative, Paddy Gallagher, declared: 'There must be no question of the small group of families who control Waterford Glass now being allowed to take the money and run.' The impotent rhetoric of the Workers' Party could not prevent the sale of Waterford and several other interests at bargain basement prices, while other concerns went bust as the recession bit deeper. *Irish Business* magazine captured the predicament facing the founding families with a report headlined 'The McGrath Fortune—Fifty Years to Build It and Five Years to Blow It!'

When it was put to him at the time of the crash that he might have been wiser to spread some of Avenue's investments into more buoyant overseas economies, Paddy McGrath agreed, but added: 'From day one our cardinal rule was that every penny earned would be invested in

Ireland. As the recession deepened we tried, sometimes against overwhelming odds, to keep business going. In the end, we paid a dear price. We could have walked away from some of them, but that is not the way we do business. I believe that you cannot put a price on integrity.'

In September 1984 the directors of Hospitals Trust released a statement claiming that the Irish Sweep was being 'slowly but inexorably' driven out of business because successive governments had refused to allow them to modernise over the previous 16 years. The criticism was made as the promoters unveiled a scheme to update the Irish Sweep by incorporating an element of Lotto, described in one report as 'the game that has become the craze of three continents'. The promoters were seeking government sanction to stage a weekly draw which allowed players to choose their own numbers and which also involved some horse racing element.

The Hospitals Trust insisted: 'Delay in granting permission is seriously jeopardizing what could be a significant contribution to government funds which, it is felt, would be swelled by capturing a large slice of the money being staked on gambling outside the State.' As usual, the promoters claimed that the proposed measure would protect existing jobs and perhaps even create new ones.

Just weeks later Hospitals Trust's directors got the answer they feared when the Fine Gael/Labour government led by Garret FitzGerald announced it was to press ahead with the establishment of a National Lottery to raise funds for sporting, artistic and social concerns. The proposed makeover for the Irish Sweeps was a non-starter. However, the first body to condemn the planned National Lottery was not Hospitals Trust but Gael Linn, which raised one-quarter of its annual income from its own small-scale lottery. A Gael Linn spokesman claimed that the National Lottery would 'gravely injure' its work promoting the Irish language.

Unmoved by all special pleading, the government invited tenders to run the new National Lottery. The main contenders to emerge included Hospitals Trust, the State postal service An Post, a syndicate comprising the Central Remedial Clinic, the Rehabilitation Institute and the Mater Hospital, and a consortium formed by Independent Newspapers and Vernon's Football Pools.

Before the full field of runners for the National Lottery franchise had been declared, the CRC/Rehab/Mater consortium held high-level discussions with An Post about the possibility of joining forces to secure the lucrative licence. In the course of these talks the CRC/Rehab/Mater representatives gave An Post a copy of the submission it had already made to the government. In a story headlined 'An Post Had Advantage Over Lottery Rivals', *The Irish Times* reported: 'The document was handed over to indicate to An Post the size of the project being contemplated and the role it might play in it.'

The Irish Times account continued: 'Contacted about the matter yesterday Mr Flannery, the Chief Executive of the Rehabilitation Institute, said that the talks had taken place "in good faith" and their submission had been made available on that basis. However, he was "disappointed" that An Post had subsequently decided to make an independent submission, but "that's life" he commented. He was confident that their proposal . . . was the best. Mister Flannery is a senior adviser to the Fine Gael Party.'

By July of 1985 a decision by the Fine Gael-led administration was imminent on the awarding of the National Lottery franchise, but 'informed government sources' were leaking the information that the competition had already been whittled down to a two horse race, with An Post and the CRC/Rehab/Mater bids the only ones with a prospect of winning.

Frank Byrne of Hospitals Trust tried to scotch the highly sourced rumours that Hospitals Trust had been relegated to the also-rans. He called a press conference and told reporters that if the Sweeps promoters did not get the licence: 'It would make life very difficult. It would make it almost impossible to continue. However, I don't see how the government could not give it to us. I don't want to sound over-confident, but there's nobody else in the business. We are the only people in the country with the knowledge, the expertise and the track record to do it.'

In this, Byrne was echoing Paddy McGrath who had earlier said he found it 'absolutely amazing' that the government would contemplate wiping out the jobs of Irish Sweeps workers. He insisted: 'The end of the Sweepstake would mean a loss on three areas to the State—lost contributions to the Hospitals Trust, loss of foreign currency reserves, and redundancies arising from the closure of the operation.' He added: 'It is vital that we get this lottery. It has been our business since 1930. It has been a good servant to this country.'

McGrath said he found it galling that An Post was a major rival for the franchise, given that it was the strike of six years earlier by postal workers that had crippled the Irish Sweeps, and given that Hospitals Trust was An Post's best customer after the Electricity Supply Board. He griped: 'I am not allowed to sell stamps and there is no way I am going to get permission to do so.'

An Post, with its nationwide network of outlets in every town and village, and its semi-state status, was awarded the franchise in October 1985. It announced it would quickly launch a scratch card game while it put in place the electronic framework for a 'more sophisticated' bingo-style game within 18 months. On the day of the long-telegraphed bombshell, the Sweeps promoters said they were 'seeking an immediate meeting with the government'. Asked about the future of the Irish Sweeps, which now seemed doomed, Finance Minister Alan Dukes bluntly replied: 'We picked the one that we felt would give us the best result and that was our concern.' Within days of losing out to An Post, Hospitals Trust announced it would be laying off its entire staff of 220 workers at its Ballsbridge HQ.

As the bill to establish the new National Lottery passed through the Dáil, the former Fine Gael Taoiseach Liam Cosgrave made a last gasp appeal for a stay of execution on the Sweeps. A long-time staunch supporter of Hospitals Trust, Cosgrave said he thought it strange that An Post, which had proved itself inept at collecting television licence fees, should be given the additional task of running the Lottery. He said he still held out hopes that Hospitals Trust would be involved, and argued that it made little sense to put 220 people out of work at the Trust in order to create 40 new ones at the National Lottery.

Cosgrave's criticisms of his own party's behaviour fell on deaf ears, as did the Trust's request to the Department of Justice to sanction a new fortnightly Sweepstake. Now installed as Justice Minister, Alan Dukes rejected the plan, reasoning that 'the operation of more than one lottery of the magnitude of the National Lottery and the sweepstake they had proposed could result in wasteful duplication'. Three months later Hospitals Trust submitted a new scheme for a series of revamped Sweeps with ticket prices hiked up to £10 and £20. Dukes judged that the ticket prices were too high, and again told the promoters he did not welcome renewed competition to the new National Lottery which was nearing its start-up date. Further exchanges followed, with the promoters asking Dukes to spell out precisely what sort of sweepstake he would sanction. He informed them: 'I could envisage sanctioning Sweepstakes indefinitely provided that they did not become an alternative to the National Lottery and provided, of course, that I could be satisfied that any proposed Sweepstakes would be commercially viable.'

After further approaches from Hospitals Trust, Dukes told them in November 1986 that he would 'consider any detailed scheme' put forward, but that the promoters would have to back it up convincingly with market research. Faced with this ministerial demand, the promoters wrote back saying they would be in touch 'at a future date when things have developed sufficiently to take the matter further'.

But Hospitals Trust had nothing left in the tank to take the matter any further. After 57 years, the promoters gave up the ghost and the Irish Hospitals Sweepstakes offices closed in February 1987 with the loss of the remaining 160 jobs. With the sale of the 11 acre Ballsbridge site expected to raise between £8 million and £12 million for the cash-strapped State which owned the land, the Federated Workers' Union of Ireland accused the government of 'asset stripping' and urged the Fine Gael/Labour coalition to 'acknowledge its moral obligation to the employees of the Sweep and to make adequate funds available to all the employees of Hospitals Trust so they can retire in dignity with adequate redundancy compensation'.

Instead, those recently made redundant and others on puny Hospitals Trust pensions found themselves cast into a financial limbo, with the government saying it had no moral obligation to make special provision for ex-employees of a private limited company and the Hospitals Trust pleading inability to pay. There was anger with the directors of Hospitals Trust who had amassed fabulous personal wealth but had left loyal staff who had clocked up decades of service to live out their remaining years in wretched poverty. John Slevin, the Trust's last financial director, later described the company's neglect of these employees as an act of 'betrayal'.

More than 3,000 miles distant from the bitter wranglings in Dublin, there was no mention of betrayal in a story carried in the *Belize Times* under the headline 'The Sad Demise of the Irish Sweepstake'. The story noted that the 160,000 inhabitants of the Central American country of

Belize had for decades been keen followers of the Irish Sweeps, and could take pride in their contribution to Ireland's hospitals.

Back home, former Sweeps staff picketed the champagne reception to launch the National Lottery in March 1987. The following year, entry to the auction for the Ballsbridge site was restricted to those who could produce a £250,000 bank draft at the door as an entry ticket. The reason given for the restriction was to keep out timewasters who couldn't show they had a *bona fide* interest in bidding. It had the collateral effect of denying entry to any impoverished former Sweeps worker who might have used the occasion to stage a protest.

In the year 2000, with the roar of the Celtic Tiger at its most thunderous, the Irish State finally raided the petty cash and paid out a lump sum of £20,000 each to 129 former Sweeps workers made redundant in 1987. If the money had been paid in 1987, it would have bought a modest house. By the time it was belatedly bestowed, it wouldn't have paid for a box bedroom.

As such, it was a closing chapter fit to bring Ireland's greatest Jekyll & Hyde saga to a suitably shabby end.

INDEX